# Your Pilot's License

# From the McGraw-Hill *PRACTICAL FLYING SERIES*

**Cross-Country Flying**
*Jerry A. Eichenberger*

**Handling In-Flight Emergencies**
*Jerry A. Eichenberger*

**ABCs of Safe Flying—Fourth Edition**
*David A. Frazier*

**The Pilot's Air Traffic Control Handbook—Third Edition**
*Paul E. Illman*

**The Pilot's Radio Communications Handbook
—Fifth Edition**
*Paul E. Illman*

**The Pilot's Guide to Weather Reports, Forecasts,
and Flight Planning—Second Edition**
*Terry Lankford*

**Understanding Aeronautical Charts**
*Terry Lankford*

**Better Takeoffs and Landings**
*Michael C. Love*

# Your Pilot's License

## Sixth Edition

Jerry A. Eichenberger

## McGraw-Hill

New York   San Francisco   Washington, D.C.   Auckland   Bogotá
Caracas   Lisbon   London   Madrid   Mexico City   Milan
Montreal   New Delhi   San Juan   Singapore
Sydney   Tokyo   Toronto

**Library of Congress Cataloging-in-Publication Data**

Eichenberger, Jerry A.
   Your pilot's license / Jerry A. Eichenberger.—6th ed.
     p.   cm.
   New ed. of: Your pilot's license / Joe Christy.—5th ed. / rev.
and updated by Jerry A. Eichenberger. 1994.
   Includes index.
   ISBN 0-07-015119-9 (pbk.)
   1. Airplanes—Piloting.   2. Air pilots—United States—Licenses.
3. Private flying.   I. Christy, Joe. Your pilot's license.   II.
Title.
TL710.E4424    1999
629.132'5217—dc21                 98-031967
                                    CIP

# McGraw-Hill

*A Division of The McGraw-Hill Companies*

1 2 3 4 5 6 7 8 9 0   AGM/AGM   9 0 3 2 1 0 9 8

ISBN 0-07-015119-9

*The sponsoring editor for this book was Shelley Ingram Carr, the editing supervisor was Stephen M. Smith, and the production supervisor was Clare B. Stanley. It was set in Garamond by Kim Sheran of McGraw-Hill's Hightstown, N.J., Professional Book Group composition unit.*

*Printed and bound by Quebecor/Martinsburg.*

McGraw-Hill books are available at special quantity discounts to use as premiums and sales promotions, or for use in corporate training programs. For more information, please write to the Director of Special Sales, McGraw-Hill, 11 West 19th Street, New York, NY 10011. Or contact your local bookstore.

# Contents

# Introduction

*Your Pilot's License* is for both prospective and beginning pilots. It is not intended to be a formal ground school text, which would normally be used in the process of learning to fly. What this book does do is explain what a newcomer to the aviation world will encounter, along with some of the basics of aeronautical knowledge that will be covered in more detail once you begin ground school.

As it surpasses the halfway point of its fourth decade of publication, this best seller among aviation books has been completely updated and expanded, and now covers not only the training steps to achieve a private pilot's license, but also discusses other options, such as the recreational pilot certificate and flying sailplanes, and many of the changes that have occurred in the flight training industry since the Fifth Edition was written in 1994. The simple, straightforward approach of previous editions is retained, so that you are not confronted with overly complicated terms and subject areas. The theory of flight, navigation, control techniques, weather basics, air traffic rules, and aircraft instrumentation are all covered in easy-to-understand language that will not intimidate even the reader with no prior exposure to flying.

Virtually anyone can learn to fly and become a safe and competent aviator, particularly with a good foundation in the basics and the willingness to expend the effort to enjoy an exciting new venture.

The world of the pilot is boundless. Through these pages you can begin to understand why most pilots say, "The worst day flying is better than the best day doing anything else." Happy flying!

*Jerry A. Eichenberger*

# 1

# The Most Frequently Asked Questions about Learning to Fly

## Why Should I Learn to Fly?

There are almost as many answers to this question as there are pilots. But, the answer depends upon you and your interests in life. Do you enjoy a challenge that is safe, yet exciting? If so, flying is for you. If you like the idea of doing something that not everyone can do, yet isn't terribly difficult, flying can satisfy that urge. If you enjoy fellowship with people who have interests similar to your own, you'll find that aviators are a very friendly bunch. Perhaps you've thought that you might like the freedom of travel that a lightplane would provide. If so, you're right. A small airplane can give you the latitude to enjoy weekend journeys and longer vacations that aren't possible by car in the same amount of time, and to go to out-of-the-way places that are difficult to reach by airline travel. Most importantly for most of us who fly, aviation is an infectious process, changing one's entire outlook on life. Come give it a try, and you'll soon have many answers to this question.

# How Long Does It Take?

The various qualifications for a pilot's license, which is correctly referred to as a pilot certificate, are stated in terms of flying hours and levels of experience. How long it will take you to accomplish the necessary training, and log the needed hours, depends on your schedule. Although the legal requirement for a private certificate is 40 hours of flying time (less at some specially licensed flight schools), most people take around 55 to 60 hours to gain the required proficiency to pass the practical flight test. When you go about learning any new skill, the keys to accomplishing it in the shortest time are consistent and frequent training sessions. If you can fly often, you'll learn in less time than if you take only a couple of lessons per month.

If you live in an area of the country that has harsh winter weather, it's often best to start flying early in the spring. That way, you can get the most advantage of the good weather to come for the next 6 months or so and utilize the longer daylight hours to fly after work if that fits into your plan. But, if the bug has bitten you in September, don't wait 6 months to start; just realize that you might get some lessons canceled due to bad weather in the winter months. If you can begin flying as the weather relents into spring, you can probably finish your training and have a private certificate by the end of the summer or early in the fall.

# What Will I Fly?

Most flight training is done in small airplanes that have two seats. There are several popular types used at flight schools, and they include the Cessna 150 and 152, Piper Tomahawk, and Piper Cherokee. If you are physically large, and find these uncomfortable, most schools have four-seat airplanes available as well. Naturally, the larger airplanes cost more, so expect to pay more for renting them during your training.

If slight increases in cost aren't vital to you, you may consider using a four-seat airplane, such as a Cessna 172 or Piper Warrior, from the beginning. After you get your license, you'll probably do most of your flying in these kinds of airplanes anyway, and there is nothing to be lost by training in them.

Instruction in a vintage or classic airplane might cost less, but you will probably sacrifice having the modern avionics that you should learn to operate. These airplanes do, however, teach the basic skills of airmanship very well (FIG. 1-1).

**1-1** *A classic airplane, the Piper Super Cruiser.*

# How Much Will It Cost?

We can't kid ourselves and pretend that flying is cheap. However, its expense can be less than many other recreational activities in which many folks engage. I've got friends, business associates, and clients who spend far more each year on their hobbies, such as golf, boating, skiing, and fishing trips, than I do flying.

Most student pilots learn to fly at flight schools where they rent airplanes in which the training is taken. As this edition of *Your Pilot's License* is being written in the winter of 1998, in the midwest, where I'm located, typical training airplanes rent for around $50 per hour at most flight schools. The fee charged for a flight instructor's time is about $20 to $25 per hour. If you do some quick math, and assume that you'll need 60 hours total flight time to qualify for your certificate, that equals about $2,400 for airplane rental. Figure that of the 60 hours total, about half of it will be dual flight instruction with the instructor, so add another $750 for instruction at $25 per hour. Then, you'll spend about $250 for a ground school at most flight training operations and probably will purchase around $150 worth of books, charts, and other supplies. Therefore, all added together, you can estimate about $3,550 for the entire training process.

If you're a quicker learner, and can fly often, you could cut this substantially by taking fewer than 60 hours to accomplish the job. Although these numbers certainly are more than movie tickets cost, in the long run, the cost of obtaining a pilot's license need not be ruinous for most folks who truly want to learn to fly.

## Can the Cost Be Reduced Further?

This answer is a qualified Yes. There is, as the saying goes, more than one way to skin a cat. In Chap. 2, you'll see that you can first obtain a recreational pilot certificate, which has fewer privileges than a private license, and therefore requires less training time. Also, you can first learn to fly gliders, which is much less expensive than flying powered airplanes. These options are covered in detail later. Another way to cut the cost of learning to fly may sound weird at the inception, but it does make sense.

When you are sure that you really intend to complete the training program, and fly after you get a license, you can emulate many aspiring aviators, including your author, who bought their first airplane very early in their flying careers. Once you make up your mind that this is really something that you intend to do, why continue to rent airplanes? Make some contacts with other pilots, discuss it with your instructor and the maintenance staff at your flight school, and give serious thought to buying the same kind of airplane in which you're doing your lessons. Airplanes have dramatically increased in value over the past few decades, and every indication is that they will continue to do so. Unlike cars, used airplanes are the norm for most people to buy, not only for their first aerial steed but most often throughout their years of flying. With good assistance from trusted advisors, you can buy a small trainer, fly it for a year or two, and probably get your money back out of it, perhaps even enjoy some appreciation during the time that you own it. We'll also talk more about this in later chapters.

## Where Should I Learn to Fly?

This question can have multiple answers, or you can be stuck with only one, depending primarily on where you live. If you live in a small town, or rural location, there probably aren't more than one or two airports close enough to you to consider as places to learn to fly. In that event, you'll learn at the local or closest airport. If you reside in or near a large city, the number of airports and flight schools will probably be larger.

Then comes a question about which the debate has gone on for years and will probably continue ad infinitum. If you have a practical choice of airports from which to fly, are you better off learning at a large or small airport? Each has its pluses and minuses, so let's go through a few.

At some point in your flying career, you'll operate at larger airports that have control towers and more traffic than you see at the local "country" airport. Learning to fly there is akin to learning to drive in the city. If you start out with a control tower, a mix of traffic between very small and larger airplanes, and more traffic, you're not intimidated by those factors later. We've all met the person who learned to drive in the backwoods and 30 years later is still hesitant to drive in city traffic. Learning to fly at a larger airport eliminates fear of the big airport environment. Like every other compromise, there are downsides to learning at the larger airport.

When you rent an airplane, conventionally you are charged by the hour. This time begins when the engine starts, and it ends when the engine is shut down after the flight. At large airports, more time is spent taxiing and waiting on other aircraft to come and go. All the while the rental charge goes on. Depending on exactly how big the big airport is, you could easily spend 10 percent or more of each lesson taxiing or waiting.

Flying into small airports can be as demanding as going into large ones. I've seen many a pilot who learned at a larger airport and is just not competent to safely handle the challenges posed by many small fields. Landing on a short or narrow runway, or operating at a small airport that has only one runway, on a day when the wind is strong and blowing across the runway (what we call a crosswind) can be beyond the comfort zone of a pilot who has done all of her flying at an airport with multiple runways, all of which are thousands of feet longer than she really needs for the airplane at hand.

Learning at a small airport can be less expensive. Generally, the taxi from the flight school's office to the runway is short, and rural airports aren't generally afflicted with heavy traffic, so you spend less time out of each lesson on the ground and more in the air. Many of these fields have only one runway, so you learn how to handle crosswinds from the beginning because you don't have the choice of two or three runways, depending on the direction of the wind. I liken this to learning to drive in a manual transmission car, as opposed to one with an automatic. When my daughter learned to drive, I insisted that she do so in a manual car. There was a little fussing, but a year later, she asked me why anyone wants an automatic, given the fact that the driver has less control over the vehicle. It's all what you're used to.

The negative aspect of training at small fields relates to the person who learned to drive on country roads and now fears the city traffic. You will have to cope with larger airports and heavier traffic someday, or your flying will be handicapped forever. You just have to face the challenge and do it.

In the final analysis, I would prefer, all things being equal, to learn at a small field. It's less costly, which is a meaningful consideration for many people. If you can dial numbers and talk on the phone, you can learn to dial numbers on a radio set and talk to a control tower after you first learn how to basically fly the aircraft. There are other reasons for my feeling, which answer the next question.

# What Kinds of Flight Schools Are There?

Basically, flight schools are of two general types, with lots of permutations. All flight instructors have to be specifically licensed by the Federal Aviation Administration (FAA) as instructors. All airplanes have to be inspected and maintained in accordance with very detailed rules set out in the Federal Aviation Regulations (FARs). But a flight school can apply to the FAA to be specially certified as what we call an approved flight school. To become so approved, the school must have certain classroom space for ground training and submit a very specific curriculum for the course of training that it proposes to offer to its students.

You can learn to fly from a licensed instructor who does not operate within the confines of such an approved school. This doesn't mean that the training will be any the less safe, competent, or complete. It just means that this instructor, and the school which employs him, hasn't bothered to go through the hoops to become an approved school. The instructor has the same license, and the airplane must have the same maintenance at either facility. There are approved schools at large and small airports, and there are flight training operations that have not sought the approval at large and small airports. My experience in flight instruction, which now covers more than 3 decades, has shown me that the instructor is the key to learning to fly, not the school.

We may as well discuss some of the problems that the aviation industry faces right now, while you're considering becoming a part of it. No one ever got rich as a flight instructor. If your school charges you $20 an hour for the instructor's time, she probably gets about $15 of that, and the school keeps the other $5. In most flight training operations, instructors can't expect to give much more than 1000 hours of instruction per year. So, given full employment, it's a $15,000 per year job, usually with no fringe benefits. Not particularly enticing as one's life work. This is an unfortunate set of facts, but true. Hence, most flight instructors are doing this work with an eye to getting out of it as soon as they can and hope to move up to a career as a corporate or airline pilot as soon as they have enough flying time to qualify for what is seen as the next career move.

Don't be surprised if you change instructors once or twice during your training. However, this effect can often be eliminated at a small airport. The aviation industry is populated with companies that we call fixed base operators (FBOs). FBO is the name we attach to the operator at an airport who often sells fuel and maintenance services, has airplanes for rent, and offers flight training. FBOs exist at all airports, large and small. At the big airport, it is common to have more than one FBO, whereas at the rural field, usually one FBO operates the entire airport.

If you do choose a small field from which to fly, you are likely to encounter an instructor who has been there awhile and who perhaps has no intent of moving on. I did most of my training at such a place. The owner of the FBO was the flight instructor and the mechanic, and he owned the operation and the airplanes. Hence, he didn't depend on his flight instruction income as his sole source of support but derived funds from maintenance services, fuel sales, aircraft rental, and miscellaneous sources. If you can find such an operation, seriously consider learning to fly there. You'll have, in all likelihood, an experienced instructor, who isn't going to an airline job next month and who will probably teach you well and wisely. In addition, you might just get the job done a little more cheaply.

Another subject deserves some attention at this point; it relates again to the type of airplane used for training. Almost all of the airplanes built today are equipped with what is known as a tricycle landing gear. This is an arrangement where the airplane has a main wheel on each side and a third wheel under the nose. All of the types of airplanes mentioned so far are tricycles.

There was a time when most airplanes were configured differently. They had a main wheel on each side, like a tricycle, but the third wheel was very small and was located under the tail, at the extreme aft end of the airplane (FIG. 1-1). Years ago, this arrangement was referred to as *conventional* gear. Because they are no longer conventional, we now call them tailwheel airplanes. Most pilots who have been trained since the 1960s will fly their entire careers without even flying a tailwheel airplane, and this is a shame.

Tailwheel and tricycle airplanes fly the same in the air but have drastically different handling characteristics on the ground. The tailwheel takes more attention and is more demanding in take off, landing, and taxiing than the tricycle. A pilot who has learned to fly in a tailwheel airplane has no trouble at all transitioning to a tricycle. But, one trained in a tricycle must undergo some time in a tailwheel airplane before learning to tame its ground handling.

The difference here is very similar to learning to drive in a car with a manual transmission as opposed to an automatic. If you know how to drive a manual, the automatic is duck soup. But, if you've never driven a manual, get some instruction first, before you go lurching down the road, alternately stalling the engine and squealing the tires by yourself. There are some qualities about tailwheel training that would make a pilot better, even in a tricycle. If you find a flight training operation that offers training in a tailwheel airplane (there aren't many that do), go for it. You'll be a better pilot in the long run.

## What If I Get Airsick?

Very few people really get airsick flying small airplanes. When it does happen, it usually afflicts passengers rather than someone who is handling the controls. I sometimes get uncomfortable in the back seat of a car, especially on twisty roads and if I'm trying to read while riding. Yet, I've never been airsick as the pilot of an airplane, even doing aerobatics.

Airsickness might be encountered early in your training, and when it happens, it's most often the product of tension that you feel. For the few who do get sick, it's usually a passing thing that goes away after a few lessons as the person becomes more comfortable and familiar with the airborne environment. If you do get feeling queasy while taking a lesson, tell your instructor immediately and go back to the airport and land. There's no shame in feeling sick, and there's no reason to let an upset stomach degenerate into the ultimate result if you don't do something to remedy the problem.

# How Safe Is Flying?

Flying is as safe as the pilot makes it. To be a safe pilot, you don't need superhuman physical skills or intelligence. During your flight training, you'll constantly be made aware of certain limitations inherent in every airplane, and you'll be taught to gain an understanding of your own limitations. Most accidents in aviation are caused by pilot error, when the pilot tries to exceed either his own limitations or the airplane's.

In my profession, I routinely defend companies and people who find themselves in a lawsuit as the result of an aircraft accident. In over 23 years of doing this, I've gained quite an insight into what causes accidents. The statistics are borne out by the facts—almost all accidents are caused by some failure by the pilot. If you are the kind of person who can accept that you do not know everything, and can't do everything, you'll be a safe pilot. If you think that you can ignore common sense rules, and common sense itself, you ought to find something else to do.

Modern light aircraft are marvels of technology and safe designs. Sure, mechanical failures do happen, but they are very rare compared with human failures on the part of the pilot. I've been flying since 1965 and have yet to bend any metal in an airplane. Learning to fly is a progressive activity; in the days gone by, instructors used to tell students that a pilot's license is a license to go on learning to fly. That's a truism that is still valid. If you view flying as an activity where you have limits, know those limits, and don't exceed them as your knowledge, skill, and experience mount as your flying career expands, you'll be safe. Another old saying is that there are old pilots and bold pilots but no old, bold pilots. Remember the essence of that one, and you'll have a fun and safe experience in aviation.

Although you probably still have some questions about the process of learning to fly, let's get into the rest of the book, and those queries will probably be answered in future chapters.

# 2

# Recreational Pilot Certificate and Glider Pilot Rating

There are several levels of pilot certificates and ratings that you can acquire and advance toward during your flight training. Before we get into a discussion of them, let's get a little jargon out of the way. Pilot licenses and privileges are governed by two basic categorizations. The first is what we call the pilot *certificate,* and the second is known as *ratings.* The easiest way to understand these terms is to view a pilot certificate as allowing the pilot to perform various levels of privileges. Ratings, except for the instrument rating, govern the various categories and classes of aircraft in which the pilot may exercise the privileges of the certificate that she holds.

The most basic and restrictive of the pilot certificates is a *student pilot* license. This is the piece of paper that every pilot must have in order to solo any type of aircraft. It is issued along with what is known as a *medical certificate* after you successfully pass the physical exam the FARs require. We'll talk about medical certificates later. When you visit the doctor who is authorized to issue medical certificates, called an *aviation medical examiner,* or AME for short, if you pass the exam, and almost everyone does, you will be issued a *third-class medical certificate* and student pilot certificate by the doctor.

The student certificate is useless for solo flight until your flight instructor endorses it, by signing in places on the reverse side, which says that the instructor deems you competent to solo, and later, to make solo cross-country flights. You don't need to have a student license to take flight instruction. The minimum age for issuance of a student certificate is 16, unless you want one that qualifies you to solo, once the instructor endorses it, only gliders or balloons. If you want to solo only those two categories of aircraft, you can get a student license at 14 years of age.

After the student level of certification, you can progress to licenses that allow you to carry passengers, then perhaps fly for hire, fly an airliner, or teach others to fly. In ascending order, after the student level, the other licenses that you can gain are *recreational, private, commercial, airline transport pilot,* and *flight instructor.* For each one of them except the recreational license, you can add ratings to the license, which can authorize you to exercise the privileges of that particular certificate in various categories or class of aircraft, such as *gliders, balloons, airships, helicopters, single and multiengine airplanes, seaplanes,* and a new one called *powered lift.* For now, let's limit our discussion to the recreational certificate and the privileges that it entails.

The recreational certificate is the newest of the various levels of pilot certificate and it has been around for only a few years. Aviation has always been a cyclical industry, with its inherent ups and downs, since the end of World War I. When the Great War ended, civilian aviation surged as military aviators came home, and the market was flooded with surplus military airplanes. Unfortunately, the heydays of the 1920s were short lived; the tragedy of the Great Depression put a screeching halt to almost all sectors of the economy, and aviation was no exception. Even though the period of the 1930s saw some dramatic increases in the capability and performance of the infant thing known as the airplane, participation in aviation was only a dream for most people outside of the independently wealthy classes.

Aviation got its next shot in the arm from another war. When World War II began in Europe in the fall of 1939, the United States started, quietly at first, preparing for the inevitable day when we would be dragged into the conflict. Even before Pearl Harbor heralded our official entry into the war, the U.S. government began what was then known as the Civil Pilot Training Program (CPT). The CPT began training thousands of future military and naval pilots for the day when the United States would be at war. During this period, which was a couple of years before the Pearl Harbor attack, the CPT utilized normal civilian airplanes and flight schools to carry out its mission. Airplane factories started humming, and flight training operations saw their first great influx of new students.

What happened to aviation after the United States' entry into the war itself is the stuff of many history books, novels, movies, and TV shows. World War II was the first war in which aviation had a material, if not deciding, influence. Although my Army buddies will always tell you that no war is won until a foot soldier occupies the conquered territory, most aviation-minded historians have championed the airplane as the deciding factor in that world conflict. In 1945, when that war finally ended, there were literally thousands of pilots and airplanes in the United States and about to come out of our armed forces.

Aviation saw a terrific boom, and horrible bust, right after World War II. Mistakenly, most of the airplane manufacturers assumed that the host of trained military pilots would come home, buy airplanes, and go on flying. This apparently did come true for about 18 months after the Axis surrender, but then the joy in our industry promptly turned to tears as the boom ended about as fast as it had begun. Why this was so is beyond our purposes here—just recognize that it happened.

During the 1950s, the lightplane industry churned along, steadily but not mightily. Factories such as Cessna, Piper, Beechcraft, and Mooney continued to build airplanes at a steady pace. New pilots came to FBOs and flight schools. General aviation, as this sector of the industry is known, was alive but not particularly growing. As the 1960s dawned, things got a little better, and general aviation started a slow growth pattern. As we moved into the 1970s, lots was beginning to change.

Flying was not immune to the inflationary pressures that beset the rest of the economy. As airline traffic grew, and corporate flying really got into high gear, more complication and regulation followed. Yet lightplane production was at an all-time high. In 1978, about 19,000 airplanes were built in the factories of the general aviation manufacturers. By the end of the decade, things were slowing slightly.

In the early 1980s, another depression hit general aviation, and it is one from which we have yet to recover fully. We'll probably never see the production figures of the mid-1980s again, but things are starting to improve. A few years ago, both the FAA and the private aviation sector took at hard look at where flying was going and what could perhaps be done to revitalize it. There were as many reasons given for the drastic decline in flying as there were reason givers. Some thought that the product liability and legal problems hampered manufacturers to the point that they couldn't build affordable airplanes any more. Others postulated that the training requirements for new pilots had grown so great that people weren't interested anymore and turned their discretionary spending to luxury cars, boats, exotic vacations, and the like. There was some truth to all of the theories, but none of them could completely explain the problem with aviation.

In an attempt to boost flight training, which in truth is the root of all gains in the general aviation field, a new level of pilot certificate, the recreational license, was created. This new level of certificate was actually an attempt to go back to a level of training, and the flying of simpler airplanes, that had existed in the years after World War II, before jets, hundreds of airports with control towers, faster and more complicated general aviation airplanes, and all of the increased training that a pilot needs to participate in that league of flying. Today, a student pilot can train to the standards of a recreational pilot and either end there or use this license as a stepping stone toward the next higher level, the private pilot certificate. One can get a recreational license cheaper, and in less time, than it takes to fulfill all of the requirements for a private certificate.

The idea behind the recreational pilot license was to allow people to achieve a level of licensure that would satisfy their needs, if they wanted to fly simpler airplanes, in a less complicated environment. Before we go in depth into the training it takes to be a recreational pilot, let's take a look at the privileges that accompany this license.

# Recreational Privileges and Limitations

First, to get a recreational license, the new aviator still goes to a flight training operation and takes flight instruction, the same as he would if his goal were to get a private license immediately. There is no need to get a recreational certificate if you don't want to; you can qualify for a private license as the next step after your student privileges if that is your desire. In August 1997 the FAA rewrote many of the rules governing flight training requirements and the privileges of the various classes of pilot licenses. When the new rules were working their way through the bureaucratic process, there was a proposal included that recreational pilots would not need to take the physical exam that private pilots have to pass. The idea was to allow recreational pilots to self-certify their medical fitness to fly, in the same manner that glider and balloon pilots can do. In the final rule, as published by the FAA, this idea was shot down, and recreational pilots still have to have the same third-class medical certificate that private pilots get.

Because the recreational pilot license was created to allow pilots to fly simpler aircraft in a noncomplex environment, the recreational pilot has more limitations put upon the exercise of that certificate than do private pilots. A recreational pilot can only fly two broad kinds of aircraft—single-engine airplanes and helicopters. He may not qualify to fly, as a recreational pilot, any multiengine airplane, powered lift aircraft, glider, airship, or balloon. The single-engine airplane or helicopter in which the recreational pilot will be certified must be powered with an engine of no more than 180 horsepower, and it can have a maximum of only four seats.

Even though the aircraft can have four seats, the recreational pilot can only carry one passenger at a time. The reason for this limitation is that the training required is less than for a private license, and the recreational pilot may not be as wise about the effects of loading and balancing the load in an airplane as is the private pilot. You will discover during your training that most small airplanes cannot be filled with fuel, have all of their seats filled with adults, and still be within their legal load limits. Every aircraft is a design compromise of some sort or another, and this is one of them. Manufacturers routinely give us the option of filling the fuel tanks and going farther between fuel stops or filling all of the seats and accepting the fact that we can't go as far on a reduced fuel load. During the training for a private license, you'll get taught how to figure how much load your airplane can carry, in terms of both fuel and people. Most importantly, you'll learn what can happen if you exceed these limits.

The recreational pilot gets less of this schooling. So, by limiting that pilot to only carrying one passenger at a time, regardless of the number of seats in the airplane, in most instances, it will be almost impossible for a recreational pilot to overload the airplane. My guess is that most recreational pilots will be flying airplanes that have only two seats anyhow, because these are the airplanes that are more often used for the casual "Sunday afternoon" kind of flying done by recreational pilots. Because of the other limitations upon their licenses, recreational pilots don't gain much from flying four-seat aircraft. There are a few very popular four-seat airplanes that a recreational pilot can fly, such as the Cessna 172 and Piper Warrior; the modern variants of these planes have 160-horsepower engines, which fall below the maximum of 180 horsepower authorized for recreational pilots. Beyond these models, there aren't very many currently manufactured four-seat planes that have engines below 180 horsepower, and no six-seat planes do.

Next, a recreational pilot receives no training in the curriculum for that license in night flying. Hence, the certificate is not valid for flying after sunset or before sunrise. Again, this limitation is not very restrictive from a practical view because recreational-type flying almost always happens during the day. Flying at night is much different from daytime operations, and private pilots who receive the required training have only scratched the surface of the body of knowledge needed to fly safely at night. Lots of recreational pilots fly older, classic airplanes that cannot be flown at night because they lack the electrical systems needed to power the lights that an airplane has to have to be flown in darkness.

One of the most restrictive limitations upon the exercise of recreational pilot privileges involves flying cross-country. This limit actually has two sublimits. First, a recreational pilot may carry a passenger on a flight within 50 nautical miles of the departure airport so long as a flight instructor has given the pilot training in operations at that airport and in the 50 miles around it. The instructor must endorse the pilot's logbook to that effect, and the pilot must carry the logbook during the flight. This limit was in effect before the change on August 4, 1997; every recreational pilot was limited to flying not more than 50 miles from the airport where she received the required training. This limitation was a severe detriment to the motivation that a prospective pilot might have to becoming licensed as a recreational pilot. Fifty miles isn't very far, but the limit exists because the training for a recreational license doesn't include training in all of the aspects of cross-country flying. In fact, to get the recreational license, the student doesn't need any training in cross-country operations. There is no required learning of the effects of changing weather en route, navigation, either by visual or electronic means, or the myriad of other subjects needed to teach a pilot how to fly cross-country.

This 50-mile limit was seen by the FAA as the practical, outside limit in terms of distance whereby one could look out the window, decide that it's an OK day to go flying, and then not go far enough away that the weather was very likely to be different than it was at the point of departure. But the 50-mile limit was so draconian, in a usefulness sense, that very few pilots actually ever got a recreational license.

Now, a recreational pilot can have this 50-mile limit removed by undergoing training from a flight instructor in the various phases and concerns of cross-country flying. In essence, the instructor will teach the recreational pilot the same cross-country skills that a private pilot would have. When that training is complete, the instructor must endorse the recreational pilot's logbook to the effect that she is proficient in cross-country flying, and the logbook must be carried in the aircraft. So, the biggest impediment to using a recreational pilot certificate has been removed by the latest changes to the applicable FARs.

Even after getting the cross-country training that will eliminate the 50-mile limit, recreational pilots aren't allowed to fly into airspace that requires communication with Air Traffic Control (ATC). ATC is the part of the FAA that operates control towers at busy airports and other control services for airplanes flying in poor weather or in the vicinity of big airports. Remember, the basic concept of the recreational level of certification is to allow flying simple airplanes in less-complex airspace. This limit exists because recreational pilots are not trained in the procedures for flying under the control of ATC or at busy airports. A recreational pilot cannot, therefore, fly into airports or in other areas where communication with ATC is required. That's all right, because the kinds of airports where recreational pilots ought to be flying are the simpler airports in rural, or outlying areas, away from big airports, airliners, jets, and other environments in which ATC services are mandated to provide safe separation between aircraft in the system.

Because of certain international agreements, recreational pilots can't fly outside of the United States. Private pilots may fly internationally because their level of training and demonstrated knowledge meets what is called for in the international agreements. This limitation isn't severe for recreational pilots in most parts of the country but could be meaningful to pilots who are based near the borders. Here in Ohio, where I live, many private pilots routinely fly into Canada. Pilots based in Florida often go to the Bahamas, and those in the southwest travel into Mexico with some regularity. If you live in these areas, and want to fly into another country, you can't do it until you progress from recreational pilot to private pilot. But if you live in Iowa or elsewhere far from the borders of another country, this limit won't have any effect on your operations.

There are other miscellaneous restrictions upon recreational pilots that don't apply to private pilots. Recreational pilots can't fly an airplane to demonstrate it to a prospective buyer. They can't fly a passenger as part of a charitable airlift. They're not allowed to fly over a cloud layer where they can't keep constant visual reference to the ground. They may not fly above 10,000 feet above sea level or 2,000 feet above the ground, whichever is higher. In addition, they cannot fly an aircraft that is towing anything, like a glider or a banner. After all of this, you might ask what a recreational pilot can do and why anyone would want a license with so many limitations.

This response is simple. If you want to fly for fun or want to cut the initial costs of your training, the recreational certificate may fill the bill. Even though I'm a qualified commercial pilot, rated to fly both single- and multiengine airplanes, helicopters, and gliders and for airplane instrument flying, as well as being a flight instructor who can teach single- and multiengine airplane training and instrument flight, my guess is that over half of all of the flying that I do could legally be done with only a recreational license. My average trip is a flight from one non-towered airport to another, in the daytime, in a Cessna 172, with only one passenger.

Many pilots want to fly in no more complicated a manner than that. Flying can serve many purposes for different people. A good number, myself included, view general aviation first as a sport and then sometimes struggle to attach a practical application to it. If your desires are met by an afternoon flight around the local area, from and to an airport without a control tower, in a less-expensive airplane, you may not need anything more advanced than a recreational license. Many pilots fly this way throughout their entire flying careers. Maybe this is just the right answer to revitalizing general aviation. Although it's certainly nice to conduct a business trip in a light airplane (another thing a recreational pilot cannot do), that isn't the reason most pilots fly.

Another benefit to getting a recreational license is to limit the cost of flight training. To get this license, you only have to have 30 hours of flight time, and the amount of dual instruction and solo practice is reduced because you don't get formal training in cross-country work, flying into airspace where you have to talk to ATC, or night operations. Therefore, you can get a recreational license and then enjoy far more freedom than a student pilot has. After some additional training, you can go where you want and take someone with you. Maybe you'll stop at this level, which is perfectly OK, or more likely, you'll view the recreational certificate as a breather in your full training and use it as a stepping stone to a private pilot's license later. Either way, getting a recreational license can be beneficial.

## Glider Pilot Rating

Flying gliders is a hoot. Before we talk about it, let's define it. A glider is an aircraft that doesn't have an engine that sustains its flight, even though there are craft known as motor gliders, which have small engines that can launch them and then are usually stowed away in the body of the glider. Also, we're not talking about hang gliders. See FIG. 2-1 for a picture of a popular training glider, the Schweizer 2-33. Gliders are also frequently called sailplanes to emphasize their ability to stay aloft for lengthy periods of time, in the right atmospheric conditions. Given the right mix of rising air, sailplane flights can go on for hours. We have one man in our glider club who has flown four separate flights that went more than 1,000 kilometers. Many of

**2-1** *A Schweizer 2-33, a popular training glider.*

my friends routinely fly cross-country trips of 50 to 100 miles in gliders. There is no real difference between a glider and a sailplane. Because the FARs speak in terms of gliders, we'll use that word to keep things simpler.

A person can qualify for a student pilot certificate, limited to gliders or balloons, at age 14. Therefore, a youngster can learn to fly a glider, and solo it 2 years before soloing an airplane. To get a private license with a glider rating, you have to be only 16. Airplane recreational and private pilots have to be at least 17. There is no recreational license for gliders. The training for a private certificate for gliders is simple enough that the FAA saw no benefit in extending glider privileges to recreational pilots.

I got into glider flying in the summer of 1994. My daughter turned 14 that year, and we joined the local glider club here in central Ohio. Although her interest waned after a few flights, just before she was ready to solo, I got hooked for good. Teenage girls often find something else more exciting to do with their Saturdays than hanging around an airport all day with dad, and mine was no exception. But she still enjoys flying with me in gliders and airplanes, so someday she may pick it back up. Even without her company, most of my Saturdays in the summer are now spent towing and flying gliders.

Glider flying has many advantages. First, it's far less expensive than flying powered airplanes. The fee structure of our club is an example. To join, one pays a one-time fee of $200, and then monthly dues are assessed at the rate of $12. Flying time includes a charge for towing the glider aloft, using a powered tow plane, and a separate charge for use of the glider. We pay $4.25 for each 1,000 feet of altitude to which we're towed, and glider pilots conventionally release from the tow at 2,000 or 3,000 feet above the ground. Most of the time, 2,000 feet is plenty. So that costs $8.50. Use of our training gliders costs $4.00 per flight. Our instructors charge $3 per flight for their services. So, a training flight costs the grand sum of $15.50, and a solo flight runs $12.50. You can't fly anything any less expensively than that. If it's a good day, with the atmosphere full of rising air, what we call *thermals,* you can stay aloft for hours for your $12.50.

Glider flying is extremely safe; that's why the FAA lets 14-year-olds do it solo. Although it's not idiot-proof, and requires competent instruction and pilot judgment, flying a glider is far less complex than flying a powered airplane. When you look at the official FAA accident statistics, glider operations always come out at the very bottom of the numbers of accidents each year, when measured per some number of flying hours.

Another tremendous advantage of flying gliders is that a glider pilot does not need a medical certificate. You can self-certify your own medical status by signing a document that says you don't have any condition of which you're aware that would make you unsafe to fly. The number of accidents caused by pilot physical problems in all forms of flying is extremely low, usually less than 1 percent across the board. That's why the FAA had originally proposed that recreational pilots in airplanes should be allowed to self-certify their medical condition as well. Even though the proposal didn't make it into the final rule in 1997, perhaps it'll be revisited some time soon, so glider pilots don't have to spend a few bucks every other year for a special FAA physical exam, like airplane pilots must do.

# Requirements for a Private Glider License

To fly a glider, you first take instruction from a flight instructor, get ground training in certain areas of aeronautical knowledge, do some solo flying, and then pass a knowledge (written) test and a flight test with an examiner. These are the same basic steps you'd go through for a private license to fly airplanes, but much less is needed at each point along the way.

If you've never flown any aircraft before, glider flying is a great way to begin. All of the cadets at the U.S. Air Force Academy get glider training during their years at the Academy. Many foreign air forces start their pilots first in gliders. By learning to fly in a glider before transitioning to powered airplanes, the new pilot learns to feel the aircraft, manage altitude and energy, and coordinate the controls. Glider pilots gain an understanding of winds, weather, and atmospheric conditions quickly.

To begin learning to fly in gliders, you need to find a glider club or commercial operation that welcomes new students and provides training. If you can't easily find one, contact the Soaring Society of America, P.O. Box 2100, Hobbs, NM 88241 for a list of glider fields in your area.

The progression any student pilot takes in learning to fly, regardless of the category of aircraft, is basically the same. You take dual instruction from a flight instructor until you are ready to solo the aircraft. Then, you fly some solo practice flights, interspersed with more dual instructional lessons. At some point along the way, you take what the FAA now calls a knowledge test, which is what we used to call a written test; it covers such things as aircraft performance, the FARs applicable to the level of pilot certificate that you're seeking, weather, flight planning, aircraft weight and balance, navigation, and similar subjects that you'll learn either in ground school or through private study of the resource materials given you by your instructor.

After you've logged the required number of flights or hours, and gained the proficiency that it takes to pass a flight check with an examiner, you take that flight check. Then, you're a licensed pilot.

To get a private pilot certificate with a glider rating, assuming that you have no previous logged time in powered aircraft, you have to do the following:

- Ten hours of flight training, and 20 training flights, of which 2 of the hours are solo, with at least 10 solo launches and landings

- Three training flights in preparation for the flight test, done within 60 days of taking the flight test

That's it for the regulatory minimum. As a practical requirement, you'll probably fly more flights than the FARs require.

Most folks who have no previous flight time will take anywhere from 30 to 50 dual instructional flights before they are ready for that all important first solo flight. Although this number may sound high, it isn't, because many flights in a glider are quite short compared to dual flights in an airplane. On days when the atmospheric lift conditions aren't good, a typical glider flight, from a tow altitude of 2,000 feet above ground level (AGL) will only last about 15 minutes, including the time spent being towed up to altitude.

As your skill level builds, you'll spend several of those presolo flights releasing from the tow at lower altitudes, usually around 1,000 feet AGL so that you can practice flying the landing approach. Because a glider can't make a go-around under its own power (it has no power), learning to judge the landing approach consumes a larger percentage of the presolo training time than it does for airplane students. These 1,000-foot tows and subsequent approaches and landings often take 10 minutes or less per flight. So even though you might fly 40 flights before you solo, the actual number of flying hours will probably be less than an airplane student spends before soloing.

At most glider fields, students get repeated flights, one after the other, to reduce training time and delays. At our club, students have first priority in the training gliders on Saturday mornings and are allowed three flights in a row or 45 minutes of flying time, whichever comes first. Then, they simply put their name on the waiting list and when their turn comes up again, repeat the process. If the glider operation runs smoothly, as soon as you land, the tow plane pulls into position, the tow rope is hooked up again, and off you go for the next flight. Lots of training can occur in a short period of time.

The goal of glider flying is to stay aloft and soar in thermals or other types of rising air. During your presolo flights, you'll be taught the basic techniques of soaring in thermals, which are bubbles of rising air. But the majority of your training flights will be devoted to learning aircraft control and how to approach the field and land. It's very common in our club to see a student soar for some time during her first solo flight and then return to the field and land.

After you solo for the first few times, your instructor will get back in the glider with you and start honing your skills to pass the flight check. When you've passed the knowledge test, and when your instructor deems you ready to pass the flight check, you'll make an appointment with the FAA examiner and take the check ride. Depending upon atmospheric conditions, and the presence or lack of thermals, your check ride might take more than one short flight.

# Glider Skills

There is more to flying a glider than simply being towed up to an altitude, releasing, flying around until you descend to traffic pattern altitude, and then landing. You need to learn how to handle the controls of the glider and how to deal with a few rare emergency situations. FIGURE 2-2 shows a picture, taken from the cockpit of a glider, of what is looks like to be towed by the tow plane. The correct position of the glider, in reference to the tow plane ahead of it, is important. As the tow plane flies, it produces a wake behind it, which is an invisible torrent of turbulent air, coming from a mixture of the propeller blast and wing tip vortices that are shed by every wing in flight. You don't want to fly in this wake, even though you could, because you'll be bounced around in it. Glider pilots in the United States generally fly the tow position shown in FIG. 2-2,

**2-2** *The view of the tow plane from a glider cockpit.*

which is called *high tow* because the glider is above the tow plane's wake. In some other countries, a tow position below the wake is used, and this is quite naturally called *low tow*.

From the tow position seen in FIG. 2-2, imagine flying in a square around the tow plane's wake, wherein you first descend through and below that wake, then move left to a position off of the tow plane's left wing. Then, you rise back into the high tow position, move laterally to the right, stopping when you're off of the plane's right wing tip. Next, you descend back into the low tow position, and move back over to the left, stopping behind and beneath the tow plane's tail. To finish the maneuver, you climb the glider back into the normal high tow position and go on with your tow to the altitude where you want to release. This training maneuver is called *boxing the wake*. Boxing the wake serves no practical purpose except that it teaches the student glider pilot the art of controlling the glider's position behind the tow plane during the tow. A side benefit of learning to box the wake is that it teaches good control coordination techniques applicable to all flying situations.

When learning to fly airplanes, students learn what to do in the very rare event that the airplane's engine fails. Modern engines can quit, but the event is so rare today that almost all pilots go through their entire aviation careers with never a whimper of discontent from their engines. In glider flying, the equivalent emergency to an engine failure in an airplane is a break of the tow rope. When the tow rope breaks, the glider pilot has to know what to do and to react accordingly, especially if the break occurs at a low altitude.

If a tow rope breaks when the glider is below 200 feet above the ground, the pilot just flies straight ahead or makes gentle turns to find a landing site. Because training gliders land at speeds around 35 mph or sometimes even less, and then roll only about 150 to 200 feet, you can land a glider virtually anywhere. Even training gliders have glide ratios around 25:1, which means that the glider will glide 25 feet forward for every foot of altitude lost. From 200 feet, the glider can go about 5,000 feet forward, which is almost a mile. With slight turns, it's hard not to find the small space needed to land within a mile.

If the rope breaks above 200 feet, the pilot is taught to go back to the runway from which he just departed and land on it. When we practice these rope breaks at 200 feet, it's amazing to see how far the glider glides down the runway, after it has been turned around, before it touches down. Above 200 feet, you're always in a position to get back to the runway if the rope breaks. When we train new tow pilots, one of the main things we teach them is to keep in mind that they are governing where the glider is going while on tow and to fly a tow pattern that always keeps the glider within gliding range of the runway if the rope should break.

Tow ropes are conventionally 200 feet long and can break for any number of reasons. Like most emergencies in aviation, tow rope breaks are almost always the result of human error. The rope can break if the glider pilot sits "on his hands" and allows the glider to get way out of position on the tow, and then jerks it frantically back into position, after a large amount of slack has developed in the rope. Glider pilots are taught how to properly deal with slack in the rope during tow, and done correctly, recovery from a slack tow rope is a no-brainer. Ropes wear out eventually because they are dragged along the ground as the tow plane lands and for a very short while during the takeoff run. Before we start flying each day, the ropes to be used are carefully visually examined along their entire length for any broken strands, knots, or other signs of wear. Examine your rope and deal properly with slack that might develop during the tow, and the problem of a rope break in flight will be purely academic to you.

# Soaring

A glider can stay aloft by using the techniques of soaring. The common way that glider pilots prolong their flights in most parts of the country is by finding thermals and then staying in them, allowing the free energy of the rising air to cause the glider to climb. Gliders can also be flown in the rising air that occurs very close to a mountain ridge because the wind blows against the ridge and is forced upward, over the ridge. This type of rising air is called *ridge lift*. Flying in ridge lift is not for new or inexperienced pilots because you have to fly very close to the face of the ridge to stay in the air that is being forced upward by the wind blowing against the ridge.

Another source of lift is found in a *mountain wave*. In this situation, wind blows against a mountain and goes over the top of it, and downwind of the mountain a cyclical wave develops because the air that was forced over the mountain continues to rise for some distance beyond the mountain and then descends again. The lift in mountain waves can be awesome, and gliders have flown higher than 40,000 feet using mountain wave lift. As the name implies, mountain waves require the presence of mountains for their generation, so in the United States they are generally found in the western states.

For those of us in the flatlands, our only source of lift is from thermal activity. Thermals are formed by the sun's rays heating certain sections of the earth's surface more than other sections nearby. Some terrain features are susceptible to being heated more than neighboring areas. Large parking lots, dark fields, major highway interchanges, and large roofs on big buildings are great producers of thermals. These features rapidly absorb the sun's heat and reflect it back upward. Because hot air is lighter than cooler air, a thermal starts rising from these sorts of generators. Thermals can be strong, weak, large, or small. If it's a hot day in the summer, if you've got a good generator nearby, and if the air is not particularly stable, you can ride a thermal for thousands of feet above the ground. If you've flown in an airplane, especially a lightplane, the turbulent air that you may have experienced was probably caused by the airplane's flying into and out of thermals. To an airplane pilot, this "rough air" can be a curse; to a glider pilot, it's the stuff of which a great flying day is made. Because gliders are light and have huge wings compared to airplanes, they ride thermals much more smoothly than do airplanes. Although a thermal can give a passing airplane a light jolt, the glider pilot generally feels only a "push" upward as the glider enters the rising mass of air.

Learning to dependably find thermals and then maneuver the glider to stay in them takes practice. Although you might accidentally stumble into a good thermal while you're on a presolo training flight, don't be fooled into thinking that it's always that easy. Finding lift is always a challenge, even for the most experienced glider pilot. One day recently, my daughter came up to our glider club for a ride with me. When she arrived, I was taking another person up and the flight lasted 45 minutes. When my daughter's turn came, just a few moments later, I couldn't find a thermal at all, and our flight lasted only the 15 minutes that it took to tow up, release, and glide back down. So goes the ever-elusive thermal.

# Controls on a Glider

Gliders have the same basic flight controls that airplanes have; they are explained in Chap. 5. Obviously, they don't have engines, and so there aren't any engine controls. A glider pilot needs a way to increase the glider's angle and rate of descent to manage the glide path of the aircraft. You'll see later on that an airplane's glide path is often controlled by adding or subtracting power, as needed; a glider does the same thing but must do it differently.

Gliders control their glide paths and the steepness of their descents by using devices called *spoilers* to vary the amount of lift that their wings produce. Spoilers come in a couple of different variants, but the effect is the same. As they are deployed from the wing's surface, they disrupt the flow of air over a portion of the wing, thereby reducing the total lift being generated by the wing. By deploying the spoilers a little or a lot, the glider pilot can greatly alter the rate and angle of descent of the craft. This is what you'll spend a great deal of your presolo training learning to do—flying the landing approach and judging when you need to add or subtract spoiler deployment to get the glider to fly a very precise approach path and land just where you want it to touch down.

Airplane pilots almost always land at an airport. Glider pilots do so less often. When you get proficient in soaring, the next big step in a glider pilot's development is to fly farther away from the airport and eventually get beyond pure gliding range of it. When you're out there, you've got to either find lift to stay up as you work your way back home or accept a landing away from the airport. These landings are called *landing out* in glider jargon. Although landing out is not the goal, it can be the outcome of a flight beyond the airport's comfort zone. Because gliders land at such slow speeds, landing out is not feared. The result is that you have to find a phone, take the wings off of the glider (they are designed to come off), and get your buddies to come after you with truck and trailer to haul you home. You might owe a farmer $100 or so for a few bushels of beans or wheat damaged by your landing out, but that's generally the extent of it. Out landings make great conversational items, over an adult beverage, at the end of a day of glider flying.

# 3

# Instructors and Flight Schools

Once someone has developed the urge to become a pilot, many questions come to mind. Typical among them are: What's this all going to cost, now and after I learn? How tough is the physical exam? Can I try a few lessons to see if I really like flying, or do I have to sign up for an entire course? How do I get a good instructor and flight school? What if I don't get along with the instructor?

Most pilots hear these kinds of questions from their acquaintances who don't fly. Unfortunately, most pilots don't really have the information to accurately field these queries because their direct knowledge is limited to their own experiences when they were student pilots. Their training regimen might have been good, bad, or indifferent, or it has become outdated with the passage of time. Although they might tell you at great length how they did it, that might not be the right approach for you. It's unlikely that the average pilot has kept abreast of the changes in flight training over the years since he was trained, and more often than not, some friend who is already a pilot will not have a current and comprehensive view of the entire flight training scene and the options available.

You have far more choices than might be apparent at first. Which one is best for you depends on many factors, including your age, goals, and the amounts of time, money, effort, and dedication that you are willing to invest in learning to fly.

# The Physical Exam

Before we get into our discussion of instructors and flight schools, let's talk a bit about the physical exam that student pilots must pass before they can solo. There are very few people who cannot qualify, physically, to become a private pilot. The FAA has three classes of *medical certificates,* which are the piece of paper that you are issued by the examining doctor when you pass the exam. A first-class certificate is required for airline pilots. Commercial pilots, such as your flight instructor, have to maintain a second-class certificate. Private, recreational, and student pilots have to have a third-class medical certificate. You don't need the certificate, which is also your student pilot's license, until you are ready to solo.

If you're in good health and don't have a history of heart disease, diabetes, or similar serious physical problems, you'll very probably pass the exam with flying colors. If you are a normally healthy person, there is no real hurry to get the exam, but you don't want to wait too long and have the lack of a medical certificate hold up your first solo flight (anyone, at any age and in any condition, can legally take flight instruction, but you have to have a third-class medical certificate and the student pilot license to solo a powered aircraft).

In Chap. 2 we talked some about flying gliders. To fly them, you don't need any medical certificate at all; you simply sign a statement when you apply for your student license saying that you have no physical condition that would prevent you from safely piloting a glider.

Not every doctor can administer the FAA physical exam. You need to go to a physician who has been designated by the FAA as an *aviation medical examiner* (AME). To find an AME, either ask your flight instructor for a recommendation, or call your local FAA office for a list of AMEs in your area. An AME has been to specific training courses put on by the FAA to earn her designation and is familiar with the regulations that cover medical standards for pilots. For a third-class medical certificate, which is what you'll get as a student and then as a recreational or private pilot, the exam is not nearly as thorough or comprehensive as you would receive from your own family doctor. The FAA is really only interested in making sure that you don't have a condition or disease that would prevent you from safely flying or might suddenly incapacitate you in the cockpit.

Eyesight standards are almost never a problem. For a third-class certificate, you have to have visual acuity of at least 20/30, with glasses or contact lenses. Even if you are blind in one eye, you can still qualify through a waiver process. One problem that does present itself sometimes, especially in men, is color-deficient vision. Most AMEs administer the color test using the little book with pages of pastel colors from which a person with normal color vision can pick out triangles, circles, or squares from the maze of dots. If you do have a color deficiency, you can take a test in which you are asked to look at a signal light from the control tower at an airport, and if you can distinguish bright red, green, and white, you'll pass. When the training requirements for a private pilot's license were changed in 1997, the FAA added certain night training regimens that didn't exist before. There is some question now about whether a person who is totally color-blind can get a medical certificate. The reason for needing some color vision is that various aircraft lights and airport lighting systems use different colors to signify which part of an airplane you're seeing at night and whether you're on a taxiway or runway at night. In the past, pilots who had no color vision could be certified, but only for daytime flying. This anomaly in the new regulations will probably be clarified soon.

You must be able to hear normal conversational-level voices, and deaf people can get a waiver. If you've ever had a heart attack, or cardiac disease, it is possible to get certified but only after some in-depth testing and review of all of your medical records by the FAA Aeromedical Office in Oklahoma City.

Diabetics were forbidden to fly, if they are insulin dependent, until 1997. Now, depending upon certain glucose-level testing before takeoff and while airborne, they can get a medical certificate. Alcoholics who have been alcohol-free for 2 years or more can qualify but only after a special review of their history and treatment by the FAA. The same goes for those people who have had a drug-dependency problem in the past.

If you've ever had a psychiatric or neurological problem, you may well be certifiable, depending on the nature of the problem, its severity, and the length of time since you suffered it.

Persons with high blood pressure can normally also obtain a medical certificate. There used to be distinct standards in the regulations that stated certain levels of systolic and diastolic readings as maximums. Now, your blood pressure is evaluated subjectively by the AME, but most people in aerospace medicine feel that a reading above 145/95 is cause for deeper investigation. If you have previously been diagnosed with high blood pressure, and are under treatment by your regular doctor, you probably have little to fear. The FAA may ask you to take some cardiac testing, and if you're cardiac system is OK, you'll have no problem. The FAA-approved list of medications for high blood pressure is quite extensive. If you are on medication, call an AME to see if your particular drug(s) is on the approved list. If not, ask your treating doctor if your medication can be changed to a drug on the list.

Other than those rare situations, you should have no problem with the physical exam.

# Flight Training Options

We touched on briefly, in Chap. 1, some of the options that are available to a person who wants to learn to fly. Let's expand on those thoughts here. At many smaller airports, usually away from major metropolitan airports, you will learn to fly in much the same manner as has been done since World War II. You just walk into the airport office and tell the operator that you want to start taking flying lessons. In this scenario, most students pay for each lesson as it is given and arrange an appointment for the next one immediately after the one they have just taken or phone later to schedule one as their time, money, and inclination permit. There is continuing debate among aviation professionals about whether this is the best way to learn to fly today. Some of us feel that modern training methods are lacking in this less formal training environment, whereas others opine that the old way has advantages not present at major airports.

At the smaller, rural airports, not much has changed since the 1960s, and the way flight training happened at the little gravel and sod runway where I learned, except for the price and a few changes in the curriculum to reflect various additions to the regulatory requirements. I am one of those instructors who see merit in the old approach and in learning to fly in less-complicated surroundings, as long as the instructor doesn't show a disdain for the newer requirements. This isn't the only good way, and people who live in major metropolitan areas needn't fear flight instruction at larger airports.

One of the primary benefits to beginning your flying at a smaller airport is cost. In Chap. 1, we talked about why those savings exist. Smaller airport operators usually don't have the overhead of the ones at the big, airline-served airports, and their prices for everything they offer reflect it. You don't spend the time taxiing and waiting for other airplanes at a small airport, and because flight instruction and airplane rental are universally priced by the hour that the airplane's engine is running, the savings are obvious.

If you do learn in the simpler environment, you've got to be careful that you don't develop a reluctance to fly into major airports. The training requirements today demand that you fly into an airport that has an operating control tower a few times before you get your license. But these few trips won't assure that you'll be comfortable flying into a place with airline traffic, corporate jets, and other airplanes all sharing the same airspace. Your instructor should expose you to high-density traffic areas if at all possible during your student pilot days. If you do become hesitant to go into large airports, you'll never get the full utilization of an airplane or enjoy all of the transportational value provided by general aviation.

# FBO Flight Schools

*Fixed base operators* (FBOs) at large airports also offer flight training and frequently provide a private pilot course as a complete package: flight training, ground school, and supplies all for a set price. These set prices do, of course, have a maximum in the number of flying hours you get for your money, with hours above the maximum charged at the normal price for those who don't choose the package option. Some of these schools have time payment plans to allow a student to pay for a course in installments over the period of time estimated to complete the course.

Many FBOs have what are officially known as *FAA-approved* flight schools. This means that they have sought and obtained a certificate from the FAA, under a part of the Federal Aviation Regulations known as Part 141, for their facilities and curriculum. This type of approval is required to teach certain programs, such as college ROTC flight training. Many foreign nationals come to the United States to learn to fly. Once you're in aviation, you'll realize that we in the United States and Canada fly far less expensively than do people almost anywhere else on earth. Foreign students can come here and get pilot's licenses at far less cost than they can in their home countries. Many of these students are training to become professional pilots in their native countries and get all of their training, up through the Airline Transport Pilot certificate here, saving tens of thousands of dollars over what the cost would be at home. To qualify to teach foreign students, the foreign airline or country sponsoring them almost always requires that the flight school be FAA-approved.

FAA approval doesn't mean that that school will necessarily teach you better than a nonapproved operation. To get Part 141 approval, a school must have certain physical facilities, classrooms, and equipment that are not really needed in an informal setting. In both situations, the instructors have to have the same licenses, the airplanes have to be maintained to the same requirements, and the students have to pass the same tests to get a license. Seeking FAA approval can be very expensive for the smaller operation. Flight instruction can be excellent or terrible at either type of school.

Flight instruction is seldom an FBO's sole source of revenue, regardless of whether it is at a large or small airport. FBOs sell fuel, maintain and sell airplanes, often fly charter flights, provide hangar space for airplanes based at their airports, and have a myriad of other income-producing activities. Some of the smaller operators might not employ instructors directly but put their students in contact with freelance flight instructors, who give instruction part-time, on an as-needed basis, and the FBO may just rent the airplane to the student.

When you first go to the airport and inquire about flying lessons, don't be disappointed if you don't get a hard sell and red carpet treatment. Sometimes newcomers to general aviation get the feeling that the operator thinks he is doing the potential student a favor by talking to her. Don't get discouraged or angry; aviators still often think of themselves as belonging to an exclusive club to which admission must be earned. This archaic philosophy is changing but not nearly fast enough.

# Flight Academies

In the last couple of decades we have seen the advent of training operations that devote themselves exclusively to flight training. They are not traditional FBOs because they offer almost none of the other services traditionally available from an FBO. Some of these large schools are even owned or controlled by airlines and exist to offer *ab initio* (literally, "from the beginning") training to students who dream of someday being a captain on a Boeing 747. Most of these aviation academies are located in the south and southwestern parts of the country, where the weather is more dependable for daily flight operations.

They do offer a good alternative for the person who can get totally immersed in flying because they usually operate in a very formal, full-time setting. For the average adult, who has a job, maybe children, and day-to-day living to contend with, this type of training is probably not feasible. If it is, you can get excellent schooling at these facilities in a really professional environment. Most of the training academies advertise heavily in aviation magazines, so finding one should not be a problem.

# Flying Clubs, Colleges, and the Military

In addition to FBOs at large and small airports, the are several other routes you can take to obtain a pilot's license, and some of them are feasible for most average people. Civilian flying clubs exist almost everywhere. There are three distinctly different setups that call themselves clubs. First, many FBOs rent their airplanes at a discounted rate to customers who pay a nominal initiation fee to join what they call a club. Really, this is no more than a way to offer a discount to regular customers who fly often at the FBO.

Second, there are clubs that are organized by an individual, or small group, who then either owns the airplanes and leases them to the club or leases the aircraft from third parties. Often, these clubs exist as a source of income for the person, or group, who owns the airplanes. Many times, the person who is the power behind the club will be a flight instructor who also gives instruction to club members. This type of operation isn't bad, but there are a few things to watch for.

These clubs usually maintain their airplanes to the standards used by a first-class FBO, but although they are mechanically safe, their cosmetics may leave something to be desired. Rental and club airplanes take a beating in everyday use, and seat covers, interior side panels, carpeting, and general appearance can suffer.

Although it's beyond the scope of this book to delve much into the subject of aviation insurance, once you get into flying, you'll need to be aware of what insurance coverage is in place on the airplanes you rent. Again, sometimes these types of clubs skimp on insurance coverage to keep costs down. Find out what program a prospective club has before you fly.

The third type of club is a true club, usually a nonprofit corporation that owns the airplanes, and members of the club therefore have at least a beneficial interest in them. Most of these "equity" clubs, as they are generally called, require a new member to pay an up-front fee that could represent the value of the member's beneficial interest in the fleet of airplanes.

Sometimes this fee is refundable when a member leaves the club, and sometimes it is not. There are basically two benefits of these true clubs.

Because the club is not profit motivated, the hourly charges to fly the airplanes are usually less than at an FBO. Second, because the members are owners of the fleet, they usually take better care of the equipment and fly the airplanes with more respect than most people treat something that they're only renting. Clubs of this type are very popular in larger metropolitan areas and offer some other advantages as well. The hourly cost of flying an airplane includes certain fixed charges, such as insurance, hangar rent, and organizational costs; therefore the more hours per year that an airplane flies, the lower the cost per hour for those items. So, in an active club, costs of flying can reach very reasonable levels.

Many of these types of clubs have a social underpinning. One of the problems with aviation is that often the family of the inspiring aviator doesn't share the same level of dedication to flying. A club with an active social calendar of fly-ins, picnics, dinners, holiday gatherings, and the like can involve the pilot's family into her sport, making it enjoyable for all. Most larger clubs have flight instructor members who can care for the training needs of the members.

If you're interested in a club of this type, look for one that has a variety of airplanes. Although you'll probably take your lessons in a two-seat trainer, that type of airplane probably won't be too attractive to you once you have a license and want to start traveling and carrying passengers. A club with aircraft of differing performance and size can meet your needs for years, perhaps for as long as you fly.

If you are still in high school, or haven't gone to college and have the desire to do so, there are many major universities that offer degree programs in aviation. Some of these are two-year institutions, but the majority are four-year degree-granting colleges. Degrees in aviation are generally of two types. One stresses the business side of aviation, and the other is more focused on flight operations, preparing the student for a career as a professional pilot.

Most major universities across the country, especially publicly funded schools such as University of North Dakota, Ohio State University, Purdue University, Auburn University, Ohio University, and University of Illinois, have excellent aviation departments and programs.

Last, those young people fortunate enough to meet the high standards of the U.S. armed forces flight training programs should consider themselves blessed indeed. There is no better flight training available anywhere than in military aviation. The requirements are tough—a four-year degree, often in the hard sciences or engineering, rigorous physical standards, and the ability to devote years of service are only the beginning. But the benefits are immeasurable. Military aviators fly the most fantastic aircraft available anywhere and are constantly on the cutting edge of developments in aviation. After one's service is completed, a military background has historically been the surest way into the cockpit of an airliner.

# Buying Your Own Airplane

There are many good books and other publications devoted to the subject of aircraft ownership, and no effort will be made here to duplicate their depth of coverage. Buying your own airplane can be a way to reduce the costs of flight training, if it's done right.

When I learned to fly in 1965, I took my first lessons and soloed in an Aeronca Champ, which was a standard trainer of the day. After I had about 20 hours of flight time, even the 18-year-old kid figured that paying the FBO to rent the airplane wasn't a very wise deal because I knew I wanted to fly for the rest of my life. So, I bought a little Taylorcraft BC-12D, which was a two-seat airplane of similar vintage to the Champ I had been renting. I flew that Taylorcraft everywhere, building my flying time on cross-country flights from Ohio to Florida, out west, and everywhere else it would take me. I only kept it about a year, but in that year, I had accumulated enough time to qualify for my commercial license.

Today, simple training airplanes like a Cessna 150 or Piper Tomahawk can be purchased for far less than most pilots spend for a car. As long as you don't get a dog, you can learn to fly in it, then build some time, and sell it, all the while flying for as little cost as possible. Used airplanes have been going up in value dramatically. My Taylorcraft, worth about $1200 in 1965, goes for at least 10 times that figure in 1998. A Cessna 170B that I bought in 1980 for about $12,000 is now worth in the range of $35,000. Examples could go on for pages. If you fly a lot, like you will do in the process of getting a license, and buy a trainer-type airplane with the advance notion that it will be sold as soon as your training is over, or a short time thereafter, flying it for around 100 hours may be the least expensive way to learn to fly. Like any other mechanical contraption, you can get stung if you charge into airplane ownership without doing your homework first and getting a thorough prepurchase inspection and advice first from a mechanic you trust. Some airplanes become holes in the sky into which the owner constantly pours money, and others reward their owners with years of economical flying. If you can afford $20,000, or maybe a little less in 1998 figures, and tread carefully, buying an airplane after your first few hours of instruction can be a great experience.

# Ground Study Options

The FAA requires that a candidate for a private pilot certificate, as well as all of the other pilot certificate levels beyond student pilot, complete two test regimens. The first is a knowledge test, which used to be called a written test. After you pass the knowledge test, and when your flight instructor thinks you are ready, you have to pass a practical test, which is a flight test, in an airplane, administered by an FAA inspector or, more commonly, by an FAA-designated examiner. The knowledge test is administered electronically, with the student sitting at a computer, reading the screen, and selecting what he thinks is the correct answer to each question from multiple choice potential answers. This test used to be given from a test booklet, with the student answering on a separate answer sheet, which was then transmitted to FAA headquarters for machine grading. Younger people take to the computer test very easily because their generation is computer literate in the first place. But even for us "old codgers," the computer format is very easy to use and not confusing at all. The beauty of the computer test is that you now get your grade instantly upon finishing the test rather than waiting a couple of weeks for a letter from the FAA, giving you your grade.

Considerable study is required to learn what you need to know to pass the knowledge test. There are several ways to study and learn the material. If you attend an FAA-approved (Part 141) flight school and participate in their approved curriculum, a ground school will be a part of it. Most of these ground schools are set up to meet for 10 or more sessions of 2 or 3 hours each. The FBOs that offer them usually schedule the classes to meet in the evenings to better fit into the leisure time of working people.

Even if you don't attend an approved school, most FBOs that offer flight training also offer some kind of similarly structured ground school. There is nothing magic about FAA approval for a ground school that would prevent a training facility that has not gone through that time-consuming and expensive approval process from giving the same ground school to its students. If your school doesn't have a ground training program, with formal classes, you could investigate other FBOs in your area to see if you could get the training there. Naturally, if you attend one of the highly structured flight academies, expect classroom study there to be very much like a high school or college class would be.

The scope of knowledge that you have to garner in order to pass the knowledge test is more thoroughly covered in Chap. 10. Basically, it covers such subjects as a working knowledge of the FARs as they apply to private pilots, weather, navigation, theory of flight, flight planning, and other academic subjects. Some people do much better learning such things in a more formal environment, where they have to prepare for a class and study for a couple of practice tests or quizzes along the way. If you're such a person, get into a ground school training program. You cannot take the practical flight test until you pass the knowledge test; therefore don't delay this step. Also, the knowledge that you gain in ground school will assist your flight training in the airplane as it progresses.

There is certainly no requirement that you go to a formal ground school. A flight instructor, or FAA-licensed ground instructor, must give you a written endorsement to the effect that she thinks you know enough to pass before you can even take the knowledge test. But, as the old saying goes, "There is more than one way to do it."

Many companies sell very good video tape courses that you can put in your VCR and play at home. Many hours are usually needed to watch the entire series of private pilot tapes. This approach has both a good and bad side to it. If you are a disciplined individual, who can set aside the time to truly study these tapes as you watch them, this option can work well. Be careful if you choose this method to make sure that you have current material. Knowledge tests change frequently because the FAA wants to preserve their security; if you buy someone else's second-hand tapes, you may not get the up-to-date information that you need.

The bad side to home study of video tapes, and the same can be said of studying the books on the market that are designed to prepare you for the knowledge test, is that you must be disciplined enough to watch them and keep progressing. If you use them as a sedative to put you to sleep, you'll never learn enough to pass the test. If you can set aside some real time, before late in the evening, to squirrel yourself away and truly study, home learning can be very effective.

It would be possible to only purchase the needed pilot supplies, like a copy of the FARs, a private pilot text book, and an aeronautical chart, and saddle up with your flight instructor for one-on-one tutoring. This option is the least attractive for a couple of reasons. First, the two persons' schedules must coincide in time and place. Then, you'll be paying the instructor for her time, and the number of hours for this approach to be successful can get very large very quickly.

There are a few companies that offer 2- or 3-day cram courses. These are usually held at a hotel someplace, and the idea behind them is to get you away from distractions and totally immersed in the material. You go at it for 8 to 10 hours a day and then take the knowledge test right there, before you go home, while everything is still very fresh. Years ago, this was probably one of the more popular options for ground study, and it can still work for the right person. If you're a busy professional or business person who has little free time, either at home or elsewhere, to enroll in a multiweek ground school or to effectively study at home, this may be the route for you to take. The more you know before you go to the cram course, the more effective it will be. If you do choose this method, still try to read one or more of the textbooks on the market or watch the video tapes before you hole up in the 2- or 3-day course.

The downside to these cram courses applies to similar ways of learning anything else. By their very nature, these course are geared to preparing you to pass the knowledge test, and oftentimes they don't have the time to get into various subjects as deeply as would be beneficial. That's why it's wise to read the textbooks or watch the videos first. Learn the material, and use the cram course for what it does best, which is put it all together so that you can ace the knowledge test.

When I was gaining my certificates and ratings at a rapid pace in the 1960s, I did all of my ground study without ever attending any ground school or cram course. But, I had several things working in my favor. I was 18 or 19 years old at the time, in college, and very used to studying, because I had done little else for over 12 years. Picking up the aviation textbooks was a refreshing interlude to reading college textbooks. Also, other than the typical part-time jobs that any college kid has, I had few other demands on my time. But now, if I were learning to fly, with a career and family, I doubt that I could do it all that way again. I cannot count the people I've known who have dropped out of flying because they never passed the knowledge test. That doesn't say that the test is difficult, which it's not. If you are a high school graduate who can do basic arithmetic, you've got nothing to fear in the knowledge test for a private pilot's certificate. You've just got to, in some way or another, dedicate the time it takes to learn the subjects.

The most basic key to aviation safety is a dedication to constantly improving your training and knowledge for as long as you fly. Once you get your private license, your learning isn't over. As was said earlier, many instructors make the point that a private license is nothing more than a license to learn to fly. While that is an oversimplification, its fundamentals are true. If you stop learning at any point, you'll become complacent and very soon, unsafe.

# Costs

In Chap. 1 we touched upon the costs of learning to fly. Flight training has two distinct components—one is the physical and mechanical handling of the airplane, and the other is the academic study we just talked about. For both of these components, one thing is certain. If you can start flying, and keep at it regularly, your learning will proceed much faster than if you drag it out.

In my 30+ years as a flight instructor, I've seen people who learned to fly and got their licenses in a matter of months, and those who took years. There is no question that you'll spend far less total money if you can keep at it. This isn't meant to discourage the person who can't fly several times a week, or even several times a month, for whatever reason, financial or something else. The person who does waste money is the one who flies a lesson or two, then doesn't come back to the airport for a month or two. With that kind of schedule, that student may never get a license.

If you can keep flying fairly regularly, at least two or three times a month, you should be able to get a license in about 60 hours of flight time, and the total cost ought to run somewhere between $3,500 and $4,000. Although that's not chicken feed in anyone's language, it can be affordable for a great number of folks. I suggest that you arrange your finances, if you can, to have a similar sum available over 6 months or so, so you can keep flying, learn in the fewest hours, and thereby keep your total cost to a minimum.

Another way to keep training costs down is to time your flying lessons in the right seasons of the year. Here in Ohio, the weather is fairly dependable from April or May through October or maybe even through November. Coincidentally, those are also the months of daylight savings time, when there is more opportunity to fly after most people's workday ends. If you begin your flight training in the spring, and couple that planning with adequate financial reserves to keep going, you should be able to get a private pilot certificate that summer or by early fall.

If you begin in the fall and don't live in the South or Southwest, you may have several days of lousy weather between lessons, and you won't be able to fly in the evening over the winter. If your schedule limits you to weekends, you might go 2 or 3 weeks between training flights. Although flying less often is certainly better than not flying at all, your total training time, in terms of hours aloft, will probably get stretched out some. In the midwest, it also tends to be windier more often in the winter, and windy days dampen flight training activity.

If you learn to fly at a smaller or rural airport, you will probably cut your costs over what they are at a large metropolitan airport. Overhead is everything in an FBO's costs, and just like other businesses, overhead is less in the country than it is in major cities. Another benefit with the smaller airport is that you may get to take some, if not all, of your training in a tailwheel airplane.

There was a time when tailwheel airplanes were the norm and were called conventional gear. Because they are far from conventional today, that moniker has fallen into disuse. Most tailwheel trainers are of the older, classic genre, like the Aeronca Champ in which I first learned. There aren't many of them around anymore being used as trainers because they have become fast-appreciating classics and are generally now in the hands of pilots who dote on them. When you find a training operation that still uses one or more of them, those airplanes generally rent for less than a newer trainer. If you can learn, at least through your first solo flight, in a tailwheel airplane, do it.

Although they can be a little more difficult to initially learn to handle on the ground, you'll be a far better pilot for the experience. The skills that you learn in a tailwheel airplane transfer easily to tricycle landing gears and will always enhance your ability to fly whatever aerial steed you use in the future.

# Instructors

Flying and teaching are two different things. A good pilot is not always a good teacher. Almost all certificated flight instructors are good pilots—all of the training and testing required to advance to that level and obtain a flight instructor's certificate make it difficult for a bad pilot to get that far through the system. But not all pilots with a flight instructor's certificate are necessarily good teachers. Flight instructors have to pass a knowledge test on the fundamentals of instruction, but the FAA can't really test anyone adequately for good communication and teaching ability.

A good flight instructor is somebody well worth searching for. He or she will be a knowledgeable, patient, and dedicated individual and will also be an experienced pilot. One of the most unfortunate aspects of the aviation industry is the fact that flight instruction is the primary method used by most aspiring career pilots, who haven't flown in the military, to build the flight time necessary to qualify for airline and corporate flying jobs. All too many flight instructors can't wait to quit instructing and get on to what they think are greater things. If you identify an instructor that your flight school has assigned to you as one of that kind, avoid him if at all possible.

Age and flying hours are not the primary indicators of a good instructor. I have flown with both young and old people who were good pilots or bad ones, great instructors or lousy ones. Aviation has always been a developing field of endeavor, and its newest changes in the rules, navigation systems, and such haven't slowed that pace nor are they likely to in the near future. Therefore, the young instructor will often be on top of things, and up to date more so than a graybeard will. Young people are just as good as teachers as older pilots, so don't be turned off by a young instructor just because she hasn't got any gray hair yet. Look first for personality, patience, perseverance, and communications skills, then age and experience.

Many pilots drop out of flying, some before they get a license, some after. Although it's hard to pinpoint all of the reasons for dropping out, I suspect that poor-quality instruction and rapid instructor turnover are two of the major reasons. Another reason, as mentioned before, to consider the smaller airport for your training is that the "one-person show," where the FBO is operated by one or a small number of people, may have a career instructor who is not aiming for an airline or corporate job at the first opportunity.

If you don't get first-rate instruction from the beginning, you might never gain the confidence to feel in total control of the airplanes at all times. Your time as a pilot could be plagued with a fear of situations in which you might find yourself in the future. It doesn't take a superhuman to fly an airplane and do it well and confidently. Flying is a skill that has to be learned, and to learn well you have to be taught well.

Some of the things that you have to do in pilot training can cause anxiety the first few times that they are performed. One example is *stalls*. When an airplane stalls, it is put in a condition in which the wings lose their ability to continue to generate enough lift to overcome the forces acting against lift, which is explained in detail in Chap. 5. Stalling an airplane has nothing to do with whether the engine is running, or at what power setting, because you can stall the wings at any power level. A stall is a normal training maneuver, is not dangerous, and occurs at the end of every flight in a lightplane when the airplane is properly landed on the runway. But some pilots go through their entire flying lives in fear of doing stalls because they never were taught how easy stalls are, and they never realized the increased confidence a pilot has when stalls are mastered.

The other extreme can also be an indication of an instructor to avoid. Your flying lessons are not the opportunity for your instructor to demonstrate that he is the greatest pilot since Chuck Yeager or that he ought to be on the air show performer circuit. If he does anything that makes you truly uncomfortable, or puts you in fear, he is not doing his job. Have a chat with the chief flight instructor at your school and switch instructors. If this person is the only instructor available, perhaps it's time to change schools.

Some instructors teach private pilot candidates certain maneuvers beyond those that are the minimum required to pass the flight test and become a private pilot. I am one of those instructors. Years ago, in the 1960s, one of my students returned from a solo practice flight with his face as white as a sheet. After I got him calmed down a bit, and he started to talk, we discovered that he had accidentally gotten himself into a spin while practicing stalls. Although a spin results from either intentional actions or gross mishandling of the controls, all he knew at the time was that he was terrified. He recovered only because he was so scared that he actually released the controls.

What he didn't know was that the training airplane in which he was flying, a Cessna 150, was designed to recover from spins by itself when the control pressures causing the spin were removed. He did the right thing without even realizing it. From that day on, every student I taught received a thorough discussion about spins, how they develop, how they are avoided, and how to recover from a spin. Then, if the student was willing, and most were, we did a spin entry and recovery together, to show how benign a spin is and how easy it is to get out of one once a pilot is armed with a little knowledge and experience. Some instructors don't believe in actually spinning a student and prefer to concentrate on teaching spin avoidance. This debate has been ongoing in the flight training profession ever since spin training was removed from the required curriculum by the FAA in the early 1950s. There's no right answer, just a difference of opinion among well-intentioned pros. I believe in spin training, just as I think you can never know too much about any other aspect of flying an airplane.

## Judging Your Instructor

How can you fairly judge the quality of your flight instructor when you don't really know much about flying yet, while recognizing that equally competent instructors differ in their perceptions of their obligations? Realizing that your attitude toward learning is an equally important factor, here are some indicators of a good flight instructor:

- It's not how much your instructor talks, but what he says that counts. Good teachers have a knack for dispensing with the superfluous and presenting a concept in the simplest and fewest words.

- Your instructor will be keenly alert to your degree of understanding. If you do not thoroughly understand what she tells you, she will sense that and rephrase it as many times as necessary. She knows that a statement that is perfectly lucid to one person can be confusing to another. We all have preconceived beliefs that tend to hinder our grasp of certain new subjects.

**3-1** *If your flight instructor is too busy to conduct thorough preflight and postflight discussions, find one who has more time. These sessions are important.*

- He will not overwhelm you with too many unfamiliar tasks or new concepts at one time.

- A good flight instructor will always explain, before each lesson, exactly what she wants you to do and how to do it. She will talk no more than is necessary during the flight because the cockpit of an airplane is actually a poor classroom. She will discuss the flight with you after landing. Most of what she tells you will be contained in these very important preflight and postflight discussions (FIG. 3-1).

- A good instructor has a well-planned, proven syllabus and uses it.

- A good instructor never pressures a student pilot but relieves as much pressure as possible. He never hurries, shouts, or displays impatience. When a student repeatedly makes the same mistake, the good instructor concludes that the fault lies with the teaching.

- She knows that humor can be a pressure relief valve. That doesn't mean horseplay or a cavalier attitude toward her obligations. A good teacher has the proclivity to laugh, rather than curse, at minor frustrations.

- He is dependable. If your lesson is at 9 a.m., he will be ready at 9 a.m., and he will expect you to be 15 minutes early.

# Mutual Respect

Your relationship with your flight instructor must be rooted in mutual respect. In many ways, the importance of the relationship should be equal to that you have with your doctor or lawyer. Lack of respect from either of you toward the other is a signal to find another instructor.

You don't have to love the instructor. A good one is going to make you as good a pilot as you can be, which means that as much will be demanded from you as you can deliver. Don't regard your instructor as an ogre for demanding that you deliver, because the day will soon arrive when you'll be in this airplane by yourself, and that helping hand of the instructor will only be there vicariously, through what you have learned. You will do yourself an extreme disservice by looking for an instructor who will demand less of you than your best.

Actually, humans aren't really taught; they learn. Your instructor cannot place a funnel in your ear and pour knowledge and skill into your head. The most she can do is demonstrate, explain, and establish attainable goals. The rest is up to you.

# The Time Problem

You won't be in the aviation community for very long before you hear other pilots lamenting that "back in the good old days" (which probably never were), aviation was a much more vibrant industry than it is today. There is some truth to that feeling, because flying activity has dropped substantially since the heyday of the 1970s. In 1978, the combined output of all of the aircraft manufacturers who made light aircraft was about 19,000 units. In 1997, probably about 1,000 light airplanes were built.

There are as many explanations for this decline as there are pundits. Some feel that flying has gotten too expensive. I don't agree with that analysis. When I learned to fly in the summer of 1965, as a freshly minted high school graduate, I earned $1.55 per hour at a local supermarket, pushing grocery carts out the door to cars in the parking lot. Dual instruction, both airplane and instructor, cost $14 per hour for the Champ in which I took my lessons. The multiple of my hourly wage that it took to buy an hour of dual was about 9. In 1998, in our part of the country, teenagers earn around $7 to $7.50 per hour for similar work. Apply the multiple, and you arrive at around $63 to $67.50—about what it costs today to buy an hour of dual instruction in a much more capable airplane. Today's trainers have electrical starters (we had to hand prop the old Champ to awaken it), radios, electronic aids to navigation, and even heaters that work so you can fly in the colder times of year without wearing a snowmobile suit. In 1965, in a Champ, we had none of these amenities.

Some other writers have taken the position that flying has become so complicated now that the fun is gone. This is pure bunk. Sure, large airports have become busier, with more airline traffic than before. Yes, you have to have a bit more equipment in an airplane now to go to the busiest airports, and the rules of the air have expanded a little. But the basic art of flying hasn't changed since World War I, when airplanes became modernized in terms of their basic design and control methods. In fact, it's become easier. Modern tricycle gear trainers are much easier to fly than the old tailwheel airplanes. Training methods have improved dramatically from the days when grizzled old instructors knew very little about how to teach people anything, even though they might have been very good pilots themselves.

Don't let anyone tell you that flying is any less fun than it ever was. Being aloft is still being aloft. The sky hasn't changed, but the airplanes have. They're now easier to fly, much more capable as transportation with modern equipment, much more comfortable, and more mechanically reliable, and therefore safer. The changes in the rules have been for good reason and aren't draconian. Thousands of people come into aviation every year, and you should be one of them.

The problem that I have identified as real deals with time. I think it's true that middle and upper middle income people today do work more hours for the same disposable income than did their parents. That's simply a fact of the modern, faster-paced world in which we live. Parents have more demands on their leisure time, because two-income households are the majority now, and kids' ball games, school functions, and precious family time all take their toll on the time people have for their own pursuits. Learning to fly does take some time.

If you are in this position, as many of us are or were, don't be disheartened. A couple of hours per week, maybe even more, for a few months, at the airport for your lessons isn't cheating your family, your business, or anyone else. Once you become a private pilot, as you'll see in the next chapter, a whole new world opens up to you. This world of personal aviation involves family trips and business travel not available to those bound to the ground.

You can involve your family fairly early in your flight training. After you've soloed, you will still take additional lessons in cross-country navigation, night flying, operating at larger airports (or smaller ones if you're learning at a big airport), and other subjects. Although it's not wise to take a passenger along on flights when you're doing stalls, or ground reference maneuvers that we discuss in the next chapter, ask your instructor if he minds if a passenger or two accompanies you on the more benign training flights. When you fly your night cross-country with your instructor, use a four-seat airplane and take some of your family with you. They'll probably feel very comfortable going along with the experienced instructor, and it's a great opportunity to show them how much fun this flying is, how beautiful the world is from the cabin of an airplane, and how well you're being taught to be a safe pilot.

Almost everything we do is more enjoyable if it can be shared with those we love. Don't leave your loved ones out of your fun. Involve them in it, and everyone will appreciate your time at the airport, rather than possibly being jealous of it.

# 4

# The Private Pilot Certificate

We're going to assume that almost all students want to achieve a private pilot certificate. Although we discussed the recreational pilot's license in Chap. 2, the history of flight training since that level of certificate was first introduced has shown that most all students want a private license. As you'll soon see, the privileges of a private pilot are very broad and quickly eclipse those available to a recreational pilot. Don't forget the recreational license though; it can be all that some pilots ever need, or it can be a break point, with the pilot just taking a breather from the training regimen and then going on to complete the requirements for a private certificate. Let's take a look at what it takes to become first a student pilot and then to get the private license.

## Student Pilot Requirements

As we've said before, you don't need a student pilot certificate until you're ready to solo. Any person can take instruction, regardless of age or any other qualifying factor. But to solo, you've got to have a student certificate. FAR 61.83 lays out the requirements to obtain a student license. These requirements are very straightforward and simple. First, you must be at least 16 years old, unless you want student privileges in only gliders or balloons, and then the minimum age is 14. You must be able to read, speak, write, and understand the English language. If you can't do any of those for medical reasons, the FAA can limit your certificate accordingly. Remember that we said that deaf people can fly? This is an example of failing the requirement to understand spoken English. The FAA will let a deaf person fly but will limit his flying to airspace where radio contact with air traffic controllers isn't required. To solo in a powered aircraft, which includes airplanes, you have to have a third-class medical certificate, which we discussed in the previous chapter. That's it; no more is required to obtain a student pilot's license.

Student pilots, once trained and once their logbooks and certificates are properly endorsed by a flight instructor, may fly an airplane solo. Your instructor must give you a presolo knowledge test of her own making that covers specified areas of knowledge. On your student license, there are places for the instructor to endorse it for solo and solo cross-country flights. Your instructor may place any limitations that she wants in your endorsements in your pilot logbook, limiting your solo privileges in any manner that she sees fit.

In addition to the limitations that your instructor may or may not put in your logbook, the FARs also limit flights by students pilots. A student may not act as pilot in command of an airplane carrying a passenger. If you take any passengers along on training flights, your instructor must be in the airplane, acting as pilot in command (PIC). A student can't carry a passenger herself.

Also, students can't make business flights. You'll see that there are requirements for certain solo cross-country flight experience before you take the flight test for your private license. The regulations prohibit business flying by students, so while you're still a student pilot, you can't legally solo cross-country in pursuit of business. But, you can always do so if your instructor is along and acting as PIC. When we previously talked about the time problem that besets so many people who learn to fly, we didn't mention some of the other many ways to help alleviate it. Asking your instructor to take you on dual-instruction cross-country flights that fit in with your travel needs is a great way to double up on the time effectiveness of your training time. Don't be put off if your instructor is hesitant at some points in your training. You may be asking to go too far, into too busy an airport or too small an airport, or just trying to push things a little too far too soon for your level of experience and skill at the moment. But, at the right time, to the right places, dual cross-country trips that fit into your other needs can be very productive, and you could even carry a passenger or two along.

# Basic Private Pilot Requirements

There are many requirements to get a private license that encompass training, knowledge, and experience standards. We'll deal with each of these separately, but let's see what the basic requirements are. Basically, an applicant for a private pilot's license, to fly a single-engine airplane, must be at least 17 years old. Private glider and balloon pilots need be only 16. Also, the candidate must read, speak, write, and understand English, just as was required of student pilots. If you can't do one or more of these for a medical reason, you can get a license limited in such a way that the deficit doesn't compromise flight safety.

Then, you have to have had the required training for the knowledge test, get an endorsement from your instructor that you're ready to take it, and pass it. You have to repeat those steps for the flight training—take the training, get an endorsement that you're ready for the flight test, and pass the flight test. Other than having a medical certificate, which is required to be at least a third-class one, that's it for an overview. Now let's break down the knowledge and flight portions of the requirements.

# Aeronautical Knowledge

FAR Section 61.105 outlines the areas of aeronautical knowledge required of a private pilot applicant. We'll touch upon most of these subjects in later chapters. Don't let this list be intimidating—it's a lot less complicated and severe than it looks at first sight. These are the basic subject matter areas covered on the knowledge test:

- Applicable FARs that relate to private pilot privileges, limitations, and flight operations
- The accident reporting requirements of the National Transportation Safety Board
- Use of the Aeronautical Information Manual and Advisory Circulars published by the FAA
- Use of aeronautical charts (maps) for navigation by various means
- Radio communication procedures
- Recognition of critical weather situations from the ground and in flight, windshear avoidance, and the procurement and use of aeronautical weather reports and forecasts

- Safe and efficient operation of aircraft, including collision avoidance and recognition and avoidance of wake turbulence
- Effects of density altitude on takeoff and climb performance
- Weight and balance computations
- Principles of aerodynamics, powerplants, and aircraft systems
- Stall awareness, spin entry, spins, and spin recovery techniques for the airplane and glider ratings
- Aeronautical decision making and judgment
- Preflight action that includes how to obtain information on runway lengths at airports of intended use, data on takeoff and landing distances, weather reports and forecasts, fuel requirements, and how to plan for alternatives if the planned flight cannot be completed or if delays are encountered

Although this list can look foreboding to the beginning student, it isn't in practice. Your ground school training, supplemented by discussions with your flight instructor, will sail you through it. This isn't rocket science; if you're a person of normal intelligence, with a reasonable degree of dedication to the task, you'll learn it all in time. We'll cover most of this material in the succeeding chapters, so just hang in there with us, and you'll see how it all comes together.

## Flight Proficiency

For the practical test, you'll have to demonstrate to the examiner that you can fly an airplane. What constitutes the ability to fly varies with the level of pilot certificate being sought and the ratings that you want. Ratings apply to the kinds of aircraft that you seek to fly and in what kind of weather you want to fly them. As you could naturally expect, a private pilot isn't required to do the things that a commercial pilot or higher is. But as you will see in a short while, when we discuss the privileges of a private pilot, private pilots have very broad operational privileges. So, the flight test is thorough, without being unduly daunting. Here's the list of what a candidate for a private license must demonstrate during the flight check:

- Preflight preparation
- Preflight procedures

- Airport operations
- Takeoffs, landings, and go-arounds
- Performance maneuvers
- Ground reference maneuvers
- Navigation
- Slow flight and stalls
- Basic instrument maneuvers
- Emergency operations
- Night operations
- Postflight procedures

All of these procedures are detailed in an FAA publication called the *Practical Test Standards,* or PTS for short. There is a PTS put out for each level of certificate from private through airline transport pilot, which is the highest pilot's license obtainable. There is also a PTS for the various ratings. We said before that a level of pilot certificate basically determines the privileges that a pilot has, and a rating describes, for the most part, either the various aircraft in which he may exercise those privileges, or the weather conditions in which he may fly. Let's use my certificate and ratings as an example.

I hold a commercial pilot certificate. That means that I can fly for hire under certain conditions, but I cannot be the captain of an airliner; that job requires an airline transport pilot certificate (ATP). On my commercial license, I have ratings for single- and multiengine land airplanes. That covers airplanes that have normal landing gear to operate from the ground. There are ratings for single- and multiengine seaplanes, which allow the pilot to fly from the water. I am also rated for helicopters and gliders, which means that I can exercise the privileges of a commercial pilots in those two very dissimilar types of aircraft. I have an airplane instrument rating, which means that I can fly airplanes under *instrument meteorological conditions* (IMCs) when *instrument flight rules* (IFRs) are in effect. While you're doing your training, and until you get an instrument rating, you'll be flying under *visual flight rules* (VFRs), which means that you must stay out of clouds, maintain certain distances from them, and have forward visibility of certain distances.

In addition, I possess a flight instructor certificate, with ratings for single- and multiengine airplanes and instruments. This means that I can teach flying in those airplanes and also instruct instrument flying.

There are many other ratings available. A pilot can be rated for balloons, airships, and a new class of aircraft called powered lift. A civilian powered-lift aircraft exists now only in experimental form. These will be aircraft that have tilt rotors or tilt wings and that can take off vertically like a helicopter and then tilt either the wings or rotors horizontal and fly like an airplane in cruise flight. The Marine Corps AV-8 Harrier is a form of powered-lift aircraft, but it has no civilian equivalent at this time. The FAA included powered lift as a new class of aircraft when they rewrote the regulations in 1997 to provide a mechanism to rate pilots in them when these advanced aircraft do become available to the civilian market.

We're not finished yet with the requirements for a basic private pilot's license, with a rating for single-engine land airplanes, which is the typical first pilot's license that a person gets. Beyond the required areas of aeronautical knowledge and flight proficiency that we've just listed, the candidate must also have a minimum level of experience to take the flight test. At this point you should understand that very few students, if any these days, can accomplish all of the needed training and get up to the performance standards in these stated minimum amounts of time.

First, you have to have a minimum of 40 hours of flight time that includes at least 20 hours of instruction from your flight instructor and 10 hours of solo flying time. Of these minima, you also have to have the following:

- At least 3 hours of cross-country dual instruction
- At least 3 hours of night instruction that includes a cross-country flight of no less than 100 miles, and 10 takeoffs and 10 landings, to a full stop, at an airport
- Three hours of instrument flight instruction
- Three hours of dual instruction in preparation for the practical test, training for which must have been received within 60 days of your flight test
- Five hours of solo cross-country flight
- One solo cross-country flight of at least 150 nautical miles total distance, with full stop landings at a minimum of three points, one segment of the flight consisting of a straight line distance of at least 50 nautical miles between a takeoff and a landing
- Three takeoffs and landings to a full stop at an airport that has an operating control tower

That's the minimum experience for a private license. Most people take around 60 hours or so total flying time to get the job done, instead of the bare minimum of 40. I've seen students take even far more hours than 60, and they have become very safe and competent pilots. Don't be discouraged if you don't take the flight test at any arbitrary number of total hours. What you learn, and retain, is far more vital than how long it takes you to do it. We aren't running any sprints in flight training; rather, view it as a lifelong marathon, paced accordingly.

## Privileges and Limitations

When you read the regulations, particularly FAR 61.113, you see that they speak more in the negative than they do in the positive concerning what a private pilot may or may not do. This is because a private pilot really has few limitations on the exercise of her certificate. The basic difference between what a private pilot can do compared to the higher commercial and airline transport pilot licenses relates to operating an aircraft for compensation of hire. A private pilot may obtain virtually any of the ratings set out in the regulations for any category, class, or type of aircraft. Theoretically, a private pilot could be rated to fly an airliner—he just can't do it for hire or in any common carriage of persons or property.

Many private pilots get instrument ratings and, in fact, that should be the next training goal for any new pilot who wants to expand her knowledge and scope of operations. With an instrument rating, and in an airplane properly equipped, a private pilot may fly anywhere that any other pilot can go, and do it in IFR weather. Although airline pilots routinely get special authorization to operate in very low ceiling and visibility conditions, from a practical point of view, an instru-mented-rated private pilot is authorized to operate in almost all flight environments.

It's not at all uncommon for private pilots to become rated in multiengine airplanes and fly light twin-engine airplanes. Coupled with an instrument rating, the multiengine-rated private pilot can operate some very exotic machinery. Airplanes that weigh over 12,500 pounds and all jets regardless of weight require what is known as a *type rating,* which means that the pilot must pass a flight test and get a special rating on her license for every such type of aircraft. I have a friend who is rated for a Cessna Citation, which is a twin-engine jet, and is a private pilot. He owns and flies this jet himself, not for hire, just in pursuit of his own business endeavors. The point is, a private pilot has the world of aviation open to him, but he cannot fly for hire.

What constitutes flying for hire has been the subject of years of debate, litigation, and court decisions. In the recent amendment to the FARs, some of this confusion was eliminated.

When a private pilot wants to take some passengers along and ask them to share in the costs of the flight, how those costs were split was a subject of intense debate until the new regulations came out. Now, it's pretty simple. If the private pilot owns the airplane, he may only collect from each passenger a pro rata share of fuel and oil consumed during the flight and incidental expenses like airport landing fees. If our private pilot rents aircraft, he must pay a pro rata share of the rental cost of the airplane. Getting anything more from the passengers is illegal because it constitutes flying for hire.

In the past, there was confusion about whether private pilots could fly tow airplanes, towing gliders, even though they weren't paid for it in the sense you and I think of paying someone. The FAA had taken the position that free flying time is compensation, so for a private pilot, flying in a glider club, towing gliders was deemed to be compensated because the flying cost her nothing. Now the regulations clearly state that a private pilot, who meets the other requirements for glider towing, may fly an airplane towing gliders, so long as he's not paid money to do it.

Private pilots may fly for the pursuit of their own or their employer's business, so long as the flight is incidental to that business, and no people or property are carried for hire. Say, for instance, that you are a regional salesperson, who travels an area of a few states for your job, and you are paid by your employer for doing that job, regardless of how you choose to travel from one place to another. The reason that you may choose to fly an airplane on your travels has nothing to do with the flying, so far as your job duties are concerned—you're just flying instead of driving or taking an airline or a bus. This is flying that is incidental to the business; the business is not flying, it's selling whatever it is that you peddle. That's perfectly legal to do as a private pilot. I would venture a guess that close to a majority of the private pilots, if not more, fly for just such a purpose.

Private pilots can also fly as an aircraft salesperson and demonstrate their wares to potential customers, as long as they've got at least 200 hours of flight time logged. The rules allow private pilots to fly in charity-sponsored airlifts, where the charity collects a donation for the airplane ride, if the pilot has 200 hours logged and conducts the flight in day VFR conditions. There are some other hoops that the charity has to jump through to make it legal, but the idea is that the pilot is not getting compensated, and the FAA blesses this activity.

You can see that a private pilot has a world of operating privileges. The big "no-no" for private pilots is getting compensated for their services as pilots. As long as they stay within that boundary, once they get the proper ratings for aircraft and weather, there is little a private pilot cannot do.

## Staying Current

Although a private pilot certificate never expires, you have to do a few things to remain current and legal to exercise the privileges of the license. You must hold a third-class medical certificate, which expires on the last day of the twenty-fourth month after it was issued. If you passed your physical exam on May 1, 1998, your third-class certificate is good through May 31, 2000. If you're less than 40 years old, the third-class medical is good for 36 months instead of 24.

Private pilots must also complete a *biennial fight review* (BFR) with an instructor every 24 months. This is an instructional session that must involve a minimum of 1 hour of ground discussion and 1 hour of flight time. The idea behind this requirement is that every pilot needs recurrent training, and the BFR is used to let a pilot get with an instructor, discuss any changes in the regulations or operating practices that have arisen since the last BFR, and fly for at least an hour to see if there's any rust that needs to be cleaned off some techniques.

To carry passengers, or to fly at night, you will also have to meet the *recent flight experience* requirements of FAR 61.57. In essence, to carry a passenger, you have to have made at least three takeoffs and landings in the past 90 days, in the same class of aircraft (usually a single-engine land airplane for most private pilots) as you will use to fly the passenger. If your flight is at night, you'll have to have done three takeoffs and landings at night within the last 90 days before flying a passenger.

# Logbook

Pilots are required to keep a logbook and enter into it all flight time that they intend to use to obtain any license or ratings. They also have to log all of the time required to show that they are current. Otherwise, there is no FAA requirement to log flying time. However, many insurance companies require that a pilot have a certain minimum amount of time in certain airplanes before they will insure that pilot in that plane. Most pilots are very diligent in logging their time. In my flying, which began in 1965, I have had fewer than a dozen hours, at most, which aren't recorded in one of several logbooks. All of your dual flight instruction must also be logged and endorsed by your flight instructor. Whenever a student pilot is flying solo cross-country, she must have her logbook with her because the FARs require that the instructor endorse, in the logbook, permission to make every solo cross-country flight.

# Legal Documents

There are a few documents that must be carried either in the airplane or on your person where you're flying. In the airplane, the certificate of registration and the airworthiness certificate must be prominently displayed. The certificate of registration is a form from the FAA's Aircraft Registry that shows who the registered owner of the airplane is. The airworthiness certificate is also issued by the FAA, and it says that the airplane met all of the certification standards when manufactured and that as long as it is maintained in accordance with the regulations, the airplane is airworthy to fly.

Also, the FAA-approved flight manual must be carried in the airplane. This manual specifies certain operating and emergency procedures and parameters, and it also shows the weight and balance limits within which the airplane must be operated.

Whenever you fly as pilot in command, you must carry your medical and pilot certificates on your person. The FARs require that you must present either or both certificates for inspection upon the request of any FAA inspector, representative of the National Transportation Safety Board, or any federal, state, or local law enforcement officer.

You have to show the requested certificate to any of those people who ask to see it, but that's all that you have to do. You do not have to surrender it to anyone without protracted legal proceedings aimed at you if you are charged with a violation of an FAR. Don't give your certificate to any of those persons who are authorized to demand to see it—just show it to them. However, you may encounter a local police officer who might never have seen a pilot certificate before and doesn't realize that you aren't required to surrender it, like you might be for a driver's license. Use common sense, and don't get into a tussle with the locals over this fine point. You can always get a duplicate certificate from the FAA if need be.

# 5

# The Airplane

Pilots have to have a working knowledge of enough aerodynamics and theory of flight to safely fly an airplane. Nobody is going to try to make you into an aeronautical engineer, and there are no fancy academics involved with what a private pilot must know. I certainly don't know the inner workings of the computer with which this book is being written. I do know enough about it to make it work and do what I need to perform on it. Look at this chapter that way; learn what you need to know to understand how the airplanes flies and how to get it to do what you want it to, but you don't have to understand all of the inner details of engineering to make it work for you, safely and efficiently.

An airplane flies on its wings. The wings produce *lift,* which is what we call the force that keeps us up. Lift overcomes, or may equal, the weight of the airplane. Think of most of these concepts as two forces, each opposing the other. Lift opposes *gravity.* Wings produce lift, and they come in a variety of shapes and sizes. Jet fighters may have short wings, gliders have long and narrow wings, and the Concorde has delta-shaped wings. Even a helicopter has wings—the main rotor blades act the same as fixed wings do on airplanes. They all have one job—to produce enough lift to oppose gravity.

Wings produce lift as a product of the air that flows over them when the airplane is in forward motion. Most wings are designed to have *camber,* which is the term used to describe the curvature of the wing when seen in cross section. The shape of the wing viewed from the wing tip is shown in FIG. 5-1. The word *airfoil* is another term used to describe the lifting surface of an airplane, and, as you'll see a bit later, the

**5-1** *Typical lightplane airfoil: The shape of the wing produces the lift. Pictured is an experimental aircraft, the Cessna XMC.*

propeller also produces lift. The curve on the upper surface of the wing is more pronounced than the curvature along the bottom of the wing.

The more difference between these two curvatures, the more lift the wing can produce at low speeds, where light airplanes operate. More lift is produced as the upper curvature becomes greater and greater than the lower surface's shape. Lift occurs because, as the airplane moves forward through the air, the stream of air is forced to separate at the leading (front) edge of the wing and then come back together at the trailing (rear) edge. The air molecules flowing over the top of the wing have to travel a greater distance, because the upper surface has the more pronounced curvature, than do the molecules that travel along the lower surface. The molecules then join up again as the stream of air reaches the trailing edge of the wing. For reasons determined by the laws of physics, the molecules that go over the top and under the lower surface of the wing must remain opposite each other as they make their trips along both surfaces of the wing. To do this, those molecules going over the top have to go faster, because they are going farther, than do the ones going under the wing.

When the molecules going over the top gain speed, they thin out, and there is more space between them. When a gas (and air is a gas) thins out, the gas loses pressure, and a partial vacuum develops. This partial vacuum acts as a suction force on top of the wing, constantly seeking to force the wing upward. FIGURE 5-2 shows this effect as it's seen in a wind tunnel.

The amount of lift that a wing produces can be increased in two ways. The first, and the least effective, is to increase the absolute speed at which the wing is traveling through the air.

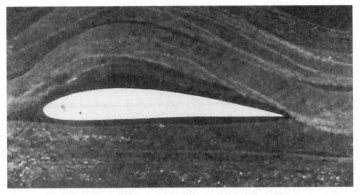

**5-2**  *Normal airflow pattern around a wing in flight.*

As the absolute speed increases, so does the differential in the speed of the air going over the top and moving along the underside of the wing. Because the partial vacuum that provides lift is a result of this differential, the greater the differential, the more lift that is produced. But, the range in operating speeds of light airplanes isn't very great. Most of the trainer types that you'll fly have minimum (stalling) speeds somewhere around 50 knots, and cruising speeds just slightly over 100 knots. So, you can only increase the absolute speed of the airplane around 50 knots or so, which isn't very much. Jets, with minimum speeds around 130 knots and maximums over 500 knots, have a much wider operating range, so differences in absolute speed through the air are much greater.

The method by which all airplanes increase the amount of lift produced by the wings is by raising the leading edge upward, which can be thought of as tipping the wing so that the leading edge is higher than the trailing edge. This causes the oncoming stream of air, which is called the *relative wind,* to strike the lower surface of the wing, generating a deflection force from underneath, which also pushes the wing upward and supplements the lift that is produced by the partial vacuum on the wing's upper surface. The extent to which a wing can be tilted upward is limited. If it's tilted too much, the airflow along the wing's upper surface is interrupted because it can no longer adhere to that upper surface. When the airflow over the top of the wing is interrupted, and loses its adherence to the surface, the partial vacuum is lost, and most of the wing's lift goes away with it. When this happens, the wing is *stalled,* and the airflow looks as shown in FIG. 5-3.

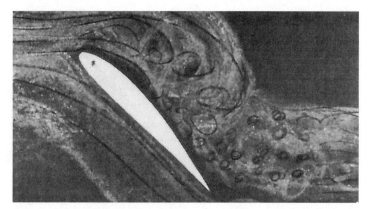

**5-3** *A stalled wing. The flow of air over the upper surface is interrupted; therefore, the lift is destroyed.*

# Angle of Attack and Stalls

Everything that an airplane does in flight depends on the angle at which the leading edge of the wing meets the oncoming stream of air. This angle is called the *angle of attack*. Angle of attack is the whole story of flight, as the relative wind meets the wing. A kite flies by the lift produced by angle of attack alone. Kites don't have cambered lifting surfaces that wings have; they fly purely because their attitude, relative to the ground, is a nose-up position, which causes the wind blowing across them to strike the underside of the kite and force it upward.

Go too slow in a airplane, while pulling the nose higher to try to maintain flight, and the wing will stall. A wing can be stalled at any speed, including the airplane's top speed. Simply increase the angle of attack past its critical point, which is normally 16 to 18° in a lightplane, causing the relative wind to strike the wing below the leading edge, and, regardless of speed, the air can no longer flow around the lifting surfaces in the smoothly adhered pattern necessary to produce lift. Then, the wing stalls. The wing can be stalled with the airplane in any attitude relative to the ground: in a turn, a climb, or a dive pull-out and with the wings level or banked. Whether the wing is still producing lift, which we call "flying" or is stalled has absolutely nothing to do with whether the engine is running or the power setting the pilot has selected. Don't confuse stalling with the engine's output of power or lack thereof. Stalling is a product of an excessive angle of attack.

Gliders have no engine, and they still fly. Their wings produce lift as the glider moves through the air just the same as do the wings of a powered airplane. In the rare case that the engine fails in an airplane, the wings still produce lift, and the pilot glides down, selects a landing site, and lands. Airplanes don't fall out of the sky if the engine quits. Stalling is what destroys lift, not the lack of engine power.

The flying characteristics of modern lightplanes are such that you have to intentionally stall them or be totally unaware of what is happening, which means that you haven't received good instruction in stalls. The airplane will give plenty of warning prior to stalling. The entire airplane will buffet, and you'll feel the controls become very sloppy and ineffective before a stall actually develops. Only very poor piloting technique results in unintentional stalls in modern airplanes. Stalls are taught and practiced repeatedly throughout your flight training. You need to know how to do a stall to properly land a lightplane because a good landing is nothing more than a stall performed just inches above the runway. The other reason that you learn stalls is so that you can recognize the conditions that lead to them and then avoid unintentional stalls.

Recovery from a stall happens only one way, by reducing the angle of attack so that the airflow can resume its normal smooth and adhered path across the upper and lower surfaces of the wings. Angle of attack is normally reduced by lowering the nose attitude of the airplane; immediately the wing starts producing lift again, and the stall is ended.

## Stall Warning Devices

All modern airplanes have some sort of device to warn the pilot of an impending stall. The first of these, which is built into to the airplane by the design engineers, is the aerodynamic warning that occurs when the engine airplane buffets, possibly accompanied by the control wheel shaking in your hands. Without either of the other two types of stall warnings, which we'll talk about in the next paragraphs, this aerodynamic warning ought to tell any alert pilot that the airplane is about to stall.

Almost all airplanes have an additional warning that is either visual or aural. There is a sensor on the leading edge of the wing, usually in the form of a little metal tab. This tab is mounted in such a way that it is forced upward, traveling about $1/2$ inch in its mounting hardware, when the relative wind starts striking the leading edge from too far below it to continue normal lift. The tab then activates an electrical switch.

This switch then either sounds a horn in the cockpit or turns on a bright red light. The horn is usually mounted in the ceiling of the cockpit, near the pilot's head. If you can't hear the horn, you've either been to too many rock concerts, or your kid plays her CD player too much at home. If your airplane is equipped with a light for a stall warning device, instead of a horn, the light is placed on the instrument panel, right in front of your eyes. When the light comes on, it dominates what you see. Regardless of which type of warning system is in your airplane, it is calibrated to activate before the stall actually is fully developed, so you have ample time to correct from the unintentional stall.

The tabs on the leading edge of the wing can get out of adjustment. When you're practicing stalls or landing, if you don't hear or see the warning device activate, have the maintenance people take a look. The tab could be misaligned, there could be a fault in the electrical connections between the tab and the cockpit horn or light, or there could be a blown fuse or popped circuit breaker in the system.

## Thrust and Drag

The engine has one purpose, which is to propel the airplane through the air. This propulsive force is called *thrust*. Propellers are airfoils and act upon the air in the same manner as do wings. When you look at a propeller from the tip of the blade, sighting down the blade toward the hub at its center, you can see that the propeller blade has increased curvature on the front side. This curvature produces lift. Because the propeller is mounted vertically, the lift that it produces is aligned with the longitudinal axis of the airplane, as shown in FIG. 5-4. This lift pulls the airplane forward.

Propeller blades are also slightly twisted, and their undersides strike their stream of oncoming air at a positive angle of attack (see FIG. 5-4). This deflection of the air pushes the propeller forward, just the same as the positive angle of attack of the wing pushes that wing upward. When you stand behind an airplane on the ground (at a safe distance from it) that has its engine running, you'll feel the "prop blast" as the air is deflected backward, away from the propeller.

As the airplane moves forward through the air, it has resistance to that motion. This resistance is called *drag*. Drag comes

**5-4** *The blade of a propeller.*

from many sources. The first source of drag is *induced drag,* which is the resistance created by the wing as it moves through the air. When we raise the leading edge of the wing and increase the angle of attack, more of the wing's lower surface is presented to the relative wind. When you increase the amount of the surface area of the bottom of the wing that is struck by the oncoming air, the amount of drag goes up, too. The pilot alters the amount of induced drag that is acting upon the airplane when the angle of attack is changed to climb, descend, or return to level flying.

To some extent, when the wing is tilted upward to increase the angle of attack, the increase in the induced drag is also caused because the body of the airplane, called the *fuselage,* naturally tilts up with the wing. Then, more of the lower surface of the fuselage also strikes the oncoming air flow and offers resistance. This portion of the induced drag changes along with the change in induced drag from the wing as the pilot varies the angle of attack throughout the flight.

The other drag that the airplane produces is called *parasite drag.* Parasite drag is the resistance to moving through the air that is caused by all of the appendages and equipment on the airplane. Things like landing gear, wing struts, and radio antennas are the main contributors to parasite drag. That's why higher-performance airplanes have retractable landing gear;

they can be raised by the pilot once airborne, getting the gear out of the airflow and eliminating the parasite drag they produce. Modern radio installations in high-performance airplanes often incorporate radio antennas that are mounted internally, either in the wings or in the fuselage.

Just as the lift produced by the wings must overcome, or in cruise flight must be equal to, the weight of the airplane, thrust must overcome, be equal to, or be less than total drag, depending on what the pilot wants the airplane to do. If he wants to increase speed, while remaining at a level altitude, he must increase thrust by increasing the power setting of the engine. If the goal is to go slower, power is reduced. In normal cruise flight, when the speed through the air is neither increasing nor decreasing, the thrust will be equal to the force of the total drag.

# Center of Gravity

In flight, an airplane is a balanced machine that can rotate three ways (on three axes) about its *center of gravity.* As shown in FIG. 5-5, these axes all converge at the center of gravity, which is the balance point of the airplane. The exact location of the center of gravity is at different points on the airplane, depending on how it is loaded with people, cargo, and fuel. The center of gravity might change a little throughout a flight, as fuel is consumed. To prevent an out-of-balance condition, there are limits on exactly where the center of gravity can be and still have the airplane be within its design center of gravity range. These limits are expressed as the *loading envelope.* The loading envelope is usually presented as a graph or series of graphs that depict where the center of gravity will be with alternative loading arrangements. The loading envelope also shows the pilot the maximum design weight of the airplane, which cannot be exceeded, regardless of how the load is distributed.

In your training, you'll be taught how to use the loading envelope. It is extremely important to always know both where the center of gravity is throughout the flight and what the entire weight of the airplane is before your begin a flight. If you take off within the total weight limit, you'll be OK for that requirement throughout your flight, because the airplane is constantly getting lighter as fuel is burned off. But, you can't make the same assumption about the center of gravity.

**5-5** *The three axes: An airplane "rolls" about the longitudinal axis (Z), "pitches" about the horizontal axis (X), and "yaws" about the vertical axis (Y).*

There are airplanes, particularly the Beechcraft Bonanza, in which you can be within the center of gravity range at take-off but fall outside of permissible limits before landing because the burnoff of fuel alters the location of the center of gravity.

*Center of lift* is a term that should not be confused with center of gravity. The center of lift is the center point of the low-pressure area on the top surface of the wing. It changes as the angle of attack changes. The center of lift has a design range of limits, too, and exceeding the permissible range results in a stall if the center of lift is moved too far forward by too great an angle of attack.

# Flight Control System

The primary flight controls that the pilot uses to control the airplane are the *control wheel* or *stick* and the *rudder pedals.* These are connected to the movable surfaces on the wings and the tail by either steel cables or tubular mechanical linkages. These controls function the same way on all airplanes, light-planes, jet fighters, and airliners (FIG. 5-6). By changing the camber of the wings and the deflection of the tail surfaces, and how they react to the changes in the relative wind that are produced as a result, the airplane will change its attitude.

**5-6** *Flight control surfaces: A, ailerons; F, flaps; S, horizontal stabilizer; E, elevators; T, trim; V, vertical stabilizer or fin; R, rudder.*

# Climbing and Descending

Some airplanes have a control stick, but most modern ones use a control wheel. When the pilot pushes the stick or wheel forward, the *elevators* (which are attached to the *horizontal stabilizer* on the tail) are deflected downward. The relative wind strikes the lowered elevators, which pushes the airplane's tail up and forces the nose down. When you pull back on the wheel, the elevators are raised, and this pushes the tail down and pulls the nose up. Because the airplane is balanced about its center of gravity, motion of the tail, up or down, forces the nose in the opposite direction.

Another way of think about the control wheel's movement and effect is that forward and rearward movement of the wheel, for the most part, controls both the nose attitude of the airplane and the angle of attack of the wings. Forward motion decreases the angle of attack and lowers the nose, and pulling the wheel back toward you increases the angle of attack and raises the nose.

# Trim

*Trim* is an adjustment of certain controls to eliminate the need for the pilot to constantly apply control pressure to hold the airplane in a desired attitude. All airplanes have trim for the forward and rearward pressures that have to be applied to the control wheel to keep the nose at a desired attitude. Some higher-performance light airplanes also have a trim for the rudder, so the pilot doesn't have to constantly push on one of the two pedals to keep the nose aligned where she wants it. Few, if any, trainers have any trim other than for the up and down nose attitude.

Nose trim is accomplished, mechanically, in one of two ways. The less-common mechanism is to have a control in the cockpit that adjusts the entire horizontal stabilizer either up or down, thus changing its angle of attack so that the tail can be made to ride higher or lower in level flight. Changing the tail's angle of attack is used to compensate for varying loads in the airplane or for different speeds at which the airplane is flying.

In typical training airplanes, elevator forces are trimmed by a device called a *trim tab,* which is attached to the trailing edge of one or both of the elevators. The trim tab on the Cessna 150 is shown as item T in FIG. 5-6. As the trim tab is moved up or down by means of a small wheel in the cockpit, the elevator rides higher or lower, with the same effect as adjusting the angle of the entire horizontal stabilizer.

Another device on many popular trainers is called a *stabilator;* it is used in place of the fixed horizontal stabilizer and hinged elevators. The stabilator is a one-piece system, which moves in its entirety as the control wheel is pulled back or pushed forward. Stabilators are generally more aerodynamically efficient, for a given size, than are the more traditional combinations of horizontal stabilizers and movable elevators. Use of a stabilator allows a design engineer to save weight by using a smaller control surface or a shorter fuselage. Regardless of how your airplane is equipped, both systems control the nose attitude and trim of the airplane through the control wheel and trim control in the cockpit. From the pilot's perspective as she flies the airplane, there isn't any difference between the two.

A properly trimmed airplane will virtually fly itself without constant control input from the pilot. But any change in power setting, such as that required to level off from a climb or to begin a descent, calls for a minor adjustment of trim. In 1997, there was stark proof of just how stable a small airplane is. A pilot was hand propping (turning the propeller by hand) an Aeronca Champ to start it, which is the only way those old classic airplanes are started. Unfortunately, the throttle was not set at idle but was pushed forward far enough for the engine to develop significant power once it caught and began running. The other unfortunate part of this story is that the airplane had no one in it when it started. It began to roll, gaining speed as it went. As it broke ground, it narrowly missed the hangar at the Urbana, Ohio, airport, where this adventure began. It took off and flew for 2 hours, covering over 90 miles, climbing as high as 12,000 feet at one point, before it ran out of gas and came to rest in a bean field three counties away.

Throughout this flight, the airplane was being chased by a helicopter and an Ohio State Highway Patrol airplane and was monitored on radar by the FAA. The end of the story allowed the entire episode to be comical because nobody was hurt. Several of us wondered how the hapless owner was explaining this to his insurance company. I'm sure your instructor will be in your airplane before you start it.

# Turns

Turning the control wheel to the left or right causes the airplane to bank in the same direction as the wheel is turned. Turn the wheel to the right and you raise the *aileron* on the right wing, while simultaneously lowering the one on the left wing. The airstream over the wings hits these deflected ailerons, and that forces the right wing down and the left wing up.

Once the wings are banked, the airplane will turn. Now is the time to dispel some confusion. Airplanes also have a *rudder,* which is attached to the vertical stabilizer and is shown as item R in FIG. 5-6. Because most of us have had at least some passing acquaintance with boats, many people think that an airplane's rudder turns it, like a boat's rudder does. This isn't so. What turns an airplane is the force of lift. Lift always remains perpendicular to the wings, regardless of the attitude of the wings, level or banked. When we bank the airplane, the force of lift pulls the airplane around in the turn. You'll see in your training that the normal stalling speed of an airplane increases as the angle of bank increases. This is because some portion of the total lift being developed by the wings must now be diverted toward the task of turning. Hence, to overcome gravity and keep the airplane flying, the total lift must increase in a turn because only part of the total lift is being used to keep the airplane up. So, the speed at which it will stall is higher in a bank because the total needed lift can't be produced at the same, slower speed that suffices for level flight.

However, the rudder does have a function to perform in turning an airplane. To produce a balanced, coordinated turn, you have to use both ailerons and the rudder. When you bank the airplane using ailerons alone, the entry into the bank is sloppy, and the nose actually slides, momentarily, to the opposite side, caused by a situation known as *adverse yaw*. If you are in normal straight level flight and you press a rudder pedal, the nose will point in the direction in which you're pressing the pedal, but the airplane will turn only slightly, if at all. Rather, it'll just *skid* through the air pointed sideways but still going almost straight ahead.

Properly executing a turn requires the coordinated use of both the wheel, to bank the wings through the action of the ailerons, and the corresponding pressure on the rudder pedal in the same direction as you're turning the wheel. For a left turn, turn the wheel to the left and use the left rudder. When you've established the angle of bank needed to turn as sharply as you desire, neutralize both the wheel and the rudder, and the airplane continues turning until recovery from the turn begins.

When you've turned as far as you want, the turn is stopped by applying wheel and rudder pressures opposite to those that started the turn. If you've been turning to the left, just roll the wheel to the right and simultaneously apply some right rudder pressure. The airplane will roll out of the bank. When the wings are once again level, neutralize the controls and fly along in the new direction.

Normally, most turns are done with a bank angle of around 30°. At this angle, the increase in stalling speed that is a by-product of every bank is very little. Also, a 30° bank is not uncomfortable for either pilot or passengers. Once in a turn, you'll find that you have to apply a little back pressure to the control wheel to keep the nose attitude level and to keep from losing altitude. Remember, total lift must increase in a turn because some of that total is now devoted to turning the airplane rather than just keeping it aloft. To increase total lift, you increase the angle of attack, and that is done by pulling back a little on the wheel.

If you bank very steeply, say 60° or more, you'll see that the needed back pressure, to keep the nose level, can increase quite a bit. In a 60° bank, most of the total lift is turning the airplane and little remains to keep us flying. So, the angle of attack has to be increased much more because much more total lift has to be generated. At some point, as bank is increased, there just won't be enough lift to keep the airplane flying, and you will increase the angle of attack to the point of stalling the wings. In training, you'll do some steeply banked turns, but probably not over 45° of bank. At 45°, everything is still quite controllable, and safe margins of stall speed versus the speed at which you're flying are maintained. Much beyond 60° of bank, you'll reach the design limit of the average light airplane, where you can't keep the nose level anymore without stalling. At that point, you have to either allow the nose to fall some in attitude or lessen the angle of bank.

Steep turns need to be practiced in training so that you can see these effects for yourself. But after you get your license, you probably will seldom, if ever, turn much more steeply than 45° of bank.

# Wing Flaps

*Wing flaps* are hinged surfaces attached to the inboard trailing edges of the wings. Their primary purpose is to allow the pilot to change the shape of the wing as they are lowered, which thereby increases the camber, or curvature, of the wing. When the flaps are extended, the new shape of the wing is more curved, and the wing is capable of producing more lift (FIG. 5-7). Because the wing is producing more lift as the flaps are extended, their use allows the airplane to fly at a reduced speed. Flaps are most often used during a landing so that the airplane can fly at a slower speed during the approach. Because the wing is producing more lift as the flaps are extended, the stalling speed of the airplane is also less than if the flaps are up. Using flaps during the landing approach enables the airplane to land more slowly because, as you now know, a good landing is a stall performed only inches above the runway.

The wing flaps on small airplanes are always mounted on the trailing edges of the wings, primarily for simplicity of design and manufacture and ease of pilot operation. But on large aircraft, usually jets, flaps are put on both the leading and trailing edges of the wing. Then, when all of the flaps are fully

**5-7**  *Extended flaps enable the wing to produce more lift, and they also add drag.*

extended, the shape of the wing is dramatically altered. Because jets operate over such a wide spectrum of speeds, compared to a lightplane, the wing on a jet has to be capable of flying as slow as 130 knots during takeoff and landing, yet also cruise above 500 knots. Radically changing its shape, with a very complicated combination of both leading and trailing edge flaps, is the only way it can be done.

The next time that you ride on an airliner, try to get a seat over or slightly behind the wings. You can watch the flaps work, especially during takeoff and landing. All of the airliner's flaps must be deployed for takeoff and landing because the wing would not be able to fly otherwise; it wouldn't create enough lift at slow speeds without the flap extension. In small airplanes, we normally take off without using any flap extension and can also easily land without flaps if we want. Flaps in a lightplane enable us to approach and land at slower speeds than if we didn't use them, but the difference isn't dramatic as it is in large airplanes.

When we discussed drag earlier in this chapter, we noted that induced drag is a by-product of lift. So, when you deploy the flaps to increase the wing's lift, you also increase the drag. Even though we don't normally use flaps for takeoff in light training airplanes, a Cessna 150, shown in FIG. 5-7, can use as much as 20° of flap extension for takeoff. If there is any more than that, the increased drag associated with flap extension will hinder the airplane's ability to accelerate down the runway and reach flying speed. Small deflections of flaps, up to 20°, are used for soft runway conditions or sometimes for short runways, when you need to lift off of the ground as soon as possible at the slowest speed practical. However, when using flaps in this manner, you'll learn that your climb out, after you break ground, will suffer as a result of the flap deployment because the drag inherent in the use of the flaps compromises the rate at which the airplane can climb.

When there is a strong *crosswind,* which occurs when the wind is blowing across the runway, flap extensions are kept at a lesser degree than when a crosswind isn't a factor. You'll see that using excessive amounts of flap extension in heavy crosswinds increases the wind's reaction upon the airplane, making it more difficult to compensate for that crosswind.

For landing, without heavy crosswinds, full flap deployment is generally used. A Cessna 150 has a maximum flap extension of 40°. When the maximum is used, the Cessna 150 descends at quite a slow forward speed and rather steeply, in terms of its angle of descent. This can be beneficial if you need to clear a power line, trees, or some other obstacle in the approach path, especially if the runway is on the short side. At times during your training, your instructor will have you make landings at all levels of flap extension, from none to the maximum available in your airplane.

# Propeller and Its Effects

We've already talked about how the propeller is shaped like a wing and produces thrust by actually creating lift in the forward direction. When we refer to the *pitch* of the propeller blades, that's another term for the angle of attack of the blades to their oncoming airstream. When the pitch is low, the angle of attack of the blades is likewise low, and when the pitch is higher, so is the angle of attack. Changing the pitch changes the thrust characteristics of the propeller and the pull that it generates.

Most airplanes with engines of 150 horsepower or less have *fixed-pitch* propellers because of the smaller airplane's limited load capacity and narrow speed range (FIG. 5-8). This class of airplane includes all of the popular two-seat trainers and most of the four-seat planes in which you might train. Airplanes of this limited performance ability could not make enough use of the more expensive *constant-speed* propellers found on larger and faster

**5-8** *This propeller is the fixed-pitch type. The landing light, engine air intake with air filter, and exhaust pipes are also visible.*

airplanes. Constant-speed propellers are much more expensive to manufacture and require overhauls and routine maintenance not requisite for fixed-pitch propellers. Therefore, small airplanes can't justify the cost of the constant-speed propeller.

The pitch of the blades of a constant-speed propeller can be changed by the pilot, within certain limits. The internal mechanisms of the constant-speed propeller also change the pitch of the blades, instantaneously, to maintain constant revolutions per minute (rpm) of the engine as various aerodynamic loads are encountered during flight. Managing a constant-speed propeller demands more pilot technique than does operating an engine that has a fixed-pitch propeller. That's another reason that trainers don't normally have them; there's nothing to be gained during initial pilot training from overloading a student with needless tasks.

Almost all modern propellers are made of aluminum, but some of the newest types are constructed of composite material. Composites are gaining fast as a material of which entire airplanes are made, and propellers are no exception. Composite materials can be stronger and lighter than metal. In the past, propellers were carved out of laminated wood stock. Wooden propellers are lighter than metal ones, but they require much more care and maintenance. Today, you generally see wooden propellers on classic and antique airplanes and on homebuilts.

When the airplane is on the ground, a propeller is dangerous to the point of being regarded as a killer. Never start an engine without *knowing for certain* that no one is in front of or approaching the airplane. You'll be taught to always open the cockpit window and yell "clear" before starting the engine. Be especially watchful for people unaccustomed to airplanes who don't realize the danger of a spinning propeller, which is virtually invisible. Of all of the ways to have an accident, allowing a person to be struck by a rotating propeller is about the most needless, and also it is always disfiguring at best and most often is fatal.

Also, be watchful for animals. If you fly into rural airports where there might be dogs or other critters around the airport, they too can get caught by the propeller. Dogs seem to be attracted by spinning propellers, and get a "deer in the headlights" syndrome. If your airport has any animals around, don't start the airplane if they are in sight. If you do ever catch anything in the propeller, immediately shut the airplane down and have a qualified maintenance technician look at it first, before any further engine operation. A propeller that is damaged to the slightest degree might be out of balance and cause severe engine damage if ignored. Also, nicks in the propeller of any significant size, usually more than one-sixteenth of an inch deep, can cause the metal to fatigue and set up a crack in the propeller, which can then lead to in-flight separation of a portion of the affected blade.

Even with the engine not running, a propeller has the potential to maim or kill. Airplane engines are normally shut down by using the *mixture* control to starve the engine of fuel, and then, after the engine quits running, the pilot turns off the ignition switch. Many pilots have neglected the final step of turning off the ignition. Even if you turn off the ignition switch, the way the system is designed can allow a short to develop. If this happens, the pilot won't normally know it, and the engine can start again if the propeller is rotated even slightly. Leaning on a propeller at rest has caused more than one engine to at least fire over a stroke or two, if not actually start running. The one doing the leaning seldom knows what hit him.

In flight, the propeller's rotation creates several forces that affect how the plane flies. Most of these forces are manifested by the airplane's "wanting" to turn. Design engineers usually design the engine mounts and vertical tail offsets to greatly eliminate most of the effects of these forces in cruising flight.

As the propeller rotates, the airflow through it is twisted. Thus, there is a *spiraling slipstream* created by the normal operation of the propeller. This spiraling nature of the slipstream leaving the propeller, and working its way aft, exerts a sideways force on the fuselage of the airplane and also upon the vertical tail surface.

Propellers on American-made engines turn clockwise when viewed from inside the cockpit. When anything rotates, it creates *torque*. Torque is a force that is generated in a direction opposite to the direction of rotation, which, in an American airplane, is counterclockwise. During operation of the airplane, torque is seldom felt by the pilot because of the design and manufacturing countermeasures discussed above.

Another of the forces associated with the propeller that causes a turning tendency is *P-factor,* which is the tendency of an airplane to swing its nose to the left when the plane is at higher angles of attack, such as when it lifts off the ground at takeoff and during a climb. This occurs because, when the airplane itself is at higher angles of attack, the propeller's descending blade (the blade on the right as viewed from inside the cockpit) has a greater angle of attack than does the opposite, ascending blade. This gives the descending blade more effective thrust than the ascending blade. Therefore, the entire circle of the rotating propeller isn't creating equal thrust on both sides; rather, the right side has more pull than is created by the left half of the propeller "disk." This unequal pull from the right side causes the nose of the airplane to be pulled to the left. This swinging of the nose is called *yaw.* To correct this tendency, inherent in all propeller airplanes, the pilot holds a little pressure on the right rudder pedal when the airplane is at higher angles of attack. When the airplane is put in a nose-down attitude, such as when making a normal descent from cruise altitudes, this effect reverses because the ascending blade of the propeller now has the higher angle of attack and therefore creates more thrust. During descents, the pilot applies some pressure to the left rudder pedal to correct this and keep the airplane in coordinated flight.

European-made engines rotate backward compared to American powerplants. For them, you apply the left rudder during takeoff and climb and the right rudder during descent. Helicopters have to have similar corrections applied by the pilot, but for altogether different aerodynamic reasons. American helicopters need the left pedal as power is increased, and European choppers get right pedal. Because you'll be flying American-built airplanes during your training and may never fly a European one and probably won't be a helicopter pilot, don't worry about the different techniques. Just remember— right pedal for takeoff and climb; left pedal for descents.

# Throttle

The throttle is the control that regulates the amount of fuel going into the cylinders of the engine just as the gas pedal does in a car. In modern lightplanes, the throttle is usually a big dark knob mounted on the instrument panel. In some airplanes, particularly those made by Piper, the throttle can be a T-shaped handle mounted on a quadrant in front of and slightly below the panel. Both configurations work in the same way. When pushed all the way in, or forward, the throttle is wide open and allows the engine to run at maximum power. Pulled all the way back, or out, the engine is at idle power.

An airplane throttle is not moved constantly as though it were the gas pedal of a car. If you have any experience with farm or industrial machinery like tractors or bulldozers, the airplane throttle is used more like the fuel control in these machines. Normally we use full throttle, or maximum power, for takeoff and climb.

If you're training in an airplane with a fixed-pitch propeller, and you almost certainly will be learning in this simpler kind of plane, you leave the power at maximum throughout the climb after takeoff. Then, when your desired cruising altitude is reached, the throttle is pulled back to set the power for cruise flight. Most of the time, the throttle is not touched again until it is time to begin a descent, when it is pulled back some, to a power setting less than cruise, which allows the airplane to descend efficiently.

You will learn in your training that the throttle, because it controls the power output of the engine, is the control that primarily determines the altitude of the flight. Pulling back on the control wheel raises the nose of the airplane and increases the lift of the wings because raising the nose also increases the wings' angle of attack. But remember, induced drag increases as lift does. So, only pulling the nose up, without increasing power, will result in a momentary gain in altitude, which is what we call a *zoom climb*. As soon as the various aerodynamic forces stabilize, the increased drag, resulting from the increased angle of attack, will slow the airplane and stop further altitude gain. To climb consistently, the pilot must advance the throttle so that the engine is putting out more power. This increase in power enables the airplane to continue climbing because the power is overcoming the induced drag that results from the higher angle of attack.

There are some airplanes, like jet fighters, that have such an excess of power that they can climb when just the nose attitude is raised. But in lightplanes, there isn't that much power available at the cruise setting, so we have to increase power in order to climb more than a few hundred feet at best.

Modern airplanes are often designed to use fuel injection rather than a carburetor to meter the fuel flow into the cylinders. Your trainer will probably have a carburetor-type induction system. From the pilot's perspective, the difference between the two systems is almost negligible, and the throttle control in the cockpit is used the same way regardless of whether your airplane is fuel injected or is equipped with a carburetor. There are some very minor differences in the technique used in certain combinations of atmospheric conditions and power output, between having a carburetor or a fuel injection system, but they are so slight as to be insignificant here.

# Engine

Airplanes have used many different powerplants over the history of aviation. Some have used diesel engines, and a few years ago, a very light airplane crossed the English Channel powered only by its pilot's muscle power as he pedaled like a bicycle rider. We all know that most airliners and military airplanes are jet powered. As a private pilot, the only powerplants that you're likely to encounter will be air-cooled, reciprocating gasoline engines, which are identical in principle to automobile engines.

Airplanes generally use air-cooled engines for two reasons. First, they are lighter than liquid-cooled engines because they don't have radiators, water pumps, the associated plumbing, and the weight of the liquid coolant. Second, air-cooled engines are more reliable because there aren't any of the aforementioned components to fail. Those of us who have been driving for some years have probably encountered a problem, at some time during our lives, with the cooling system of our car. A broken water hose or pump or a leaky radiator is an inconvenience on the highway. It's a more significant problem at 5,000 feet above the ground. Lately, we have seen a resurgence of liquid-cooled airplane engines, as the sciences of engine design and metallurgy have advanced. So, you might have a liquid-cooled engine in your aviation future. Liquid-cooled engines are more efficient than are air-cooled ones, and the price of fuel is driving aviation engine manufacturers to try to improve efficiency. These liquid-cooled engines are designed to run for an extended period of time even after all of the coolant has leaked out, matching their safety to that of the air-cooled engine.

Most of the engines you'll encounter are equipped with horizontally opposed cylinders, similar to the engines that powered Volkswagen Beetles and older-style Porsches. FIGURE 5-9 depicts a typical lightplane engine manufactured by Teledyne Continental.

## Ignition System

Unlike automobile engines, airplane engines have two complete and separate ignition systems supplying power to the spark plugs in the cylinders. In an airplane engine, there are even two spark plugs in each cylinder, each powered by one of the two ignition systems. The electrical energy needed to provide power to the spark plugs is derived from two magnetos, each of which powers one of the separate systems. In this way, reliability and safety are enhanced in several ways.

First, magnetos, or *mags* as they are commonly called by pilots and maintenance technicians, are totally separate from the airplane's electrical system. The electrical system consists of a battery and either a generator or alternator, and this electrical system supplies the power to start the engine and run the radios, night-flying lights, and other electrical options. But the electrical system has nothing to do with keeping the engine running. An airplane can suffer a complete electrical failure; its battery can short out, its generator or alternator can cease to put out any electricity, or the voltage regulator can break, and none of this will have the slightest effect on whether the engine runs. Auto engines have a different system that does rely on the car's electrical system to keep power going to the spark plugs. That's why, if your car's alternator fails, you can drive only a short distance because you're then using up the stored charge

**5-9** *This is a six-cylinder, opposed-type, air-cooled engine manufactured by Continental. Shown are: C, carburetor; E, exhaust; M, magnetos; O, oil cooler; P, propeller hub; S, spark plugs; and T, starter.*

in the battery to power the ignition. As soon as the battery runs dead, the car stops. Not so with an airplane, for the obvious safety reason.

The magnetos that power the airplane's engine are very old technology. In fact, your power lawn mower has a magneto to run its engine's ignition. Although some pundits have criticized aviation manufacturers for not employing the latest and greatest new advances in airplanes, I prefer the old saying, "If it ain't broke, don't fix it."

Then, because there are two magnetos on an airplane, and each one powers a totally separate and unconnected ignition system, including one of the two spark plugs in each cylinder, one entire ignition system can fail, and the engine will run properly on the other system. So any of the components in one system can fail, from the mag to a spark plug lead or the plug itself, and we can continue flying. When the engine is running on only one of the ignition systems, it loses a tiny bit of efficiency and can't produce quite all of its rated power. But this decrease is so slight that it is barely noticeable even to experienced pilots. You will learn that before takeoff, there is a simple check that pilots perform to ensure that both ignition systems are working properly. If one is not, we certainly don't take off, even though we could, because if we did take off on only one of the systems, we'd be depriving ourselves of the significant safety margin inherent in having redundant ignition systems in the first place.

The ignition switch in the cockpit has five normal positions: OFF, LEFT, RIGHT, BOTH, and START. The START setting is just like in a car; you turn the switch to that position to start the engine, and it's spring-loaded to return to the running position when you release the pressure on the key as the engine starts. The BOTH position is the normal position for flight, and it allows both of the ignition systems to operate, again, totally separate from each other. The LEFT and RIGHT positions, when selected, energize only the respective ignition system and disable the other one. Before takeoff, you push the throttle until the rpm of the engine is at a setting that the manufacturer specifies, usually around 1,700 rpm, and then switch from the BOTH position to either LEFT or RIGHT.

Then, you'll see that the engine keeps right on ticking, using only the chosen ignition system, while the other one is switched off. You'll also see that there is a minor decease in rpm, usually around 75 to 100 rpm, because the engine does lose some efficiency running on only one of the systems. The next step is to go back to the BOTH setting momentarily, and then switch to the other separate position. Again, the engine runs and loses a tiny bit of rpm. Go back to BOTH and your check of the ignition systems is complete. When you switch to only one of the two systems, you can immediately tell if there is a problem with any aspect of that chosen system. If the rpm drop exceeds the manufacturer's specification, or if the engine runs rough, taxi back to the hangar and have the maintenance folks take a look at it. It's that simple to have, and check, the safety factor that comes with two separate and independent ignition systems.

## Primer

Unlike cars, airplanes have a primer system that is activated with a push-pull knob on the instrument panel in the cockpit. This primer injects raw fuel into the intake manifold as an aid to starting. Some engines need lots of priming to start, especially in cold weather, whereas others need little or none. Your instructor will teach you the proper starting technique for the airplane in which you're training. Every modern airplane has a *Pilot's Operating Handbook* (POH) published by the manufacturer. The POH describes virtually every technique and procedure the pilot needs to know or be able to find to properly operate the airplane. Priming procedures are covered in the POH, and these vary from one airplane to the other.

The POH is a vitally important document. You will commit some portions of it to memory before you take your flight test for your license. If you're the kind of driver who has never opened the owner's manual for your car, your proclivity will change as you become a pilot. You can't ignore an airplane's POH.

## Flight Instruments

The basic flight instruments shown in FIG. 5-10 are the *airspeed indicator, altimeter,* and *turn coordinator* (or its predecessor, the *turn-and-slip indicator*). Most training planes that you will fly also have an *artificial horizon,* also called an *attitude indicator,* a *vertical speed indicator* (VSI), which many pilots also call a *rate-of-climb indicator,* and a *directional gyroscope* (DG).

The airspeed indicator is actually a pressure instrument that measures the velocity of the air moving past the airplane. To measure this impact pressure, a small tube is placed outside the cabin with the open end of the tube facing directly into the oncoming stream of air but outside of the propeller blast. This tube is called the *pitot tube,* pronounced "pea-toe" (FIG. 5-11). *Pitot* and many other aviation words and terms have French origins: fuselage, nacelle, chandelle, aileron, empennage, and the like. When aviation was in its infancy, and after the Wright brothers had first flown a powered airplane, the French quickly took over

**5-10** *The Cessna 150 instrument panel: 1, turn coordinator; 2, airspeed indicator; 3, directional gyro; 4, attitude indicator or artificial horizon; 5, clock; 6, vertical speed indicator; 7, altimeter; 8, G-meter; 9, VOR course indicator; 10, communication transceiver and VOR navigation receiver; 11, automatic direction finder receiver; 12, tachometer; 13, fuel gauges; 14, ADF bearing indicator; 15, ammeter; 16, vacuum gauge; 17, oil pressure and oil temperature gauges; A, parking brake; B, engine primer; C, combination magneto and starter switch; D, electrical system master switch; E, toe brakes; F, rudder pedals; G, glove box; H, carburetor heat; J, fuel mixture; K, throttle; L, elevator trim; and M, transceiver microphone.*

as the leaders in aircraft development. Most of these terms had been solidified in the jargon of aviation before World War I.

Don't confuse the airspeed indicator with your car's speedometer. The airspeed indicator is not a speedometer because the airspeed indicator merely shows the speed at which the airplane is moving through the air; it is actually measuring the speed of the air moving past the aircraft. The airspeed indicator cannot take into account the movement of the air mass supporting the airplane and through which it is flying. The movement of the supporting air mass is the wind aloft, and the presence of wind aloft will always make the *ground speed* of the airplane different from its airspeed. The ground speed is the speed at which you're actually moving across the ground. We'll cover this distinction completely in Chap. 9.

**5-11**  *Pitot tubes are usually heated to prevent ice blockage.*

Airspeed indicators do not tell the whole story about airspeed because the type of indicator used in lightplanes is a pressure instrument that cannot compensate for the varying density of the air in which it is flying. As an airplane climbs higher, or as air becomes warmer, the air is less dense. When the airplane is moving at the same absolute speed through less-dense air, the airspeed indicator shows a slower speed than if the air were denser. This occurs because the only thing that the airspeed indicator can measure is the impact of the oncoming stream of air into the open end of the pitot tube. Because less-dense air has fewer molecules for a given volume than does denser air, the airspeed indicator is "fooled" into measuring a slower speed than the absolute speed when flying in this less-dense air.

Because lightplanes, especially trainers, seldom fly very high, almost always below 10,000 feet in altitude, this inherent error does not generally cause the pilot much concern. The error can be corrected when the need arises, through the use of a pocket computer. You'll find many uses for an aviation computer, and many of them will be discussed in Chap. 9. When I learned to fly, we used a circular slide rule, marked off in miles per hour, knots, gallons per hour, and other aviation-related gradations. Today, most pilots use an electronic calculator, again modified

**5-12** *An electronic aviation calculator simplifies flight planning and provides accurate time, speed, and distance computations.*

to display aviation information, like the one shown in FIG. 5-12. I still use my circular slide rule because there aren't any batteries to die. It truly is hard to teach an old dog new tricks. You'll need to acquire one of the two types during your training because you can't do the navigational problems on the knowledge test or properly plan a flight without one.

Some airspeed indicators have a means for correcting for the varying density of the air and the resulting display on the indicator. This is done by a rotatable ring around the outside of the dial on the indicator's display. The pilot can rotate this ring to compensate for both the altitude at which she's flying and the temperature of the air outside of the airplane. When the ring is correctly rotated, the needle of the airspeed indicator then points to the *true airspeed* at which you're flying through the air. Without this correction, the indicator can only show your *indicated airspeed*. You must remember that when the indicated airspeed is corrected into true airspeed, either with the ring around the instrument or with a computer, you are still only seeing airspeed, not ground speed.

The altimeter really is a barometer, with its dial calibrated in feet (FIG. 5-13). All barometers measure the density of the air, and the altimeter is no exception. It works on the principle that air density, and therefore the pressure of the air, steadily decreases as you rise in altitude. The altimeter's readings need to be corrected for air temperature because the instrument can't

**5-13** *The altimeter has three hands. The longest hand indicates hundreds of feet; the middle hand, thousands; the shortest hand, ten thousands. The altimeter at left is showing 2,500 feet; at right, 6,000 feet. All readings are altitude above sea level.*

adjust itself. This adjustment normally isn't critical at the altitudes where lightplanes fly, but when necessary, the pocket computer can make this adjustment.

Air pressure, the result of the density of the air, constantly varies as a result of one or more of three variables. First, air pressure decreases as we rise in altitude. Second, as air warms, it gets less dense and therefore has less pressure. Lastly, the more humidity there is in the air, which means that the more water vapor is in the air, the less dense that air is. These last two factors influence the pressure of an air mass at a constant altitude. Along with these three variables, the atmosphere contains air masses that are less dense than an arbitrary norm, and also, there are air masses with pressures above the norm. These air masses are called *highs* and *lows*.

As an airplane flies through the atmosphere, it encounters changing air mass pressures almost from the moment of takeoff to the point of landing. The air is seldom totally stable over much of a distance. As these various weather systems and differing air mass are traversed, the altimeter must be adjusted, or "set" to the barometric pressure of the air mass in which the airplane finds itself from time to time. The altimeter has a little rotatable knob to make the adjustment and a little window to display the barometric pressure to which it's been set.

In practice, when you make local flights to and from the same airport, you'll make the altimeter setting correspond to the local barometric pressure very easily. Altimeters, when set to the local barometric pressure, read altitude above mean sea level (MSL). If you know the local altimeter setting, say, if it's given to you by a control tower, you just rotate the knob until the stated pressure appears in the window. Then, while you're still on the ground, the altimeter should display the airport's elevation MSL.

If you're flying from an airport that doesn't have a control tower, a *nontowered* airport, you rotate the setting knob until the elevation of that airport appears on the display. The elevation of every airport is shown on the aeronautical chart (a fancy word for map). Of course, you'll soon memorize the elevation of your home airport. Then you can read the airport's actual barometric pressure in the setting window. These are two ways to do the same thing—adjust your altimeter to the local barometric pressure.

When you fly away from your home base, you need to set the altimeter from time to time as your flight moves along so that you are reading the correct altitude. All altitudes below 18,000 feet are stated in MSL. If you look at your altimeter and see that you are at 5,500 MSL, you can look at the aeronautical chart and see the elevations of airports and obstacles such as radio towers and power plant stacks that are beneath you and quickly determine how high you are above them. If your altimeter hasn't been properly set, your display of altitude won't be accurate.

Every FAA radio facility, such as control towers and flight service stations, with whom you communicate will automatically give you the barometric pressure at its locale. That way, you can periodically set your altimeter and keep up with the inevitable changes in air pressure as you fly from one place to another.

The VSI is another barometric instrument. Its dial is calibrated to show whether the airplane is ascending or descending, and the display shows you this altitude change in hundreds of feet per minute (fpm). VSI readings are not instantaneous; rather, the instrument lags several seconds behind what the airplane is actually doing. For that reason, a VSI cannot be used to maintain level flight, and if you try to so use it, your flight profile will look like a roller coaster's. The VSI is used to establish a constant rate of climb or descent, if that becomes necessary during a flight. As a private pilot, you won't need to do this very often. But once you progress to the training for an instrument rating, you'll find the VSI very useful.

The turn-and-slip indicator is one of the oldest instruments in your panel, dating back well into the infancy of flight instrument development. You may hear older pilots call it the turn-and-bank indicator, but that term is a misnomer. This instrument is actually two separate instruments in the same case. One part of it looks like a carpenter's level, but it has a ball suspended in the fluid rather than an air bubble. When the ball is in the center of the tube, the airplane is in coordinated flight, which means that it is neither skidding nor slipping through the air. If the ball is off to one side, your flying isn't coordinated. There's an easy way to correct this situation. If the ball is off to the left, add a little left rudder pedal pressure; and if it's off to the right, press on the right rudder. There's an old saying to describe the corrective action, which is, "Step on the ball."

The other instrument that makes up the turn-and-slip indicator is a gyroscope that is connected to the needle on the face of the instrument. This immediately senses any turning of the airplane and deflects the needle in the direction of turn. When the airplane is on a steady path, and not turning in either direction, the needle stays centered.

The newer type of instrument, which gives the same information, is the turn coordinator. It still has the tube filled with fluid and the little ball to tell you if you're in coordinated flight. Instead of the needle to show turning, it has a little airplane symbol that banks in the direction of turn. There are some inherent deficiencies in this newer turn coordinator's presentation.

First, the little airplane symbol only shows the turn, not any information about whether the nose is level, high, or low. Some inexperienced pilots can confuse it with the artificial horizon, which we'll discuss next. Second, this instrument shows *only* turning. Although normal turns are made with the airplane banked, it is possible to cross-control an airplane, turning with just the rudder pedal and using the aileron to keep the wings nearly level. That isn't the correct way to turn, but it can be done, usually inadvertently. Just remember that when you see the little airplane symbol banked, it is only telling you that the airplane is turning in the direction of the displayed bank, and nothing more.

The artificial horizon, now more commonly called the attitude indicator, is another gyroscopic instrument. Today, it is a primary and required instrument for instrument flying. It displays the attitude of the airplane by using a small airplane symbol superimposed upon a level line on the face of the instrument. This line represents the horizon outside of the cockpit.

Depending on the precise make and model of the instrument, either the airplane symbol moves up, down, or banks left and right or the line does the moving while the airplane symbol remains stationary. In either type, the same information is displayed to the pilot. It tells whether the wings are level or banked, and if banked, in which direction. It simultaneously shows whether the nose attitude is level, high, or low relative to the horizon. It will take you a short while to be able to interpret the attitude indicator's display. Once you master reading this instrument quickly, it is a very useful tool because it senses attitude changes and displays them almost instantly, with no perceptible lag.

The DG is yet another gyroscopic instrument. It does not have any ability to actually sense direction, like the *magnetic compass* does. The DG has a display that is calibrated in the form of a circle, with the degrees of the compass direction inscribed on the face. The pilot must set the DG to correspond with the compass. This task is a part of the various pretakeoff checks that you'll learn. Setting the DG is very simple; you look at the compass and then grasp a rotatable knob on the DG and twist it until the DG's reading is the same as that shown by the magnetic compass. Once set, the DG is extremely stable, and it changes its displayed direction, what we call the *heading* of the airplane, just as fast as the airplane turns.

If you were a scout as a child, or have been a boater or hiker, you've probably got some memories of using a magnetic compass. The compass is anything but stable and must be held still to give an accurate reading. If it is jostled about by a shaky hand, or in airplanes, by any air turbulence, its readings are approximate at best. In rough air, the compass in an airplane can swing around so much that it becomes virtually useless. The DG isn't affected at all by turbulence or by the turning or pitching of the airplane. Therefore, in modern airplanes equipped with them, DGs are used by the pilot for primary indications of the airplane's heading.

There is a problem of which every pilot must be aware. All gyroscopes are subject to *precession,* which is their tendency to drift from a preset and stable setting. To make sure that the DG hasn't precessed too far, it is normally reset about every 20 minutes or so in flight. Pick a stable moment during your flight, when the airplane is established in straight and level cruise and then use the setting knob to make the DG's indication match the magnetic compass. I've seen DGs that didn't drift off of a set heading more than a degree or so in as long as an hour. I've seen others that had to be reset every 10 to 15 minutes. Usually, when you find one that drifts a lot over a short period of time, it's because that instrument is about ready for replacement. These gyroscopes spin at tremendous rates, as high as 30,000 rpm. The little bearings in them do wear out. When you see one start to precess at a faster rate than normal, that's a good sign that it's about at the end of its useful life. This instrument is then removed from the panel and sent to a certified instrument repair shop for overhaul.

Both the attitude indicator and the DG are usually powered by vacuum, which creates a stream of air through them, and this jet of air spins rotors inside the instrument, which in turn spins the gyro itself. The vacuum is created by a pump that is attached to the engine in most training airplanes. As soon as the engine starts, the vacuum pump starts producing the vacuum, which goes to the instruments through small hoses. Air rushes in one side of the instrument's case, as it is sucked in by the vacuum. Then, the instrument may take a moment or two for the gyroscope to spin up to operational rpm and for the instrument's indications to be reliable. By the time you taxi to the runway and perform your pretakeoff checks, your gyroscope instruments are ready to go.

Some older airplanes don't have vacuum pumps. Some airplanes have funny looking little hornlike devices attached to the side of the fuselage. These are *venturi tubes,* which create a vacuum as the air moves through them. A venturi, or maybe two, can provide the vacuum needed to power gyroscope instruments. But, because a venturi operates by air moving through it, the airplane must be flying for a sufficient amount of airflow through the venturi to exist. The only problem with a venturi is that the gyroscope instruments won't get spun up to operational rpm and stabilize until a few minutes after takeoff. A venturi also creates a small amount of drag because it protrudes into the airstream. The good side of a venturi is that it is very reliable. Unless its opening is blocked by some obstacle, such as ice or a bug nest, it can't fail. Vacuum pumps do break, and when they do, you have no gyroscope instruments until the faulty pump is replaced.

# Engine Instruments

There are three engine instruments that are common to all lightplanes; in fact, they are required by FAA regulation. In higher-performance airplanes, you'll find some additional gauges to tell you about what and how the engine is doing. In trainers, you generally see only the three required engine instruments.

The *tachometer* indicates the rotational speed of the engine, expressed in rpm. Tachometers are now standard equipment in most cars, so you should have seen one prior to flying an airplane. If you haven't, don't worry about it. The tachometer (often abbreviated as *tach*) is a simple instrument to read and use. Most of the tachs found in lightplanes are driven by a flexible cable that comes right off of the rear case of the engine. Some newer airplanes are equipped with electrically driven tachometers, but they are not very common in trainers. Because you'll almost certainly learn to fly in an airplane that has a fixed-pitch propeller, you'll learn to rely on the tach as the indicator of the engine's power output. Because an engine equipped with a fixed-pitch propeller can only have its power adjusted by the pilot changing rpm, you'll see that there are various rpm settings called for by the manufacturer that will, in turn, produce varying amounts of power from the engine. To increase power, increase the rpm by advancing the throttle; to decrease power, do the opposite, which will decrease the rpm.

The second of the three required engine instruments is the *oil pressure* gauge. This device tells us whether the engine's oil lubrication system is functioning properly. Every modern engine has an oil pump that pumps oil throughout the innards of the engine, under some pressure that the pump produces. Oil is the lifeblood of any engine; without constant lubrication, an engine will run only a few minutes at most before it tears itself apart internally and eventually seizes. Unless there is pressure circulating the oil, there won't be lubrication.

The oil pressure gauge has a green-colored range of readings, which is the normal range of proper oil pressure. Within a few seconds after the engine is started, you should see the oil pressure move up into the green range. In very cold weather, when the oil is very thick and somewhat congealed, it may take a minute or two for the pressure to come up. Your airplane's POH will specify the maximum amount of time it should take for oil pressure to develop. If it doesn't come up within this time, immediately shut down the engine to prevent any internal damage and have a qualified maintenance technician take over. Running the engine without oil pressure will soon destroy it and will cost someone thousands of dollars.

The last of the three engine instruments that we're discussing is the *oil temperature gauge*. This instrument does exactly what its name implies—it shows you the temperature of the oil inside the engine. Because the airplane's engine is air cooled, if the engine is cooling properly, the oil temperature will remain within normal limits. This gauge also has a green-colored range of normal temperatures. A rapid rise in oil temperature is a specter of a serious problem. The engine may be losing its oil supply, making the remaining oil increase in temperature. If you ever see your oil temperature rise suddenly, or rise above the normal operating range, discontinue the flight, land at the nearest airport, and have a maintenance technician find out what's happening.

# 6

# Flying the Airplane

Almost everyone has some sort of opinion about how safe or dangerous lightplanes are to fly. The truth can be summed up in a few words: Airplanes are neither safe nor dangerous—pilots are. Like most other areas of human endeavor, flying is what you make of it. Remember that machines are inanimate objects that can't make mistakes—only people can. If you have common sense, a degree of self-confidence without foolish bravado, and normal physical coordination, you can learn to be a very safe pilot and enjoy an entire career in aviation. If you like taking risks, get a rush out of the dangerous, or think you are immortal, stop right now and find another pursuit for your leisure time; stick to the airlines for transportation.

For those who want to be able to fly around the local area on nice days and maybe take a passenger, the training for a recreational license is within the grasp of almost anyone. But if you want to go on, and use an airplane for transportation, fly regularly at night, go into large metropolitan and unfamiliar airports, and even fly in instrument weather conditions, you will spend a substantial amount of time training for a private certificate and an instrument rating. Regardless of what level of certification, skill, and competence you want to eventually achieve, no good pilot ever really stops learning.

From the very beginning, the two most important things you can do in an airplane are to think and relax. Flying takes a good amount of planning and thought. No one can fly very well without being relaxed at the controls. Relaxed doesn't mean being inattentive; it means not being tense.

An airplane wants to fly and is, by its design and nature, a very forgiving machine. Remember the true story in the last chapter about the little Aeronca Champ that flew about 90 miles without the benefit of anyone in it. When your airplane is properly trimmed, it takes very little effort to fly it in cruise flight. There is another true story about a pilotless airplane—during World War II a B-17 bomber was so badly damaged from combat that the entire crew, pilots as well as the other crew members, bailed out, thinking that their bomber was doomed. It then did the same thing as the Champ; it flew on, across the English Channel, and back over England. When it finally ran out of gas, it glided down to a passable forced landing in a farm field, all without a soul on board.

Because airplanes are so inherently stable, pilots can get lazy and fall into sloppy flying habits. They forget the admonitions of their instructors to always think ahead of the airplane and have a plan ready. Laziness and thoughtlessness can and will eventually lead to trouble.

In aviation, you're not allowed the luxury of a great deal of time to defer a decision. When confronted with uncertain weather ahead or, perhaps, a dwindling fuel supply as darkness approaches and you're over unfamiliar territory, you can't procrastinate about what to do. In even the simplest of lightplanes, you're still moving along at around 100 mph, and you can't pull into a truck stop or rest area to ponder what to do next.

The solution is to have your options already identified and planned before you let things go that far. Pilots who tell of hair-raising adventures in airplanes are those who usually bring the situations upon themselves. They are poor planners, not good thinkers. This is one personality trait that is needed by every pilot—the ability to think out options first, before crunch time comes when events may make your decisions for you. Then, a pilot has to evaluate those options, make a reasoned decision, and execute it properly.

Your instructor will tell you, and then remind you more than once, to relax. If your muscles are tensed, you won't be able to feel the multitude of sensations of flight in a way that they will be helpful or enhance your learning. Controlling an airplane in a coordinated fashion is a learned feel. You can't feel anything very well while tense.

Don't confuse alertness with tenseness. A pilot should always be alert. I have found that relaxation and alertness are perfect partners. Some of my most alert moments, whether flying or doing anything else, come at a time when I'm otherwise relaxed. I can then devote my attention to flying an airplane, staying alert, and letting my brain work at peak efficiency, unimpeded by tenseness.

When you actually put your hand on the control wheel and take control of the airplane, you'll quickly learn that it takes very little physical force on the controls to produce the desired input. Your instructor might do what I have often done over the years, which is to have you grasp the wheel with only two or three fingers at first, to prevent you from applying too much force to it. Airplanes are flown with fingertip pressures on the wheel, not with large movements of the hands and arms like we have to do when making large turns in the average car. Pilots refer to this as *control pressure,* which is the term we'll use in this book. Don't think of the control wheel moving as you fly; just think of your applying pressure to it.

This same idea of pressure rather than control movement also applies to the rudder pedals. It's best not to wear heavy-soled boots while flying because you won't have the sensitivity in your feet that you will have if you wear thinner-soled shoes. I once knew a pilot who took his private pilot check ride in the early winter, wearing heavy leather boots for the first time in an airplane. He nearly failed the test because his control coordination was very poor because he couldn't feel the pedals. This fellow went on to become my mentor in aviation. I could not imagine his control technique ever being poor; when you flew with him, it was apparent very quickly that the control surfaces of the airplane were extensions of his fingers and feet.

Now let's go out to the flight line at a typical general aviation airport and become acquainted with a popular training airplane. In this book, we'll use the Cessna 150 as our trainer. Cessna made a newer version of it, the Cessna 152, for a few years before production of two-seat Cessnas ceased in the mid-1980s. Basically, a 152 is the same as a 150, except the 152 has a different engine, made by Textron Lycoming, in place of the Teledyne Continental engine used in the 150. The only other meaningful difference between the two is that the wing flaps on the 152 have a maximum extension of 30°, whereas the 150's flaps can go down to 40°. Properly handled, the 150 is a pure joy. Although not particularly difficult to fly, the Cessna 150 does demand enough of its pilot to teach good control technique.

If your flight school has Cessna 152s instead of 150s, don't worry. They fly virtually identically, but the newer 152 may rent for a few dollars more per hour than an older 150.

Piper and Beechcraft also made two-seat trainers. Piper manufactured an airplane called a Tomahawk and made trainers out of their Cherokee line of airplanes. Piper Cherokees usually have four seats, but to make a trainer, Piper put a smaller engine in one model of the series and restricted it to two seats. Beech made the Skipper, but it did not sell as well as the Piper trainers. All of the Piper and Beechcraft trainers are low-wing airplanes, which means that their wings are attached to the lower part of the fuselage, and the occupants sit above the wings. Cessnas are high-wing designs, in which the wings are mounted at the top of the fuselage, and the people inside sit below the wings.

Most pilots have an intense devotion to either high- or low-wing airplanes, and this feeling is usually rooted in whichever type they initially flew as a trainer. My preference is for high-wing airplanes, even though I've flown thousands of hours in both types. A high-wing airplane is usually easier to land, but it is harder to taxi, especially in much wind, than a low-wing plane. In flight, cockpit visibility out of a high-wing is excellent looking ahead and down but lousy in a turn when the wing blocks your vision in the direction of the turn. The low-wing airplane has poor visibility downward, but in a turn, you can see very well into the turn because the banked wing is out of your line of sight. My preference for a high-wing plane started because I learned to fly in one and didn't fly a low-wing for quite a while after my initial training. Plus, have you ever seen a low-winged bird? It just seems natural to me to sit in the shade and have the wing on top.

Let's begin with some familiarization facts about the Cessna 150. This is a two-place airplane, meaning that it carries a maximum of two people. Its empty weight is about 1,000 pounds, depending on how each particular one is equipped, and it will carry about 600 pounds of people, baggage, and fuel. This weight of occupants, baggage, and fuel is called an airplane's *useful load*. Every airplane has a *maximum gross weight* that is the most the entire airplane can legally weigh at takeoff. To find the useful load, you start with the gross weight, subtract from it the airplane's empty weight, and the result is the useful load. The useful load varies a bit from airplane to airplane of the same type because each one's empty weight is a little bit different, due mainly to optional equipment installed in one and not the other.

The Cessna 150 cruises between 110 and 117 mph, or between 95 and 100 knots. Today, we express all speeds in knots. I'm not sure why; to me miles per hour registers better in my head. But when we get into navigation in Chap. 9, you'll see that using knots makes things a bit easier when computing the effects of wind on your flight. This airplane has a fuel capacity of 22.5 usable gallons out of a total of 26 gallons. Almost all airplanes carry some fuel in their tanks that cannot drain out into the fuel lines that go to the engine. This is called *unusable* fuel. The 150 burns about 5 gallons per hour (gph) at cruise, and that gives the airplane a range of about 400 miles. That's not bad fuel efficiency, even in these times of fuel-consciousness.

# Preflight Check

Observe the airplane as you first approach it. This is where and when the *preflight check* should begin. Some instructors refer to this phase as the preflight inspection. See if the airplane is resting in a level attitude. If it isn't, a landing gear strut may need air or oil or a tire may be low or flat. There could always be damage to the landing gear that could have occurred during the previous flight that wasn't reported by the pilot.

There is no more important part of every flight than the preflight check. Only fools omit it, even if they own their own airplanes and no one has touched it since the last flight (FIG. 6-1). In your flight training, you'll almost certainly be flying rental airplanes at your flight school. Although flight schools do a very good job, on average, of maintaining their equipment, rental airplanes, because students and rental pilots are flying them, take more abuse than does the average airplane that is owner flown and is that owner's pride and joy.

For this reason, you should be taught, during your first few lessons, how to do a very thorough preflight inspection. If you arrive early enough for your next trip on an airliner, you'll see the copilot (called the first officer in airline lingo) do a walk around inspection of even the biggest airliner. No pilot is ever too advanced, or too knowledgeable, to perform the preflight check.

In the POH for your airplane, the manufacturer will provide a checklist for the preflight inspection. Some POHs refer to this as a *walk around* inspection. Whatever you call it, preflight check, preflight inspection, or walk around inspection, the process is the same, and so is the goal: to ensure, the best a pilot can in an exterior visual look-see, that the airplane is airworthy and safe for flight. The best way to conduct the preflight inspection is to begin at the same point on the airplane each time. You can

**6-1** *Preflight check. Look the airplane over carefully.*

modify your POH's checklist to begin at a point most convenient for you as long as you check each item covered in the checklist.

I usually start a preflight inspection at the pilot's door for several reasons. First, I've approached the airplane with my headset, flight case full of charts (maps), and probably some other stuff in my hands. So, the first step for me in almost any flight is to unlock the pilot's door and put those things inside the airplane. While I'm doing that, I usually plug my headset into the jacks in or under the instrument panel and remove the *control lock*. The control lock is a device that most often fits through the shaft in the control wheel and has a metal sheet, usually about 2 by 4 inches, or thereabouts, in size, which goes over the ignition switch.

When an airplane sits on the ground, the control surfaces such as the ailerons and elevators can be blown up and down by the wind or the propeller blast of passing airplanes. If they are left unlocked, this can severely damage the control mechanisms and hinges of the control surfaces. The control lock immobilizes these control surfaces, eliminating this threat of damage. The control lock has a little plate that fits over the ignition switch to prevent you from inserting the key and starting the airplane with the control lock still in place. But a few pilots manage to take off every year with the lock installed. I've never figured out how they do it, but a few people will always find a way to do some things unimaginable to the rest of us. So, when you get the door open and get your briefcase and other carry-ons stowed inside the airplane, remove the control lock as the first step in your preflight inspection.

While your head is still in the cockpit, make sure that the ignition and electrical master switches are turned OFF. Then, turn the master switch ON just long enough to do two things. First, look at the fuel gauges. In our Cessna 150 there are two fuel gauges, one for each tank, mounted one in each wing. Second, grasp the flap switch and run the flaps down to their full extension. Then, turn the master switch back OFF. When the switch is ON, you're running the battery down, and there's no need to leave it on while you do the rest of the preflight check. Lastly, while still inside the cockpit, look at the floor area right ahead of and between the two seats. There you'll find the fuel selector handle. Make sure that it is in the ON position. In the Cessna 150, you cannot direct fuel to the engine from the two fuel tanks independently; they both feed the engine simultaneously.

Because the pilot's door is on the left side in all single-engine Cessnas, the next step is to start walking toward the tail. While you're approaching the tail, look at the fuselage side. The metal skin of the fuselage should be inspected. If you see a wavy or wrinkled skin, call a maintenance technician; this condition almost always means that here is some hidden structural damage inside the fuselage. Assuming that the fuselage is OK, go on back to the tail.

Once there, squat down and untie the tie-down rope that is securing the tail. At the tail, you'll check three general areas. First, look at the elevators, and check both their top and bottom surfaces. Look for bad or missing rivets and wrinkled skin. Inspect the hinges very carefully where the elevators attach to the fixed horizontal stabilizer, and check the stabilizer, top and bottom again, for wrinkled skin or rivet problems.

Second, do the same inspections on the rudder and the vertical stabilizer. While you're located directly behind the airplane, you can see and check the connections of the control cables to both the elevators and the rudder. Check the trim tab on the trailing edge of the elevator, especially its hinge and control cable attachment.

Lastly at the tail, while squatted down, look at the underside of the fuselage. Here, you're looking for a couple of things. Check the skin for dents, wrinkles, or other obvious signs of damage. Also, look for any oil stains. If an airplane develops any but the most severe oil leaks in the engine, the oil will stream under the fuselage and be apparent if you look for it.

Continue around the tail, and proceed up the right side of the fuselage, repeating the inspection that you just made of the left side. The next step is to inspect the trailing edge of the right wing.

Now your first point of interest will be the extended flap. Look at the flap itself and the roller tracks upon which it extends and retracts. Grab the flap's trailing edge and shake it a little. It will have a small amount of play it in, but with experience you'll be able to detect if the flap is loose or if there is excess wear in the rollers or tracks. Next, look at the right aileron. Check its general condition, freedom of movement, hinges, and control cable attachments, just like you did for the elevators and the rudder. Now walk around the tip of the wing and look at it. See if there is any damage to it or the small light, called the *navigation light,* that is mounted on the wing tip. Next, walk on around the tip to the leading edge of the wing. Disconnect the tie-down rope, and check the leading edge for dents or other damage.

While at the leading edge, we need to inspect the fuel tank mounted in the right wing. Because the Cessna 150 is a high-wing airplane, and because the fuel tank filler opening and fuel cap are on top, we'll need a small step stool to get up there, unless you've recently played professional basketball. Most flight schools keep these stools or small stepladders in their trainers. Get up on the stool where you can remove the fuel cap and look directly down into the filler opening. You should be able to see that the fuel is full, and then put the cap back in place and twist it until it's properly closed. This is one of the more important parts of a preflight check and should never be omitted.

Never trust fuel gauges or ground service crews to make sure that you have fuel in the airplane. Remember when you looked at the fuel gauges in the cockpit; the reading you saw on them ought to match what you see when you actually look in the tanks. If not, get the gauges fixed. FIGURE 6-2 shows this part of the preflight properly performed. The ground service folks won't be along with you if you run out of gas. They will be sorry if it happens to one of their customers, but they won't suffer the physical consequences that you and your passengers will. No competent ground server will ever be insulted because you checked the fuel and caps, even if it's right after the air-

**6-2** *Always visually check the fuel tanks for quantity and correct type of fuel.*

plane was fueled and the gas truck driver is still right there. The best of these folks, and the most caring, will offer you the opportunity to do so just as they finish fueling your plane, even to the extent of leaving their ladder in place for you to use. Availing yourself of this offer will indicate to the FBO that they have a competent pilot renting their airplane.

While you're in this position ahead of the wing, it's good time to inspect the right landing gear. Check the tire for the appearance of proper inflation, and see if the tire's tread looks good, if there are any cuts in either the sidewalls or tread, or if there is excessive checking in the sidewall surface. Our Cessna has a spring leaf or spring tube (in the later models) for the landing gear leg. Not much goes wrong with them, and if it does, it's immediately apparent. While there, look at the brake on the wheel. There is a metal or flexible line running out of the fuselage and down the gear leg that carries brake fluid to the brake. Look for any leaks or fractures in this brake line. Disc brakes are used on all modern airplanes and the brake pads are exposed; check their thickness. You can also plainly see the brake disc, sometimes called the rotor, and see if it's cracked. If you don't recognize these parts, ask your instructor to point them out to you.

Now open the access door of the engine cowling. First, take a good look around the interior of the engine compartment. See if there are any oil streaks inside the cowling; they are evidence of engine oil leaks. Look for any broken or loose wires

**6-3** *Always check the oil before each flight.*

inside the area and around the engine. Check the exhaust system pipes and muffler for holes and large stains. Stains indicate either an engine oil or exhaust gas leak.

The next step is to check the quantity of oil in the engine (FIG. 6-3). Nobody checks the oil in a car each time it's driven, but we do check the oil each time we fly an airplane. Air-cooled engines, by their nature, consume some oil. Often flights last several hours, so we want to make sure that the oil is at the proper level before we begin a trip. You check the oil by pulling out the dipstick, just like in a car. Your POH will specify a minimum oil level for flight. If the oil is more than a quart or quart and a half below the full mark, ask your instructor to look with you. Many airplanes burn so little oil that such a reading is just fine; others go through so much that you might want to add oil if you're going on a cross-country flight away from the local area. FBOs often fill rental airplanes' oil supply to about a quart below the maximum reading because airplane engines often throw the first quart overboard quickly if they are filled to the maximum.

While you're still looking inside the engine compartment, you'll notice a small pull knob that opens the fuel strainer. You will want to use it to check for the presence of any water in the fuel. Because water is heavier than gasoline, and doesn't mix into solution with gas, this is easy to check. Pull the knob out for about 4 seconds and allow fuel to drain out into a transparent plastic cup; then you can hold it up and visually examine the contents. The fuel sump that is opened by pulling out on the knob is at the very bottom of the fuel system, so any water in the fuel will collect there and run out when you perform this fuel check. When you release the knob, be sure that the flow of fuel out of the strainer stops.

Look carefully at the cup of gas. Water, if any, should sink to the bottom, and it may form globules. Aviation fuel is colored on purpose so that its grade can be visually determined. The Cessna 150 runs on either grade 80 or 100 low-lead (100LL) aviation gasoline, which is abbreviated as avgas. Grade 80 is red, and 100LL is light blue. Water is naturally clear, so water will show up in a fuel sample if it is present. In the past, when we were finished looking at a fuel sample, we just dumped it on the tarmac. In these environmentally conscious times, dispose of it properly. Many 150s also have a gas drain on the bottom of each wing tank, near the cockpit doors. It your airplane has them, check the quality of the fuel in each tank with the cup. In the winter, if the airplane has not been stored in a heated hangar, the water in the fuel, if there is any, may freeze into ice balls. Then, little or no flow comes out of one or more of the strainers. If you experience this condition, don't try to fly the airplane. Have a technician look at it because the flow of fuel is probably blocked by ice.

The most common ways that fuel gets contaminated by water are either ill-fitting gas caps that allow rain to leak into the fuel tanks or through condensation. Overnight most of the year, water vapor condenses out of the atmosphere and forms water droplets, which are seen as dew on the grass, on the surface of the windshield of your car, and on any other solid surface. Unfortunately, this condensation also occurs on the inside walls of fuel tanks and not just in airplanes. The best way to avoid water condensing on the inside of the fuel tanks is to fill them with fuel after each flight, and especially after the last flight of the day. This way, there's no room for water to condense. If the airplane is stored in a heated hangar, the chances of condensation are reduced somewhat, but the threat is still there.

It is possible for contaminated fuel to arrive at the airport in the tanker truck that delivers it, and some fuel farm systems at airports are more susceptible to contamination than others. These are less common causes of water in fuel than are leaky gas caps and condensation. Regardless of the cause of its presence, engines won't run on water. So, always check the fuel for contamination.

After you've performed all of the inspections inside the engine compartment, close the cowling access door, and make sure that it's closed properly and tight. These doors can come open in flight, rip off, and possibly bang into the windshield if they're not closed properly. The next thing to check is the propeller.

Stand directly in front of the nose and look at each blade of the prop. Run your fingers lightly down the leading edge of the blades. You're looking for nicks in the blade. If you find one, no matter how small, have a technician look at it before you fly. There are some allowable small nicks, but if one is too deep, it can set up a stress point in the metal of the propeller. Stress points are where cracks begin. If a crack starts in a propeller blade, it can very quickly propagate until a piece of the blade breaks off. During flight, the propeller absorbs tremendous forces and stresses in normal operation, so make sure that it is free of defects. Also look at the back and front sides of the propeller too, looking for any signs of damage. If the bolts that secure the propeller to the flange of the engine's crankshaft are visible (they often aren't), check them too. Look here to see if they are present and look at the safety wire that connects all of the bolts together so that one cannot back off.

While still at the front of the airplane, the next item to check is the nose gear. The Cessna 150 has an air and oil shock strut, and you should plainly see some of the strut exposed. The POH describes the amount of strut that should be visible. If the proper length of strut is not exposed, have a technician add the needed air or oil to it before you fly. Also, look at the nose tire, checking for apparent proper inflation and the absence of any physical damage to the tire. There is no brake on the nose gear, so we inspect only the strut and tire up here.

Proceed on around the nose to the pilot's side of the cowling area. Here there is a tiny hole in the side of the fuselage, just behind the cowling. This hole is the *static air vent*. The pressure instruments that we described in Chap. 5 depend on the functionality of this air vent, and they won't work if the vent is blocked. These holes are so small that they can get clogged with wax when the airplane is cleaned, and they make very attractive homes for nesting insects. If you find it blocked, maintenance people will have to clean it before you proceed, or your airspeed indicator, altimeter, and vertical speed indicator won't function properly, giving you erroneous readings.

From here, walk along the leading edge of the left wing. Near the point where the strut attaches to the underside of the wing, you'll see another vent tube, which is the vent for the fuel system. It too must be clean and free of obstructions. If it's clogged, the fuel may not drain out of the tanks properly into the engine.

Check this fuel vent very carefully. Just outboard of the fuel vent is the pitot tube, which we talked about in Chap. 5. This is the tube where the ram air enters to operate the airspeed indicator. The airspeed won't work at all if the pitot is blocked. Like the static air hole, the pitot is very attractive to insects as a place to build a nest.

From here, go down the leading edge of the left wing, around the wing tip, to the trailing edge. Inspect the aileron and flap on the left wing in the same way you did on the right side. When those tasks are done, so is your exterior preflight check of the airplane. And, you're standing right beside the pilot's door, where the entire process began moments ago.

## Getting Started

Now you know that the airplane is safe to fly, because everything was checked out during the preflight inspection. Now it's time to get in. You'll sit in the pilot's seat, on the left, starting with your very first instructional flight. The airplane has fully functioning dual controls at both pilots' seats, even down to the brakes. Therefore, your instructor will sit on the right, where he can fly the airplane until you learn. The Cessna 150 is not the easiest or most graceful airplane to enter. The cockpit is a bit cramped but not overly so. The door is a bit small, so you'll be tempted to look for something inside to grasp to assist your getting in. Don't grab the control wheel or instrument panel. Rather, there is an assist strap on the forward door post that is there just for that purpose.

Both of the seats are adjustable fore and aft, just as they are in a car (FIG. 6-4). They slide on tracks, with the release located at the front bottom of the seat. Adjust the seat into a position so that you're comfortable and can reach all of the controls. Push the rudder pedals, one at a time, throughout the full length of their travel to make sure that you can get full rudder deflection if you need it. The FARs require that the seatbelt and shoulder harness be worn by those in the pilot seats during takeoff and landing. Get into the habit of adjusting and fastening both of them right now, before you even start the engine. It's such an ingrained habit in me that I "belt up" even if I'm only going to taxi an airplane from one spot on the airport to another, with absolutely no intention of flying. We still have a few more things to do before we start the engine.

**6-4** *Adjust the seat for comfort. Using a modern headset will make communications much easier and will save your hearing too.*

Before engine start, it's smart to set the parking brake. To do that, push down on both of the *toe brakes,* which are the top halves of each rudder pedal. While you keep both brakes depressed, pull out the parking brake knob to its fullest extent of travel. Then, take the pressure off of the toe brakes, and release your pull on the parking brake knob. Cessnas have independent brakes on each wheel, activated by the toe brake on the respective rudder pedal. If you've ever operated a tractor, or other such machinery, you'll know about independent brakes. If you haven't, the knack of using them comes very quickly. On the ground, airplanes are steered by an interconnect between the rudder pedals and the nose gear. Pushing a rudder pedal turns the nose wheel in the same direction. The independent brakes allow a pilot to turn in a tighter radius than can be done using the nose wheel steering alone. It's a very bad habit to turn by using the brakes unless absolutely necessary. If you lock a brake, you can turn the airplane around in its own wingspan distance, but that is very hard on the tire that isn't rotating.

Once you're in your seat, the instrument panel is directly in front of you. There are several electrical switches on a sub-panel. Look at each of these and make sure that they are all OFF. Then, look at the floor, and check once more to see that the fuel selector is in the ON position. Even though you checked the fuel selector during the preflight, make sure that neither you nor the instructor kicked it to the OFF position as you got into the cockpit. If you start the engine with the fuel selector OFF, there is likely to be just enough fuel in the lines to allow you to taxi to the runway and commence the takeoff. As you lift off, things can get mighty quiet if the selector isn't ON.

To the right of the subpanel where the electrical switches are you'll find the three primary engine controls, the *carburetor heat, throttle,* and *mixture* knobs, in that order as you move from left to right. First, ensure that the carburetor heat (abbreviated as carb heat) is pushed all of the way into the panel, in the COLD position. We'll talk a lot more about its use in a little while. Move your hand to the right of the throttle, and you'll see the red mixture control knob. Make sure that it too is pushed all of the way in, which will be in the RICH position.

Next, lay your right forefinger along the shaft of the throttle, with the knob of the throttle in the palm of your right hand. If you position your forefinger with the nail about $\frac{1}{4}$ of an inch from the stop, you can then push the throttle in about $\frac{1}{4}$ of an inch. That's about all the throttle opening you need for engine start. Never try to start an engine with the throttle opened much more than that for a couple of reasons. First, the engine is cold, so we want it to start running at a low rpm to allow it to begin to warm up and the oil to start circulating throughout it. It's very damaging to any engine to run it at high rpm before it and the oil have warmed. Second, if the parking brake isn't set properly, or if there is any other problem with the brakes, we don't want the airplane to start moving rapidly across the ramp. If you start the engine at this throttle opening of around $\frac{1}{4}$ of an inch, the airplane probably won't move at all even with the brakes off. If it does move, it will be slowly, and you'll have time to shut the engine down before trouble strikes.

Before starting the engine, it'll need to be primed most of the time. If the weather is warm and the airplane has just returned from a previous flight, maybe you won't need to prime; your instructor will tell you. The primer is located on the subpanel, over to the left. To use it, you rotate it until it can be pulled out and then pull it out all of the way. Push it in slowly and repeat the process once. That will give the engine two shots of prime, which should be sufficient unless the weather is cold. It's always better to be conservative about priming because overdoing it will flood the engine. If the engine doesn't start readily with two shots of prime, you can always prime some more. But clearing a flooded engine is a nightmare of a job, and it sometimes runs the battery down if it's weak.

Now, turn the *master switch* to ON, which will energize the airplane's electrical system and enable you to use the starter. It's a red button or rocker switch, located near the throttle or near the primer (the exact location and type of switch changed from year to year during production of the 150). Open the window and yell "Clear." Yell it loudly so that anyone near the airplane will hear you and know that you're about to start the engine. Wait a moment and look out the windshield and around the airplane to see if anyone is nearby.

Once you've assured yourself that no one is near the airplane, turn the ignition switch to the START position, and as soon as the engine catches, release the key just as you do when starting your car. The ignition switch is spring-loaded to return to the BOTH position as soon as the starter is released. Some older 150s have a pull handle to engage the starter. If you're learning in one of them, you turn the ignition switch to BOTH, pull the T-handle out to engage the starter, and release it as the engine starts.

We want to idle the engine at about 1,000 rpm (FIG. 6-5). As soon as the engine gets going, look at the tachometer and make whatever fine adjustment is needed with the throttle to achieve that idle rpm. An rpm of 1,000 is enough to allow the alternator to kick in and start recharging the battery and powering the electrical system, yet it's slow enough not to unduly strain a cold engine. Immediately look over at the oil pressure gauge. The needle should come up out of the red zone within 30 seconds, sooner if the weather is warm or if the airplane has been recently flown. If the pressure doesn't move up into the green zone within that time frame, immediately shut the engine down to avoid any further damage from running it without oil pressure.

If the engine is running properly and the oil pressure came up within limits, we're ready to begin taxiing and move out of our parking spot. If the flaps haven't already been retracted from your preflight inspection, do so now. A tap of your toe on each toe brake, simultaneously, will release the parking brake. Keep your feet up on the rudder pedals so that you can steer and be able to apply the brakes if needed. If the airport has a control tower, we'll have to contact ground control for permission to taxi from the parking area onto taxiways.

Applying a little power by pushing the throttle in a little is all it will take to start the airplane moving. Keep the same hand position on the throttle that you did for starting, using

**6-5** *Adjust the engine idle after starting with your forefinger along the throttle shaft. Notice the transponder in this airplane, below the navcom unit.*

your forefinger along the shaft, with the knob in the palm of your hand. That way you can make fine adjustments in the throttle setting. If we need to turn, pressure on the rudder pedal in the direction of desired turning will get that job done. The connection between the rudder pedals and the steerable nose gear is a bit sloppy. It is not nearly as positive and precise as is the steering in a car. In Cessna airplanes, the steering linkage disconnects as soon as the airplane lifts off of the runway, and the shock strut in the nose gear extends. If you ever find that your 150 won't steer on the ground, check the extension of the strut in the nose. If it's got too much air in it, it is possible for it to be extended beyond the point where the steering disconnects. That's why the POH will specify a minimum and a maximum amount of extension on the ground, when you do your preflight check. Too little, and there's not enough shock absorption; too much and there's no steering.

The control wheel has no direct steering at all. During your first couple of flights, your instructor may ask you to taxi with your right hand on the throttle and your left hand in your lap. This is often done to get a student used to steering with the rudder pedals and to eliminate the natural tendency, at first, to rotate the control wheel in an attempt to steer while taxiing.

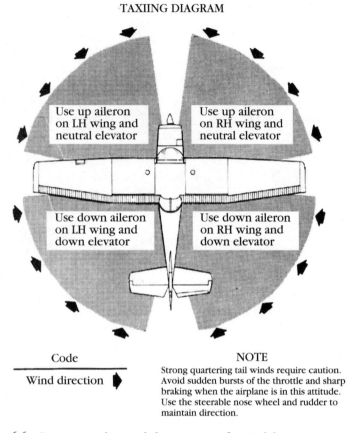

TAXIING DIAGRAM

Use up aileron on LH wing and neutral elevator

Use up aileron on RH wing and neutral elevator

Use down aileron on LH wing and down elevator

Use down aileron on RH wing and down elevator

Code

Wind direction

NOTE

Strong quartering tail winds require caution. Avoid sudden bursts of the throttle and sharp braking when the airplane is in this attitude. Use the steerable nose wheel and rudder to maintain direction.

**6-6** *Proper control inputs help compensate for wind during taxi operations.*

Later on, the instructor will show you that the wheel does play a part in taxiing if there is any appreciable wind (FIG. 6-6). If you have to taxi over any rough ground, unless the wind is very strong from behind you, pull the control wheel all the way back to take weight off of the nose wheel.

The tricycle landing gear is a wonderful invention. It has made ground handling of airplanes far easier than was the case with tailwheel airplanes. A tailwheel configuration results in different geometry and taxiing techniques than you'll learn in a 150. But, the nose gear is inherently weak by the nature of its placement under the heaviest part of the airplane, right beneath the engine. When you have to taxi over sod, or other rough areas, pulling the wheel back will lighten the weight that the nose gear is carrying. If the sod is at all soft, the little nose tire can act like a knife and cut its way down into the mud to the point that you can get stuck, or worse, strike the propeller on the ground. Don't taxi on sod as a student until your instructor and you talk about the techniques to use and you get her OK to do so.

If you're operating at a nontowered airport (we used to call them noncontrolled airports), it's up to each pilot to proceed on a see-and-be-seen basis. There is nothing inherently unsafe about nontowered airports. If you drive on the Los Angeles freeway system, or in any other areas of congested auto traffic, you certainly don't have a control tower telling you what lane to be in or when to speed up or slow down, or making any of the other decisions that a driver makes every few seconds. For some reason, people not accustomed to aviation think at first that every airport needs a control tower. That just isn't so.

At nontowered airports, we still use the radio, which is discussed further later. As you roll down the taxiway, keep your speed to that of a fast walk. If you creep along, it'll take forever to get to the runway, and you'll probably have difficulty steering the airplane because the response is a little sloppy. If you careen along, that's unsafe. While taxiing, we have an opportunity to talk about the carburetor heat control and its use.

The throat of the carburetor has a device called a *venturi,* which is shaped like an old-fashioned soda bottle. It's a tube that is narrower in the center of its length than it is at either end. Due to some laws of physics and fluid mechanics, a stream of fluid moving through a venturi undergoes a loss of both pressure and temperature as it leaves the narrow part of the tube where it was first compressed. As the stream of fluid (air and gasoline are both fluids) leaves the compression zone in the venturi, it rapidly expands as it is sucked into the intake manifold of the engine. This expansion results in the loss of pressure, and more importantly for this discussion, it's temperature can decline dramatically. This decrease in temperature of the mixture of fuel and air flowing through the venturi in the carburetor can be as much as 40° Fahrenheit (F).

Air always has some water vapor, which we think of as humidity, in it. Because of the temperature drop that occurs in the carburetor, this water vapor can freeze, and ice can form in the carburetor throat when the outside air temperature is between 25 and 70° F. If this happens, the mixture of fuel and air going to the engine can be reduced or completely blocked by an accumulation of ice in the carburetor's throat.

Carburetor ice usually occurs when the engine is running at relatively low rpm because the flow of the fuel/air mixture through the carburetor is going relatively slowly, allowing more time for the ice to form. If your car has a carburetor, rather than the newer fuel injection, your engine may have stalled at stoplights in cool, rainy weather or at least have a hesitancy to accelerate away from the stop. Now you know why— you may have had carburetor ice.

In normal cruising flight, carburetor ice isn't too much of a concern. With the engine running at or above the cruise power settings, the flow through the carburetor is sufficient to deter ice formation, unless atmospheric conditions are really favorable for icing. Carburetor ice at cruising speeds usually only occurs when the humidity is really high or if you're flying IFR through clouds or rain, where there is obviously lots of moisture in the air. The symptoms of icing are easily recognizable— the rpm will start to drop, sometimes very slowly, over a period of several minutes. If the pilot doesn't know what's happening, and he surely should if he's awake, the engine will start to run rough as more ice forms in the carburetor. If the pilot is really asleep, the engine will probably stop running.

Before the situation gets to the point of even rough running, you will have noticed that the rpm has fallen off a little and taken the curative measure, which is to pull out the carb heat knob. Almost instantly, the ice will melt; the carburetor heat system sends very hot air, taken from a muff around the exhaust pipes, directly into the carburetor. The induction of this hot air drives the temperatures in the carburetor throat up to a point where the ice melts very quickly. When the ice melts, the slug of water that results goes only one place, through the engine. For that reason, the engine will run rough for a second or two as it ingests the water. Even if you delay taking remedial action until the engine is running rough from the presence of carburetor ice, the heat will still cure it. However, if you procrastinate until the ice blockage in the carburetor kills the engine, you're now in a glider. Without the engine running, there is no source of hot air to melt the ice.

We almost never apply carb heat for takeoff. The hot air is much less dense than cold air. Therefore, two things happen. The ratio of fuel to air in the normal mixture of the two gets very rich, which means that there is less air in the mix than there should be, because the hot air is so much less dense. Another product of running the engine with the hot, less dense air going through it is that the engine can't produce its normal amount of power. Engines take loads of air to run properly, and when the air is less dense, the power production falls off. This also happens at higher altitude, where the air is just less dense, regardless of temperature. Naturally, the hotter and higher you are, the less power is produced. At takeoff, we use full power in piston-powered airplanes that don't have turbochargers. We need all of the power we can get for take-off and don't want part of it robbed by using carb heat.

The red mixture control knob controls the ratio of fuel to air in the mix that is fed from the carburetor into the intake manifold and then into the cylinders of the engine. When the airplane gets very high or even at fairly low cruise altitudes on hot summer days or anytime that the carb heat is left on for an extended period of time, the pilot can correct the overly rich fuel mixture by using this control. The time-honored way to set a proper mixture is to *lean* the mixture by pulling out slowly on the control knob until you begin to note that the engine is just starting to run a little rough.

This signals that the mixture is getting too lean; there is not enough fuel in the mix. Then, you push the mixture control knob back in, again slowly, until the engine runs smoothly again. Leave the mixture there until you either change power setting or altitude, when you'll have to repeat the process to accommodate the new conditions.

We've finally arrived near the runway after a good taxi. Gently apply the brakes and we'll stop the airplane on the *runup pad,* which is an area just short of the runway. Here we can go through our final pretakeoff checks.

If we were flying at a towered field, the ground controller would have given us the barometric pressure so we could set the altimeter. But because we're flying from a nontowered airport, we set the altimeter so that the face of it reads the elevation of the airport, in feet above MSL. Because this is our home base, your instructor knows the elevation and will tell it to you on your first instructional flight. When you go to another airport, you can get the information by looking for a sign, which is often posted near the ends of the runways; if there aren't any such signs, just pull out your aeronautical chart and look up the airport symbol, and you'll find the elevation in the printed block of data about that airport. Never fly without the chart that covers your area, even for local flights.

Turn the little setting knob at the bottom of the altimeter to move the indicator hands on the face of the instrument until they read the field elevation. Here at our airport, the field elevation is 905 feet MSL. When you look in the window for the barometric pressure, you'll see 30.00" Hg (30 inches of mercury). That's the barometric pressure right now. If we had a control tower here, the controller would have given us the pressure information, and we would have twisted the same setting knob until 30.00 showed in the window. Then, the hands on the altimeter's face would have shown 905. Like other measuring devices, an altimeter can and will eventually get out of calibration, to the point that the correct elevation won't show when the right barometric pressure is dialed into the window. For VFR flying such as we're doing, an acceptable difference is about 50 feet, maybe as much as 75. If there is more than that, the altimeter needs to be removed from the airplane and sent to an approved instrument repair shop for calibration.

Because we're flying in warm weather, we've taxied with the cockpit windows open. Now it's time to latch them prior to takeoff and also to give each door a little push to make sure that it is properly closed and latched. Check your door and the instructor's too. As the pilot, you're responsible to see that a passenger has a safe flight. A good instructor wants to be treated as a passenger to the extent possible so that you'll develop good habits now, for the day after you get your license and fly with folks who don't know all of these things.

Your airplane's POH contains a checklist for every phase of flight, including the pretakeoff checks that we're now doing. *Always* use it. Most flight schools and FBOs copy the checklists and put them in laminated plastic sheets, often bound together with a ring at the top of the pages, so you can easily flip from one checklist to the other. If there isn't a bound group of checklists in the airplane you're flying, take your copy of the POH, which you'll have to purchase for a nominal sum, and create this flip page bound checklist for yourself.

The items on the checklists are too important to risk to memory. Later in your flying, you will advance to more complicated airplanes, and the checklists will get more involved too. If you fly more than one type of airplane, which many pilots do, you can't remember several different checklists. Now is the time that you will be forming the habits that will make you either a careful, safe pilot or a risky one, just as a child forms his or her personality early in life. Make the habits you develop now the kind that will bode you well over the entire spectrum of your flying career. The rest of the steps we'll describe now for the pretakeoff checks are normal ones in most airplanes. If your checklist differs either in content or in the order in which items are done, follow the checklist.

We'll first check the flight controls for freedom of movement. Many serious accidents have resulted from the pilot's failure to remove the control lock or to discover a problem with the flight controls that would have been easily discernible had they been checked. On some airplanes, control locks consist of blocks that are attached to the control surfaces and clamp the rudder, elevator, and ailerons so that they can't be moved. You don't have any indication inside the cockpit that these clamps are in place until you try to move the controls throughout their complete range of movement. Roaring down the runway on takeoff is no time to discover that your controls are still locked. You should have seen these external clamps when you did the preflight inspection, but we're not leaving anything so important to chance.

Take the control wheel and rotate it fully from one side to the other and then pull it all of the way back. Next. Push it all of the way forward. While you're doing this exercise, turn your head and look at the control surfaces to ensure that they're actually moving. Do the same with the rudder pedals.

The elevator trim is controlled by a large black wheel that protrudes from the instrument panel below the throttle (FIG. 6-7). It has a pointer that moves as the wheel is turned. There is a setting where the pointer will be opposite the word TAKEOFF printed beside the pointer. Rotate the trim wheel until the pointer lines up with TAKEOFF.

Next, we'll check the operational health of the engine. Hold the brakes firmly down all the way and advance the throttle until the tachometer reads 1,700 rpm. Look outside for a moment to make sure that the brakes are holding. Because it's summer, we don't have to worry about the airplane sliding on snow or patches of ice that may be on the runup pad. Put that possibility away in your memory banks for winter flying. With the engine running at 1,700 rpm, grasp the key in the ignition switch and rotate the switch from BOTH to the R position and watch how many rpm's are lost now that the engine is running only on the right magneto.

It should drop about 75 rpm or so because the engine is slightly less efficient when running on only one of the magnetos, when only one of the two spark plugs in each cylinder is firing. A larger drop than that should be checked by the maintenance

**6-7** *Set the elevator trim prior to takeoff.*

folks before you fly. If there is no drop, that indicates that the switch might be faulty and might not be switching off the left magneto, another thing that needs to be fixed right now. A switch that doesn't turn a magneto off is very dangerous because the engine is "hot" at all times on the ground and could fire or even completely start if someone rotates the propeller on the ground, even slightly. After you've checked the right magneto, turns the switch back to BOTH for a few seconds.

When running on only one magneto, the plugs normally fired by the other one aren't firing and slightly foul as carbon builds up in their electrodes. Turning the switch back to BOTH allows them to fire and clear up any of these deposits. Then, turn the switch to L and check the rpm drop when running only on the left magneto. Many POHs also have a specification for the maximum differential in the rpm drop between what you see on one magneto, and the other. Our engine has thus far checked out OK, so let's go to the next step.

Return the switch to BOTH; we're finished with the magneto check. Pull out the carburetor heat control knob all of the way. Again, there should be some rpm drop because the hot air robs the engine of some of its power. If the engine runs more than a little bit rough, that's cause to get it looked at. If there is no rpm drop, that also means a trip to the maintenance shop; when the carb heat is functioning normally, there is some drop, usually also about 75 rpm. While you're doing this, glance over at the oil pressure and temperature gauges to make sure that their readings are both within the green, normal operating range. Then, reduce the throttle to our 1,000-rpm idle setting. Pull the throttle out all of the way to make sure that doing so doesn't reduce the setting so low that the engine quits. With the throttle all of the way out, the engine should idle smoothly, usually at around 650 rpm. The alternator warning red light may come on, and that's all right so long as it goes back off when you put the power back up to 1,000 rpm.

Also look at the vacuum gauge, which tells us if the engine-driven vacuum pump is providing the vacuum needed to run the attitude indicator and the directional gyroscope. It should read about 4 inches of vacuum. Although we don't actually need these instruments for VFR flying, if the pump isn't working, get it fixed. You may someday stray into IFR weather and have to avail yourself of the emergency instrument flying training you'll receive as a part of your training. You can't do that if the instruments aren't getting the vacuum that they need to operate.

Your instructor will show you how to position the airplane on the runup pad to perform these pretakeoff checks. If there is any appreciable wind blowing, the airplane should be heading into the wind for a couple of reasons. First, we have an air-cooled engine, so heading into the wind allows a flow of air into and over the engine to cool it. Sitting with the engine running, especially at the higher power settings that we used for the magneto and carburetor heat checks, can lead to higher than desired engine temperatures if we have the nose pointed away from the wind. Second, if the wind is blowing hard, it's much safer to have the nose pointed into that wind because that way the airplane is more easily controlled and far less likely to blow around or over.

After all of these checks are completed, the last thing to do before takeoff is to visually assure yourself that no one else is in the way of your take off. The FARs and common sense both provide that landing aircraft have the right of way over those waiting to take off. You don't want to be in the takeoff position on the runway until you're certain that nobody is landing on the runway or even on a different runway at a nontowered field. If you have the physical room on the runup pad, turn the airplane completely around in a 360° circle and look out of the windshield to see the entire traffic pattern all of the way around the airport. The *traffic pattern* is a planned and prescribed rectangular course around the airport that airplanes follow when landing or departing. We'll talk about it more later. A towered fields, the controllers are supposed to provide separation between airplanes under their jurisdiction. But all humans make mistakes, and controllers are no exceptions. Even though you may be cleared by a tower to take the runway, certainly look around yourself first, and taxi off of the runup pad only when both you and the controller are satisfied that it's safe to get onto the runway.

# Ready for Takeoff

Now we know that there isn't any other traffic, so we're ready to fly. Taxi the airplane onto the runway, and line up in the center of it. Smoothly push the throttle all of the way in to the full power position. You maintain a straight course down the center by using the rudder pedals to steer the nose wheel (FIG. 6-8). Be careful that your feet aren't planted up high on the pedals, because you don't want to be apply any pressure on the brakes at this point. As you roll down the runway, the airplane picks up speed rapidly.

After we've rolled about 800 feet, the airspeed indicator will have swept past 50 knots. You'll also realize that, in the meantime, the flight controls have "come alive," which means that enough air is flowing over them and that they are now effective. Ease back on the control wheel so that the nose rises a bit to give the wings a positive angle of attack. Initially, you'll need

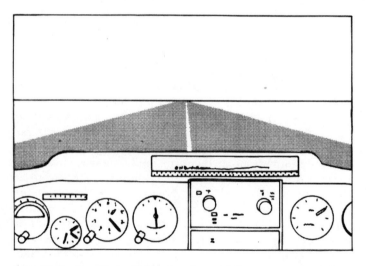

**6-8** *Beginning of takeoff: The throttle is at full power; use the rudder pedals to keep the airplane tracking down the runway.*

to pull back a little bit more than you have because most people are a little tentative on the first takeoff. As soon as you have the nose tire off of the ground, the airplane will become airborne. Hold the nose right where it is, relative to the outside horizon, and we'll start climbing away from the runway.

The nose will start swinging a little to the left, due to the P-factor of the propeller. Apply a bit of pressure to the right rudder to keep the nose going straight, and use the control wheel to keep the wings level. You'll soon develop the habit of selecting a reference point beyond the end of the runway at which to aim the nose, and that will keep you going in a straight line during the climb out.

Now it's time for your first lesson in how to control an airplane's airspeed. In lightplanes, pilots usually control the airspeed with a combination of nose attitude and power setting.

Whenever we have a fixed power setting, such as now while we're climbing at full power, the desired airspeed is maintained by adjusting the nose attitude up or down, as the need arises. There are many airspeeds at which we could climb. The POH sets out a certain climbing airspeed that would get us up over any obstacle in our path in the shortest distance over the ground. This is called the *best angle of climb* speed. Another predetermined climbing airspeed will give us the most altitude gain in the shortest period of time, and this is the *best rate of climb* speed.

Here at our airport we don't have short runways, nor do we have any obstacles in our path right after takeoff, so we don't need to climb at the best angle possible. We could climb at the best rate, which would get us at altitude in less time than if we climb at any other speed. But, even at the best rate of climb speed, the nose will probably be riding high on the horizon, somewhat blocking our view straight ahead. Develop a habit right now of thinking about where other airplanes might be, and always being alert to keep an eye out for any collision hazard. Few pilots ever survive a midair collision. So, we'll use a compromise airspeed in our climb that gives us a decently good rate of climb and also allows the nose attitude on the horizon to be low enough that we can easily see if there are any other airplanes in our path. Experience has determined that around 70 knots is a good speed, and we call this a *cruise climb* airspeed. Using the cruise climb speed also allows more airflow through the engine compartment. On a hot summer day, this might be important, because we don't want to see the engine temperatures get too high during a climb.

As we approach 400 to 500 feet above the ground, we'll make a 90° turn, usually to the left, although at some airports, local rules call for a right turn if there are obstacles off to the left or if there are noise-sensitive areas over there. Once we make this 90° turn, we can climb out, away from the airport. Most flight schools use a designated area somewhere near the airport but far enough away that training maneuvers don't present a threat to airplanes coming and going into the traffic pattern. This is called the *practice area*. We'll climb to our practice area, and level off from our climb when we're about 2,000 feet above the ground.

To level off from the climb, first put the nose level on the horizon by applying a little forward pressure on the control wheel. The first few times that you do this, look out at the wingtips on both sides of the airplane. When the undersides of the wings are roughly level with and parallel to the horizon, you'll be fairly close to a nose level attitude. Now the attitude of the nose will only need minor adjustments to achieve level flight. You can see by looking at the altimeter whether we're continuing to gain altitude, losing it, or staying level. Don't chase the altimeter; rather, use it only as a reference. If we're still going up, lower the nose a little more, wait a few seconds, and see if that stops all climbing. If you have overcorrected, and we start going down, raise the nose a little, wait, see what happens, and make whatever final adjustment in the nose attitude that is needed. Learn now not to chase the instruments' indications—you'll never fly level that way.

After we level off, and as the airspeed builds to around 90 knots, we'll pull the throttle back to cruise power. If we were going on a cross-country flight, we'd run the engine somewhere between 2,350 and 2,500 rpm, depending on how high we were, how far we needed to go, and a few other factors. But for training flights, we aren't interested in flying as fast as practicable, and there is no need to burn fuel at any higher rate than we need. Additionally, even though we are wearing headsets and have a voice-activated intercom to enable us to talk to each other, we don't want any more cabin noise than is necessary. Headsets do a good job of reducing the otherwise high cabin noise level, but any reduction in the ambient noise only makes it quieter and easier for us to talk to each other. And, we are going to be talking almost constantly during these first few lessons. A good compromise power setting for training in our Cessna 150 is 2,350 rpm.

Your instructor will show you how to use a friction control knob on the throttle. Lightplanes have enough engine vibration in flight to cause the throttle to creep, sometimes in, sometimes out, during cruise. There is a knurled circular knob around the throttle shaft that can be tightened to prevent the throttle from unwanted movement. Tighten it down to keep the power at 2,350 rpm. Lastly, now that we're all leveled off, reach down to the elevator trim wheel and rotate it, usually forward, so that you don't have to keep constant pressure applied to the control wheel to keep the nose level. The goal is to trim the airplane for level flight so that it will stay level when you totally take your hands off of the wheel.

You'll quickly get the hang of the effects of each of the flight controls. It's best, now, to forget mechanically using the controls. Don't think about moving them but sense the pressures that you need to apply to achieve a desired attitude. All performance from an airplane results from the combination of attitude and power that the pilot has selected. Just think of what you want to happen. Think in terms of left wing down, right wing down, nose up, nose down, and the like rather than trying to translate the desired attitude into mechanically moving the controls. Let the controls become extensions of your limbs and mind. If that sounds a bit confusing, consider it this way. Your nervous system masters the techniques of physical movement quite easily. When you throw a baseball, you don't mentally break down the action into the many muscle movements involved in the task. You just pick up the ball and throw it. When you teach a child to throw a ball for the first time, you don't analyze the action to any great extent. Rather, you teach the child to get the "touch" and "feel" of throwing.

Control handling is a technique that is difficult to verbalize precisely. You drive a car in the same manner, making constant small control inputs to do what you want to do without conscious thought about each tap on the brake, increase in pressure on the gas pedal, or small correction with the steering wheel.

At first, you'll probably have a tendency to overcontrol the airplane by using too much movement of the controls. Don't worry about it. It's natural and is a habit developed from driving cars and operating other machines that are less sensitive to control inputs than airplanes are. Your technique will quickly improve as you get accustomed to the light control forces needed to fly. Most often only fingertip pressures will suffice, especially in making the small corrections necessary in straight and level flight.

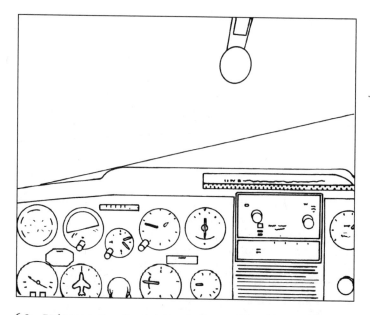

**6-9**  *Right turn: Coordinated use of aileron and rudder together produces a proper turn.*

Entering a turn in an airplane is different from turning a car. In your car, you use the steering wheel; in an airplane you use both the control wheel and rudder pedals (FIG. 6-9). To begin a turn, simultaneously apply pressure on the wheel in the desired direction, to begin banking, and also use your foot to apply pressure on the rudder pedal in the same direction. For a left turn, it's wheel to the left and left rudder at the same time (FIG. 6-10). We refer to this simultaneous use of wheel and rudder as *coordinating* the controls. As soon as the angle of bank reaches what you want, release the pressure on the controls and return both the wheel and the rudder pedals to neutral. Now, the lift of the wings, which always acts perpendicular to them, will continue to pull the airplane around in that turn until you either recover from the turn or the airplane runs out of gas.

If, instead of returning the controls to neutral after the turn reaches the desired bank angle, you continue the control pressure in the direction of the turn, the angle of bank and rate of turn will get steeper and steeper until the bank angle goes beyond 90° and the airplane makes an inverted roll. If you progress in your training beyond your private license to aerobatic flying, you'll see what we mean. But for now, we don't

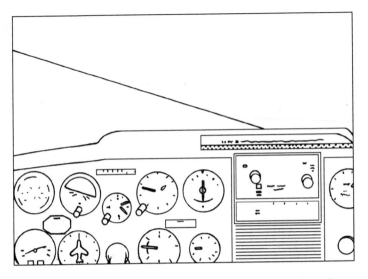

**6-10** *Left turn: Return the controls to neutral after the bank angle and rate of turn are established.*

want to see the bank angle exceed 45° for most operations, sometimes 60° but no more. To recover from the turn, and reestablish straight and level flight, just apply control wheel and rudder pressures opposite to the direction of turn. Wait a second or two while the airplane rolls out of the turn. When the wings are level again, return the controls to neutral and fly straight ahead. That's all there is to entering a turn, allowing the airplane to turn until it gets headed where you want it, and recovering back to straight and level flight.

Because part of the total lift generated by the wings is pulling the airplane around in the turn, we need to increase the total lift while turning. If the airplane weighs a certain amount, we will always need lift equal to the weight in order to stay at a level altitude. Whenever we turn, we have to add some back pressure to the wheel to keep from losing altitude during the turn. Pulling the wheel back a little increases the angle of attack of the wings, enabling them to increase the total lift that they are creating. So, as you roll into a turn, your instructor will show you that you'll pull the wheel back at the same time as the wings are banking. The steeper the bank, the more that you need to pull back. When you return the airplane to wings-level flight, you need to release the back pressure on the wheel as you roll the airplane out of the turn. Otherwise, your nose will pop up as the airplane levels, resulting in a little climb. Coordinating all of these control pressures will become second nature after only a few hours of instruction.

# Stalls and Stall Recovery

We've already talked some about stalls and how you know that the airplane is about to stall. Most modern airplanes are equipped with a stall warning indicator that either lights up, beeps, or whistles. Our Cessna 150 has a warning horn that sounds like a mournful cry when it is activated. There are also aerodynamic signs of an impending stall.

As the stall approaches, the controls in the cockpit get a mushy feeling to them. They are losing effectiveness close to the stall, so the pilot has to use more control movement than is used when at normal flying speeds to accomplish a result. When close to the stall, the airplane starts buffeting. The buffet may come from the tail surfaces, the wings, or both. It's hard to ignore. Lastly, there is an airspeed indicator right in front of you, and unless you've caused a very unusual stall, called an *accelerated stall,* by overenthusiastic yanking of the control wheel back, or unless you're in a very steep bank, you'll see that the airspeed is getting very slow as you get closer to stalling.

The modern lightplane is designed to have a gentle stall that is easy to avoid or manage if intentionally entered. Gone are the days when stalls developed without aerodynamic warning and quickly and violently degenerated into what is known as a *spin,* which lay people incorrectly call a tailspin. Our Cessna 150 has pretty good stall characteristics, particularly for teaching stalls. It has excellent aerodynamic warnings, and the stalls are easy to manage. Yet, if the stall is ignored, or if grossly incorrect recovery techniques are used, you'll know it. Some other trainers have stall characteristics that are so benign that the student who trains in them barely learns anything about stalls. Heavier and faster airplanes have stall behavior that is a bit more sudden and quirky than does the 150. As you get your license and checkout in different airplanes, you should always practice a few stalls, with an instructor onboard, in each type of airplane that is new to you. Let's go through the process of doing a stall and recovering from it.

The first thing that we want to do before performing any maneuver that takes our attention away from constantly looking for other airplanes is a *clearing turn.* Enter a turn in either direction and continue it for 90° of change of direction. Look around, above, and below your airplane. Then, do a turn in the opposite direction, scanning all around for other traffic. After these two turns, you'll end up flying in the same direction as you were before the first turn. Now, pull the throttle back to idle, and raise the nose to the normal climbing attitude. It'll take several seconds for the airspeed to bleed off, during which you'll have to add continuing back pressure to hold the nose up. Soon, you'll have the control wheel nearly all of the way back in an attempt to keep the nose in the climbing attitude.

The nonevent is about to happen. The airspeed has fallen back to about 43 knots and the indicator is bouncing and is hard to read precisely. The airspeed indicator isn't exact in this attitude anyway because the relative wind is coming from below the leading edge of the wing and is therefore entering the pitot tube at an angle instead of head on. This inherent inaccuracy of the airspeed indicator at high angles of attack is called *position error.*

Now that the wings are stalled, the airplane is just mushing along, not doing anything remarkable or scary. The nose is bobbing up and down a little as the wings are doing what they are designed to do—trying to unstall themselves. A glance at the vertical speed indicator and altimeter will confirm that although we are keeping the wings level and the nose high, the airplane is actually descending and losing altitude. We are no longer truly flying; the wings' lift isn't overcoming gravity.

Modern lightplanes are designed so that their wings don't stall, all at once, over the entire wingspan. What is now happening is that the inner portions of the wings are stalled, while the outboard sections are still producing lift. This enables us to keep some control by using the ailerons to some extent. If we jerk the wheel back all of the way, we could probably get the angle of attack high enough to stall the outer section of the wings, but for now, we don't need to do that. All that we need to do to recover from the stall is to lower the angle of attack to restore airflow over the entire wing. To do that, just lower the nose a little, and the wings are flying again. If you add some power as the nose is lowered, the recovery comes a little more quickly.

The whole story to recovering from a stall centers about reducing the angle of attack to a point where airflow is restored over the wings. Power can hasten the process, but adding power will not end the stall until a positive control input is added to lower the angle of attack. Some jet fighters and aerobatic aircraft have so much excess power that they can fly straight up, with the power sufficient to overcome the weight of the airplane. Our Cessna 150 isn't in that league.

If you learn to fly in a glider before transitioning to airplanes, you'll practice stalls in much the same way as we've just described. Except, a glider has no engine, so you learn from the beginning to lower the angle of attack to effectuate a stall recovery. Flying gliders teaches a lot to any pilot. I highly recommend that every pilot take a few instructional flights in a glider; even if you don't fall in love with the sport of powerless flight, your aviation education will be far more complete.

We can also perform a stall with the flaps extended, instead of retracted, as they are for normal cruising flight. With the flaps hanging out, the stall speed is reduced some, and in the 150, the stall with occur at about 38 knots will full flaps. The behavior of the airplane will be a little more dramatic at the point of stall, and the nose will "fall" more definitively than it does when the flaps are fully up. Also, when the flaps are fully extended, a stall is accompanied by more aerodynamic buffeting.

So far, we have been discussing stalls from a wings-level attitude. Stalls can also be done from turns, and they are more abrupt when the wings are banked. In a 30° bank, which is about normal for most turns, there is more buffeting, and the break, which is the point of stall, will be more pronounced. The nose will fall into a nose-down attitude. Quite possibly, the airplane will "fall off," which is airplane jargon that means that the bank angle may increase as the stall occurs.

To recover from this situation, the first thing to do is to stop the yawing of the nose. Apply rudder pressure opposite to the direction of the turning movement. The turning will stop almost instantaneously. Now, lower the nose and get the wings level. The wings will already have begun leveling from the rudder input that you used to stop the yawing. Also, apply power to hasten the recovery, and in less time than it took to read this paragraph, the airplane is flying once again.

The big difference between a stall from turning flight and one from a wings-level attitude is that more altitude is lost in the maneuver and in the recovery during a turn. That's why unintentional stalls while turning can be dangerous. You'll see that after a little practice, you can recover from a straight and level stall with almost no altitude loss. But not so for a turning stall. If you accidentally get into a stall while turning, especially at very low altitude in the traffic pattern while landing or just after takeoff, you may become a statistic. Low-altitude stalls, especially from turns, are one of the greatest cause of accidents in lightplanes. Now you know how to avoid a turning stall because you've practiced them at a safe altitude and know what they're like.

There are more old sayings and cliches in aviation than the contents of the proverbial bottle of little liver pills. One of the time-honored concepts is that there are three things that never do a pilot any good: the altitude above him, the runway behind the airplane, and the fuel in the truck back at the airport. Practice stalls a lot; they are fun and provide great training. But remember that stalling is safe only when done at an altitude high enough to permit a recovery before any loss of that altitude becomes critical. As a general rule, be about 2,500 feet above the ground when initiating an intentional stall. If your instructor wants you higher than that, all the better.

# Landing

Approaches and landings in our Cessna 150 can be made with power on to some degree, with the power at idle, without any flaps extended, or with the flaps out at any angle of deflection up to the maximum of 40°. There isn't any "normal" approach configuration because the POH allows any of these variables to be used by the pilot. The determining factors that dictate the type of approach and landing to be made and the configuration of the airplane's flap setting are primarily the surface wind conditions, the turbulence of the air, and the size and kind of airport into which you are going.

When I learned to fly, we learned to make our approaches with power off, gliding the airplane all of the way around the traffic pattern, and then to land in a fully stalled condition. Today there are fewer gliding approaches made because airports are larger and generally have more traffic going into and departing from them. However, unless strong surface winds prohibit a full stall landing, that is the only correct way to land a single-engine lightplane, especially a trainer. Gliding approaches, made with the power at idle, are still a valuable skill for any pilot to master. If there is no traffic ahead of you in the pattern, my advice is to make every approach with power at idle. If and when the day comes that you need this technique, such as when performing a forced landing after engine failure, it'll be old hat. If you've always approached the runway carrying some power, you're not well trained for the day when you don't have any power to use.

Another benefit of learning to fly a glider comes into play right here. Because a glider has no engine, every approach is made while purely gliding. There are controls in gliders that the pilot uses to vary the angle and rate of descent on the landing approach, such as spoilers, speed brakes, and flaps. Although

no typical training airplane has anywhere near the glide performance of a glider, landing without power in an airplane is not
much of an event for a glider pilot. A glider pilot learns to judge
the approach while making it and to vary the angle and rate of
descent as needed to land at the intended spot. The pilot of a
lightplane can and should be able to do the same, all without
having to add power, once the throttle is retarded to idle.

Typically, we aim to touch down somewhere in the first third
of the runway. Naturally, this rule of thumb varies to suit the
conditions at hand. If we're landing at a large airliner-type airport with 12,000-foot runways, and the turn-off to the area
where we'll park is 8,000 feet down that runway, we don't
need to land at the approach end and then taxi for well over a
mile before leaving the runway. Conversely, if we're going into
a 2,000-foot strip, we don't want to let the first third of it
(almost 700 feet) go needlessly underneath us and get ourselves into a position where we either have to use aggressive
braking to get stopped, or worse, overrun the end of the runway. Judgment has to be developed and used. Let's assume
that we'll be landing at a typical general aviation airport, where
the runway is adequate, without being either excessively long
or short.

Take a look at FIG. 6-11 and learn the names and locations of
the downwind and base legs of the pattern. After you roll out
of the base leg, aligned with the runway, you're on what's
called *final approach,* or just *final* for short. At most small airports, plan to be at 800 feet above the ground as you enter the
downwind leg. Plan your approach to the pattern so that you
are at this altitude, called the *pattern altitude,* before you actually arrive on the downwind leg. Don't enter downwind high
and then descend while flying this leg; you might descend right
into another airplane below you who did it right. Realize now
that the most difficult airplane to see is the one below you. It
doesn't contrast very well with the terrain that is in your visual
background. An airplane at the same altitude as yours is easier
to see, and the one above you is easiest of all to pick out.

Aim for a point along the downwind leg that is at the halfway
point along the runway as the place where you'll turn into, and
become established on, the downwind leg. Plan to turn about
45° from your heading as you approach the airport onto the
downwind leg. Normally turns in the traffic pattern are all made
to the left, as the FARs require. But, at some airports the traffic
pattern uses right turns. *Right traffic,* as the pattern with right
turns is called, is used at airports where tall buildings or other

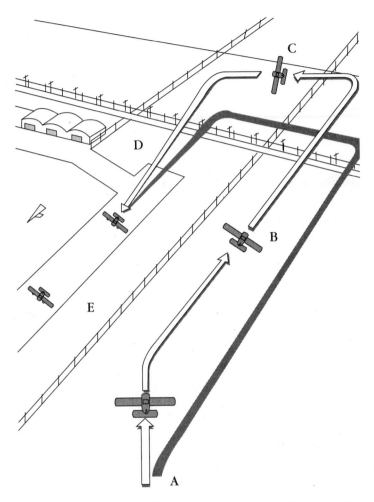

**6-11** *Normal left-hand traffic pattern: Enter (A) at a 45° angle so that you can see other traffic. Lengths of the downwind leg (B) and the base leg (C) are determined by wind conditions and other traffic. Touch down at (D), and roll out on the runway (E).*

structures, noise-sensitive areas, or other justifications dictate flying on the other side of a runway than you would if you were making left turns.

As soon as you get established on the downwind leg, keep looking around for any airplanes ahead of you in the pattern, taxiing toward takeoff, or taking off from the runway(s) below you. Make sure that the mixture control is in the RICH position.

Now, pull the carburetor heat knob out all of the way, and leave it in that position until just before we land. As you pass the approach end of the runway, pull the throttle all of the way back to idle. Hold the nose up until the airspeed reads about 65 knots and then lower the nose just enough to maintain that airspeed. Leave the flaps up for now, and the airplane will begin a gentle gliding descent.

The time to turn from the downwind leg onto the base leg is never the same on any two approaches, and this timing is something that you'll learn to judge. Generally, the turn onto the base leg occurs when the intended landing spot is about 45° behind you, as you look at the runway over your left shoulder. If there is a strong wind blowing down the runway, you'll learn to turn sooner than if there is little or no wind. With a heavy wind in your face while on the final, you'll want to be in closer to the runway on base so that your time on final isn't protracted by the slow speed you'll have over the ground.

As soon as your turn to the base leg is completed, add about 20° of flap extension. Unless the wind is strong, we'll soon put the flaps all of the way down, but not yet. Because the flaps are now partially deployed, they'll be adding drag, and you'll need to lower the nose some more to maintain the gliding speed of 65 knots. Your instructor will harp about maintaining airspeed in many of your maneuvers, and none of them is more important than now. Remember, stalls are great at altitude and within a few inches of the ground as we land; but we don't want to risk a stall in the pattern.

Flaps should not normally be applied all at once even by an experienced pilot. At the training stage, periodic application of increased flaps allows you to see how the airplane reacts and to maintain your airspeed and attitude in better control. The flap switch on newer 150s is an electric switch shaped like a paddle, just to the right of the mixture control on the panel. When flaps are extended, the angle of descent increases, and you have to lower the nose to keep the proper airspeed.

As we fly the base leg, time the turn to final approach so that we roll out of the turn lined up with the runway. Don't worry if you overshoot this turn and aren't lined up for the first several times you fly the pattern (FIG. 6-14). The timing of this turn is also a product of judgment that takes a little while to develop. Because we're making a power-off, gliding approach, we'll add the rest of the flaps as we fly down the final. We're also assuming that there aren't any adverse winds on this approach that would require our landing with only partial flap

**6-12**  *Here it is for real: Entering the pattern at 800 to 1,000 feet above ground at a 45° angle to the downwind leg. The wind indicator is in the segmented circle in the foreground.*

**6-13**  *Downwind (parallel to the runway) is flown at 800 or 1,000 feet, depending on local requirements.*

**6-14** *Turning from the base leg onto final approach. The base leg is usually about a quarter mile from the end of the runway.*

extension. As soon as more flaps are selected, the nose attitude will have to be lowered more to maintain our 65-knot gliding airspeed. The angle of descent will steepen more, and the visibility over the nose now gets to the point where you can easily see the entire runway environment right in front of you.

While gliding down the final approach, pick out the spot on the runway where you think you'll touch down (FIG. 6-15). Watch this spot for a few seconds, and put it into relation with a fixed position on the windshield, which we'll call our windshield reference point. If the spot on the ground starts moving up the windshield from the windshield reference point, we're not going to be able to glide, in the present configuration, to that spot on the runway; we'll touch down short of it. To cure that, add some power. By adding power, the angle of descent will flatten out, and the airplane will go farther along the ground before it reaches landing height. If your spot on the runway is moving down the windshield, away from the windshield reference point, we're not descending at a steep enough angle, and we'll touch down beyond the point on the ground that you picked out. Depending on the length of the runway, this may be OK, or we may be setting ourselves up for a trip into the weeds off of the end of the runway. If we're *overshooting* the runway, we have to descend at a steeper angle, which we do by either

**6-15** *Final approach. In this view, we're a little to the left of the runway centerline and correcting to get back in line with it.*

reducing power, adding flaps, or both. In an extreme circumstance, where we've done all that we can to steepen the angle of descent and it looks like we'll still overshoot, the only remedy is to add full power, climb out, and fly the entire pattern all over again.

The use of the windshield reference point in relation to a fixed point on the runway is a time-honored way of learning to make precision spot landings. But for now, don't worry too much about touching down exactly on a desired spot on the runway. Greater precision will come with practice. During the training stage in which you're now involved, use the windshield reference point simply to determine that your approach is going to take you safely to the runway, and not result in an over- or undershoot. For now, we'll be happy to use all of the runway that is safely available. The student pilot's major task at this point is to learn to fly the pattern, get the feel of the airplane, and just learn to land it.

When the airplane is throttled back to idle power and established in the glide for landing approach, the weather conditions and the laws of aerodynamics have established the maximum distance that the airplane can glide before reaching the ground. With the engine idling, there is nothing that you can do with the wheel or rudder pedals to increase the gliding distance by even 1 inch. The only normal way to glide farther is to add power. Because we have flaps extended, we could increase the gliding distance somewhat by retracting them partially or all of the way. But this can be dangerous. The total lift being generated by the wings drops when the flaps are pulled up, and therefore, the stalling speed increases. We're fairly low when on final, usually between 400 and 0 feet, so this isn't the place to put the airplane into a condition where the stalling speed goes up. If you've got flaps deployed on final, which you normally will have, add power when you need to glide farther, and leave the flaps alone, except in abnormal situations, which your instructor will demonstrate further along in your training.

When you see that your glide is going to result in a touch-down short of the runway, the natural human tendency is to pull back on the wheel to try to stretch the glide. This won't ever work and will actually have the opposite effect. When you raise the nose by pulling back on the wheel, you increase the angle of attack of the wings. As we've already discussed, a by-product of an increase in angle of attack is an increase in induced drag as a result of the greater lift. Assuming that you don't add power, pulling the nose up only increases the total drag, and the angle of descent just steepens some more and you end up reaching the ground at a point even shorter than you would have without pulling the wheel back.

So, once you're on final and decide that you need to glide farther, the only way to do it is by adding power. How much power to add is determined by how much farther you need to travel in the glide, how late you were in recognizing that your existing glide wasn't going to take you safely to the runway, and therefore how low you allowed the airplane to get before corrective action was taken. This whole sequence is one of the best examples of the maxim that the control wheel controls pitch and therefore to a great degree also controls airspeed, whereas the power is the primary control of altitude.

When a landing approach does go sour, and many will in your career as a pilot, don't hesitate to shove the throttle in. Then safely establish a climb out as though you had just taken off, and go around the traffic pattern for another try. Early recognition of the need to abort a bad approach, coupled with an early deci-sion to execute a go-around, is important to ensure a plentiful margin of speed and altitude. There is nothing embarrassing or amateurish about going around. Many accidents have occurred because pilots have either not recognized that the approach had gone south on them or for some silly reason motivated by ego instead of common sense tried to "salvage" a landing. Another of the wise sayings in aviation is that a good landing is the product of a good approach. It's very difficult to make even a passable landing if the approach isn't nailed down early and properly. There is enough to do while performing a good, stable approach and subsequent landing. Don't overload your mental or physical limitations; just go around if anything about the approach gets out of the ordinary or becomes questionable.

Transitioning from a landing approach to a climb isn't difficult or dangerous in any airplane, but it's simpler in a Cessna 150 or similar trainer. Learn now to make the decision to go around when it first seems prudent. A bad approach won't get better, so solve the problem properly. Most instructors will command a go-around when you aren't expecting it, even if the approach is going properly. The day will come when another airplane, whose pilot isn't on the ball, will taxi out onto the runway as you're on final approach to land, an animal will intrude into the runway area, or a host of other such calamities will arise to prevent your safe landing. Some of the major airlines require their pilots, the most highly trained and competent anywhere, to go around if the approach isn't stable at 500 feet above the ground. Even though you're not flying a jet, which takes longer for the engines to spool up and reach climb power than we spend in an 150, you might want to adopt the same parameter for yourself. If the approach isn't suitable at 500 feet, abort and go around.

Now, back to our landing. As we come in over the end of the runway, and when we get down to about 10 to 12 feet above the runway, we'll start a maneuver called the *flare* or *roundout* (FIG. 6-16). This is done by applying some back pressure on the wheel to lessen the rate of descent. From here on down to touchdown, we'll continue to add more back pressure as the airplane continues to sink. We don't want to stop the descent entirely; what we want to do is gradually reach a point about 3 inches above the runway when we have the wheel all of the way back and the airplanes stalls. This is done by constantly increasing back pressure during the flare and allowing the airplane to sink at an ever-decreasing rate until the stall occurs.

During your training, you'll spend a few hours in the traffic pattern doing many landings. Old-time pilots refer to this phase of learning to fly as "bounce drill." Don't get discouraged when you don't get the timing down for several hours. You'll start to stall high, and you'll try to drive the airplane into the pavement without a proper flare. Your instructor is there, and she's been through this many times before. She'll save the day with appropriate nudges on the wheel at the right time to avoid any damage.

**6-16** *The last stage of the final approach, about ready to begin the landing flare.*

As the airplane nears the runway during the flare, you'll notice that the rate of sink lessens due to a condition called *ground effect*. Ground effect is a cushion of slightly compressed air that develops between the wings and the ground, and it usually extends up from the runway about half the distance of the wingspan of the airplane. We're flying a high-wing airplane, so the ground effect isn't as pronounced as it is in a low-wing airplane because the wing on our Cessna sits higher above the ground even after we've landed. When you start flying low-wing airplanes, like the modern Pipers, Beechcrafts, and Mooneys, you'll see what ground effect is. It simply prolongs the flare a little bit because the cushion of compressed air delays the onset of the stall.

After we touch down on the runway, continue to hold the wheel back where you have it, and steer straight down the runway with the rudder pedals. Be careful that your feet aren't on the tops of the pedals, where you'd be applying braking force. As the speed dissipates, the tail surfaces will lose aerodynamic effectiveness, and the elevator won't be able to keep the nose wheel off of the ground. The nose wheel will settle gently to the runway. Keep the wheel back until you've slowed completely and turned off of the runway.

A proper stall landing occurs with the main wheels touching down several seconds before the nose wheel settles. Don't allow the nose to come down early. Remember that it is an inherently weak structure, and premature "slamming" of the nose onto the runway can easily cause damage to the nose wheel mounts and the engine firewall or mounts to which it's attached. When you land properly, you'll hear the stall warning horn sound just before you make ground contact. This whole process involves many elements of feel, sight, and sound. But it is like it was when you learned to ride a bicycle as a child. You thought you'd never do it, but then, magically, it all came together one day, and it has been second nature ever since.

As we steer down the runway, leave everything alone. Don't raise the flaps until we've taxied off of the runway. We train this way for a very important reason. Someday you'll probably fly an airplane with retractable landing gear. If you learn right now to leave well enough alone during the roll out after landing, and do not start raising switches and fooling around with things in a hurry, when you should be occupied with rolling out, you won't reach over, raise the wrong switch, and pull up the landing gear at a very inopportune moment.

Assuming that the runway is of normal length, allow the speed to drop as much as practical before applying the brakes (FIG. 6-17). Don't ride the brakes, and don't try to use them until well after the nose wheel has settled onto the runway. Even though you're flying a rental airplane, treat it now as though it were your own. Every pilot dreams of the day when he owns his own airplane, and many do. If you start flying by abusing airplanes, you won't know better, and you'll abuse your own someday and increase your maintenance cost immeasurably.

**6-17** *The landing roll. Allow the airspeed to dissipate. Use the brakes only as necessary to be able to turn off of the runway at a convenient intersection. Never "hog" the runway with excessive taxiing.*

Now that we've slowed to a comfortable taxiing speed, the next job is to get off the runway at the next available intersection. Runways are for taking off and landing; taxiways are for taxiing. Don't tie up runway space with prolonged taxiing. Someone in the traffic pattern behind you might have to do a needless go-around because you didn't exercise one of the common courtesies that pilots should extend to each other by not getting off of the runway when it was safe to do so. Courtesy seems to have a partner in many aspects of life, and that is safety. Flying is no exception.

# Weight and Balance

Flying an airplane safely and legally means more than just having undergone the proper training and having a pilot certificate. It also means putting that training and knowledge to work before and during every flight. A safe flight begins before you even get to the airport. In later chapters, we'll talk about weather information and cross-country flight planning. For now, let's chat about loading the airplane.

One of the most important tasks in planning a flight is to make sure that the airplane is properly loaded. Loading isn't much of a concern in two-seat trainers, assuming that the occupants are of normal weight, say about 170 pounds or less. Airplanes like the Cessna 150 don't carry all that much fuel. On training flights, little if any baggage is routinely carried. Even with all of these levels of comfort, you need to know how to figure your load and how it is distributed.

That's because the day will come, shortly after you get your license, when you'll want to check out in a four-seat airplane so that you can carry more than one passenger with you. Four-seat airplanes generally carry lots more fuel, have a total of four seats, and have large baggage compartments. When you advance to these larger airplanes, weight and balance become real concerns. There are very, very few airplanes that can legally, safely, and sometimes even physically fly with all of the seats full of adults, a full fuel tank, and baggage. You can do this with a car, but almost never with an airplane. Airplanes offer many options and compromises in loading. If you have to carry four adults, you'll find that you may have to take off with less than full fuel and accept the fact that you may have to make a refueling stop along the way. If you need maximum range, you can't carry four adults and the kitchen sink too.

There are two concerns when you calculate the airplane's load. The first is called *maximum gross weight,* and the second is the airplane's *center of gravity* (CG). The maximum gross weight is a figure that the manufacturer has established in the design and testing of the airplane, and it is the maximum amount that the airplane can weigh at takeoff. Larger airplanes often have a maximum ramp weight that is a little heavier than maximum takeoff weight. This accounts for the fuel that will be burned during engine start, taxi, and the pretakeoff checks. For the kinds of airplanes you'll fly as a private pilot, you will generally only see a maximum gross weight specified in the POH.

The CG is the balance point of the airplane. If you could hypothetically suspend the airplane in the air from a string, the CG is the point where you would attach the string, suspend the airplane, and have it in a level flight attitude. The manufacturer also specifies, in the POH, a range within which the actual CG must fall. It is very possible in many airplanes to have the total gross weight below the maximum, yet have the airplane loaded in such a fashion as to cause the CG to fall outside of the limits.

When the maximum gross weight is exceeded, several things happen, and they're all bad. The stalling speed increases, which also increases the landing speed. The aircraft's rate of climb suffers because the engine is trying to climb with more weight than it was designed to handle. The struggle to climb when overweight results in increased fuel consumption and possible engine overheating. As can be expected, takeoff distances can increase dramatically, and if the gross weight is high enough, the airplane won't fly at all. Also, at weights higher than allowed, the structural strength of the airframe is compromised, and the airplane no longer has the safety margins that have been designed into it.

Excessive weight reduces the airplane's tolerance to gravity (G) forces. Assume, for the sake of discussion, that your airplane has the normally designed maximum load factor of 3.8 Gs. This means that at the maximum legal gross weight, the structure of the airframe, wings, and all can support 3.8 times the actual maximum gross weight. During accelerated flight, which is encountered in pull-ups, turns, and rough air, the actual load on the wings is greater than just the gross weight of the airplane. If an airplane's legal gross weight is 2,400 pounds, when 3 Gs are encountered, the wings are supporting 7,200 pounds, which they can still do. Keeping the same assumed

2,400-pound gross weight, the design factor of 3.8 means that the wings can support about 9,120 pounds before there is risk of failure. If you overload the airplane by 600 pounds and get the actual gross weight up to 3,000 pounds, look what happens. The wings can support only 9,120 before you risk breaking something, so the increased G factor is reduced to 3.04, from the normal 3.8. That a reduction of 20 percent in what may keep you alive in very rough weather, and I don't take those kinds of chances and neither would any other competent pilot. Overloading can cause popped rivets, permanent distortion of the airframe, and even complete structural failure.

The allowable gross weight is composed of two elements— the airplane's *empty weight,* which together with the *useful load* equals the maximum gross weight. The empty weight is just that—what the airplane weighs empty, with only the unusable fuel added. Every airplane, even of the same type, has a slightly different empty weight, which is influenced not only by the design but also by the various options installed and the slight variations in manufacture. There is always some small amount of fuel that is not usable but remains in the tanks after the useful supply is exhausted. Once an airplane first gets gas put in its tanks, this amount of unusable fuel is with it for life.

When you start with the maximum gross weight and subtract the empty weight, you then have the useful load. This is the maximum weight of all usable fuel, occupants, oil, and baggage. This useful load must be distributed in such a manner that the CG falls within the allowable limits. Even if the airplane is loaded below maximum gross weight, if it's out of balance, its flying characteristics are adversely affected. Even a slightly out of balance condition will be unsatisfactory. If the CG is too far forward, you may not be able to pull the nose up enough to flare to land. If the CG is too far rearward (aft), the airplane can have very dangerous stall characteristics, and it will be difficult to keep nose down in level flight. If the CG gets too far out of whack, the airplane is impossible to fly.

Because baggage compartments are large, there's a tendency to overload them. Just because your baggage area is large enough to accept a certain item or items, don't assume that it's OK to put them there. Baggage compartments in typical single-engine airplanes are the most aft of the places that you can place any part of the useful load. Therefore, the loading of the baggage area has the most telling effect on where the CG is eventually located. The floor of the baggage area is a piece of the airplane's structure and has a loading limit, too. It is often quite possible to load the airplane below maximum gross weight, within the allowable CG range, but exceed the floor limit of the baggage area. You have to be cognizant of all of these factors.

A few airplanes have another loading scenario of which the pilot must be aware. As an airplane flies, it naturally loses weight (too bad we can't say the same for people as we travel through life). As fuel is consumed in flight, the weight of the airplane goes down. Due to the location of the fuel tanks in these airplanes, notably some models of the Beechcraft Bonanza, the CG shifts as the fuel is burned off in flight. It's possible to take off within all of the applicable limits and then have the CG go out of the allowable range before landing. Pilots of these airplanes then have to calculate their CG both at takeoff and at the end of the flight to keep everything safe.

Many POHs provide a shortcut method of calculating the location of the CG. You merely fill in some blanks on a form with the known load being taken aboard, figuring gasoline at 6 pounds per gallon, oil at 7.7 pounds per gallon (not per quart), and the actual weight of people and baggage. While we're on the subject of the weight of people, watch out to be sure that you use the actual weight. Most of use weigh ourselves on home scales when we're scantily attired. That's fine for our egos, but if we're flying in the winter and are loaded down with heavy clothing and boots, you'd better add a good fudge factor to accommodate for everyone's dress. Also, make it clear to your prospective passengers that you need to know their real weight, not what they wish they weighed or what their high school yearbook pictures would lead one to believe.

You also need to know how to mathematically calculate weight and balance without a shortcut form and to fully understand what is being determined. The math involved is not complicated; it's only arithmetic. When prospective pilots have asked me over the years about what level of education is required to be a pilot, my response is that if you can read at a junior high school level and do basic arithmetic and a wee bit of geometry, that's all it takes. Many of my military and airline pilot friends were history and English majors in college and aren't mathematicians.

The longhand calculation of weight and balance starts with adding up the empty weight and proposed useful load to see if you're going to exceed the maximum gross weight. Assuming that you don't, now you only have to figure the CG. Because the CG is going to fall someplace along the fuselage of the airplane, we need a reference point from which to measure, and that is called the *datum*. This datum point might be someplace on the airplane, or it can be an imaginary point out in front of the propeller. On many single-engine airplanes, the datum is the firewall at the rear of the engine compartment, but wherever it is, the location is clearly shown in the POH. What we want to find out is where the CG will fall. The POH will show us the allowable range, usually measured in inches aft of the datum, where the CG must be located.

The placement of weight affects the CG; 20 pounds of weight right over the CG affects it little, but the same 20 pounds put back in the tail can move the CG dramatically. Think of it this way: Most adults can lift 40 pounds up over their head if they keep the weight in close to their body on the way up and then hold it up straight above their head. But there aren't many who can fully extend their arms, grab the same 40 pounds, and then hold them out in front of their face, with arms extended. We are going to calculate the leverage exerted by a given amount of weight. The rule is weight × arm = moment (leverage) (FIG. 6-18). The arm is the position of the weight from the datum.

Let's figure the CG for a six-seat place Cessna 310, which is a high-performance twin-engine business airplane. If you see how it's done for this class of aircraft, doing the same calculation for a single-engine plane is duck soup. Assume that the CG limits are given in the POH as 35 to 43.1 inches aft of the datum. This is the envelope, or range, in which the CG must fall for the airplane to be within its design balance limits. Further assume that the empty weight is 3,450 pounds, and the maximum allowable gross weight is 5,100 pounds. A sample calculation would look like this:

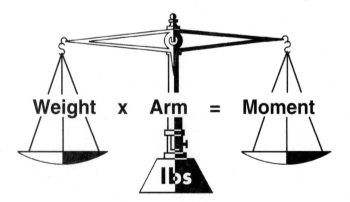

**6-18** *The basic weight and balance formula.*

| Item | Weight (pounds) |
|------|----------------:|
| Aircraft empty weight | 3,450 |
| Pilot and front passenger, 155+165 pounds | 320 |
| Two passengers in middle seats, 160+200 pounds | 360 |
| One passenger, rear seat, 170 pounds | 170 |
| Baggage in nacelle lockers | 200 |
| Baggage in aft cabin compartment | 160 |
| Fuel, 130 gallons | 780 |
| Oil, 6 gallons | 45 |
| Total gross weight | 5,485 |

First, we see that we're 385 pounds over the maximum gross weight. Something must be left behind, either fuel, passengers, baggage, or some of all. For the sake of example here, let's reduce the fuel load to 90 gallons, which lessens the load by 240 pounds, and eliminate 145 pounds of baggage from the lockers at the rear of the engine nacelles. That will bring us down to the maximum legal gross weight of 5,100 pounds.

Now, we'll determine whether the load is distributed in such a manner that the CG limits are not exceeded. Using the arms given in the weight and balance section of the airplane's POH, and the known weights as shown above, we obtain the following:

| Item | Weight (pounds) | × | Arm (inches) | = | Moment (inch-pounds) |
|------|----------------:|---|-------------:|---|---------------------:|
| Aircraft empty weight | 3,450 | | 36.5 | | 125,925.0 |
| Pilot and front passenger | 320 | | 37.0 | | 11,840.0 |
| Two middle passengers | 360 | | 71.7 | | 25,812.0 |
| One rear passenger | 170 | | 105.0 | | 17,850.0 |
| Baggage in nacelles | 55 | | 63.0 | | 3,465.0 |
| Baggage in aft cabin | 160 | | 124.0 | | 19,840.0 |
| Fuel (90 gallons) | 540 | | 35.0 | | 18,900.0 |
| Oil (6 gallons) | 45 | | 3.5 | | 157.5 |
| Total | 5,100 | | | | 223,789.5 |

The equation is center of gravity equals total moment divided by total weight. When we do the arithmetic, 233,789.5

divided by 5,100 equals 43.88. In this example, our CG is 43.88 inches aft of the datum, which is out of limits again. We are 0.78 inch behind the aft limit for this airplane, which is 43.1 inches. Some of the load will have to be moved forward. Let's shift 145 pounds of the baggage from the aft cabin compartment to the engine nacelle lockers.

Now the nacelle baggage will weigh 200 pounds, have an arm of 63.0 inches, and have a moment of 12,600.0 inch-pounds; the baggage in the aft cabin will weigh 15 pounds, have an arm of 124.0 inches, and have a moment of 1,860.0 inch-pounds. Substituting these new figures, the total moment has changed to 214,944.5 inch-pounds. Of course, our total gross weight of 5,100 pounds is the same.

So, when we divide 214,944.5 by 5,100, we get a new CG location of 42.15 inches aft of the datum, which is within limits. Now we're ready to fly this load in this airplane. We've intentionally done one of the more complex loading problems that a private pilot is likely to ever encounter. Few private pilots fly twin-engine airplanes with multiple baggage areas and six seats. When you're at the airport for your next lesson, ask your instructor to let you see the POH for a Cessna 172 or Piper PA-28 series airplane, which is what you'll probably fly after you get a license. You'll see that the calculation for these airplanes is much simpler than our example for a Cessna 310.

Doing the weight and balance calculation is one part of a pilot's preflight planning. In Chaps. 8 and 9, you'll learn about weather decisions and navigational planning, which also must precede every flight outside of the airport's local area.

# 7

# Control Techniques

There are two primary techniques that you'll need to master to control an airplane. First, you need to know what to do with the airplane, in terms of what controls need to be adjusted, and in what manner, to achieve a certain performance from your airplane. The second part involves gaining the skill to physically manipulate the controls in the desired way. Experienced instructors usually develop methods of teaching that contain useful explanations that student pilots can understand and comprehend. Some students learn best if everything is put into short, concise phrases, and others want and appreciate a long-winded explanation of everything.

If your instructor is the type who prefers short, simple explanations, and you want to know more, speak up. When I taught at a major university's flight department when I was in undergraduate school, I often encountered student pilots who were Ph.D.'s in engineering or were otherwise highly educated, who wanted things explained in the greatest detail possible. The next hour I might be instructing a fellow undergraduate student, majoring in history, as was I, who didn't care about the advanced aerodynamic principles of things like boundary layer separation during stalls or exactly why you might get detonation within the cylinders of the engine if the mixture was grossly improper for a given power setting at a certain altitude.

I've always believed that a pilot can't know too much about the airplane and why it does what it does in all regimes of flight. I also understand why some people don't care about the advanced details. But the problem with not caring is that you have to be careful that you don't ignore something that really is important. There is a difference between learning the essential and casting aside what you think at this stage may not matter, only to be ignorant of a fact or concept that is vital to safe flying. If your instructor can't, or won't, explain something in detail when you ask, change instructors. You may have been paired with someone who doesn't know and tries to mask that lack of knowledge with indifference.

Sometimes an explanation can be condensed into a cliche. But cliches should be accepted for what they are: reminders of the basics. Before you accept a cliche as a reminder, you need to know the whole story behind it. For instance, we said in Chap. 6 that the whole story of flight is the angle of attack. That's true, but it assumes that, for an airplane, the engine is running properly. When we talk about emergency procedures later in this chapter, we'll see the situations that arise when the engine fails and how control techniques have to be altered to accomplish what we want the airplane to do.

Another of these training cliches is "Pitch plus power equals performance." This is totally accurate, again assuming that the engine is running. Yet, even this saying requires additional explanation and elaboration. Within limits, some performance values are interchangeable. It's possible to make some trade-offs among altitude, airspeed, and vertical speed.

Let's do a simple experiment in our Cessna 150 to demonstrate this idea. Assume that you are flying along in normal cruising flight, with the power set at 65 percent and the airplane properly trimmed for hands-off flight. Now, without moving the control wheel or rudder pedals, push the throttle in to increase the power setting. What happens?

When you trimmed the airplane in cruise, you had really trimmed it to maintain an airspeed, which was whatever airspeed that the 65 percent power setting generated. When you increase the power, without doing anything else, the airplane will still maintain the trimmed airspeed. The result is that, with the increased power, the nose will pitch up slightly, and you'll begin to climb. We now have excess power being produced by the engine, over that amount of thrust necessary to maintain the trimmed airspeed. Hence, the airplane climbs because the trim, attempting to maintain the trimmed airspeed, pitched the nose up and increased the angle of attack. The greater angle of attack generated more total lift from the wings, and that lift is more than what is needed to stay in cruise flight, at a constant altitude, so the airplane climbs.

Let's look at another example. Go back to normal, stable cruising flight with the power set at 65 percent. Then, pull back a little on the wheel, without adding any power. Initially, the airplane will climb some because raising the nose increases the angle of attack, which produces more lift and causes the airplane to climb. But remember, every time that you increase the angle of attack, you also increase the induced drag as a result. If more power is not added to overcome the greater drag inherent in an increased angle of attack, the climb won't last for very long. The forces acting upon the airplane will soon reach equipoise again, and you'll be flying along with the nose higher, at a slower airspeed, and with a constant altitude. Everything eventually balances out, but before the balance occurred, there was a short climb. The cliche that you can "trade airspeed for altitude" applies to what we've just done. We gave up some airspeed from what it was before we pulled the nose up and gained some altitude in the short climb before all of the forces balanced out again.

The reverse can also be accomplished. While in stable cruising flight, if the pilot pushes forward a little on the wheel, several things will happen. As the nose lowers, the angle of attack does also, which results in less total lift from the wings. Unless the power is reduced, the airspeed will start to increase because, with a lesser angle of attack, less power is needed to overcome the drag because there is less drag. When the power setting is unchanged, the airplane now has an excess of power over what is needed to overcome drag, and the speed goes up. This is what is known as "trading altitude for airspeed," which is a valuable technique. Assuming that you are high enough to give up some altitude and still be safe, this is a way that you can quickly increase airspeed if you've gotten yourself into a situation where the airspeed is too low or if you need to maintain a gliding speed if the engine gives up its labors for the day.

These foregoing examples illustrate the notion of "limited interchangeability" of altitude and airspeed. In the real world of everyday flying, you will often make very minor altitude corrections with pitch—forward or back pressure on the control wheel—because the resultant airspeed changes will be very minor and insignificant.

When you advance to flying larger airplanes, those that have more excess power available, especially when lightly loaded, than does our Cessna 150 trainer, you'll be able to make greater trades of airspeed for altitude and control wider variations of altitude with the control wheel alone. All of this adds up to the fact that pitch and power are not separate in controlling the airplane but are, rather, interdependent. Until and unless you understand this interrelationship, aircraft control will be confusing.

# Load and Air Density

To safely fly any airplane, every pilot must understand two critical factors that influence performance: the load that the airplane is carrying and the density of the air.

Given the same amount of power, and therefore the same thrust being produced, a heavily loaded airplane must fly at a greater angle of attack than when it is lightly loaded. More weight must be supported by more lift, and the only way to get more lift out of the same wing is to fly that wing at an increased angle of attack.

Although an increase in power setting, if possible, will somewhat compensate for a heavier load by flying the wing at a faster airspeed and getting the needed lift in that manner, normally this excess power isn't available in light airplanes because the bigger engines that it would take to produce that much thrust cost more to manufacture, buy, and maintain. They burn more fuel, which means the fuel tanks would have to be larger, and that fuel burn costs more too. The design of every airplane is a series of trade-offs of many traits of performance, weight, and cost. In lightplanes, the compromises are many.

So, smaller airplanes are simply trimmed to fly at an increased angle of attack when heavily loaded. Their pilots have to accept the trade-off of reduced airspeed because the increased angle of attack needed to produce the lift necessary to carry the load means more drag. The more drag, with the same power setting, the slower the airspeed will be. Another by-product of heavier loads is that the airplane will stall at a slightly higher airspeed because it needs more lift to fly than it will when loaded with less weight.

Air density affects aircraft performance in two ways. As air density goes down, the wings produce less lift and the engine produces less power. The density of the air lessens as altitude increases, the ambient temperature goes up, and the air becomes more humid. The effects of decreased air density multiply as two or all three of these factors combine at a given time.

An engine loses its ability to produce power as you climb to higher altitudes because the volume of the fuel/air mixture flowing through the carburetor, and into the combustion chambers, is steadily reduced. At somewhere around 7,500 feet MSL, normal lightplane engines can only produce about 75 percent of their rated horsepower when the throttle is pushed all of the way in. As the airplane climbs higher than that, the output of power diminishes markedly. By the time a Cessna 150 has struggled up to 14,000 feet MSL, it has reached its *service ceiling,* which by definition is the altitude at which its rate of climb has eroded to a meager and tentative 100 fpm. Shortly after we took off from our home airport, where the elevation is only 905 feet above sea level, the airplane was climbing at more than 600 fpm.

Some four-seat and larger lightplanes have engines that compensate for this inherent loss of power with increasing altitude by using a *turbocharger* to compress the air before it is fed into the carburetor, through the intake manifold, and on into the cylinders. A turbocharged engine is capable of maintaining a much larger percentage of its maximum rated power output at much higher altitudes. Turbocharged airplanes can cruise at altitudes up to 25,000 feet, and occasionally higher. But turbocharging an airplane engine has some penalties. The engine runs hotter because compressing the intake air also heats it. This makes for more critical engine management techniques on the part of the pilot. The turbocharger itself adds cost to the airplane and increases the pilot training needed to fly it. Turbocharged engines suffer greater internal stresses, which reduce their overhaul lives and which add increased maintenance costs in other ways. When flying up at the altitudes where a turbocharger gives some benefits, the airplane's occupants need supplemental oxygen, and a whole new host of weather and flight planning concerns present themselves. A turbocharger is a classic example of another old saying, "There's no free lunch."

Today, many popular automobiles also use turbocharging, but for different reasons. In cars, the object of using it is to extract more power from a smaller engine than it would take to produce the same power if there were no turbocharger installed. The smaller engine allows the car to be smaller and weigh less and still have the horsepower output that, before the advent of turbochargers, was only obtainable from larger engines. Car engines have an entirely different set of design criteria than do airplane engines. First and foremost, airplane engines are designed for reliability and long service lives. Although we all want our cars to last as long as possible, the result of a car quitting on the freeway isn't the same as an airplane engine quitting on takeoff at night.

Our Cessna 150 is not turbocharged. Its engine is *normally aspirated,* which means that the aspiration, the feeding of air into it, is normal and not augmented with a turbocharger. Hence, our little 100-horsepower engine will start running out of steam as the airplane climbs. Although it's not capable of producing its full rating of 100 horsepower at any altitude above sea level, the effect isn't very dramatic until we climb several thousand feet high.

Air density also decreases as the air becomes warmer. Warmth means the air molecules are more active, with increased molecular motion. The molecules are more spread out, and a given volume of air contains fewer molecules when warm than when cold. Hence, warm air is less dense than cold air. At the same absolute altitude, the airplane will suffer more from the effects of lessened air density when the temperature is higher than when the air is cooler.

Next, humid air is less dense than dry air because some of the space in a given volume is taken up with water vapor, not air molecules. Because there are fewer air molecules in a volume of humid air than are present in the same volume when the air is drier, that humid air is less dense, and the performance of the airplane suffers accordingly. Fortunately, the adverse effect of higher humidity is not nearly as pronounced as are the problems associated with increased altitude and higher temperatures.

The atmosphere also varies in density from one day to the next or in times of rapidly changing weather conditions, even from one hour to the next. The sea of air that surrounds the earth is in a constant state of change, as high pressure areas, lows, and fronts move across the world. The density associated with weather changes is expressed as barometric pressure. There are times when, at a given geographical location, the barometric pressure won't change much for a day or so, but these conditions aren't encountered very often. Especially in the winter, any airplane in North America can see a wide variation in barometric pressure, and the air density that it measures, in the course of a cross-country flight covering a few hundred miles.

To give us a means by which to calculate the effects of high altitudes and variations in temperatures, the aviation world has created the concept of *density altitude*. Density altitude results from a calculation that simultaneously takes into account the effects of absolute altitude, ambient temperature, and the atmospheric density of the air, the last of which is expressed as barometric pressure.

Figuring what the density altitude is at any given time and location is very easy because your pocket computer, whether of the electronic or circular slide rule type, will do it for you. To arrive at the density altitude, you have to know the elevation of the airport above sea level. You can determine that by looking on the aeronautical chart for that area; the elevation of every airport is printed on the chart, right beside the airport symbol. Next, you need to know the temperature. If there isn't a thermometer outside of the office building at the airport, you can either call the *flight service station* (FSS) that has jurisdiction over the area, assuming that your airport reports its weather into the national network, or go to your airplane, which usually has an outside air temperature gauge built into a corner of the windshield. Lastly, you need to know the barometric pressure. Again, you can get this from the FSS if it is reported. If not, go to the airplane again, set the altimeter to read the field elevation, and read the barometer setting from the little window in the altimeter.

Plug this data into your computer, and in a flash you know the density altitude at that airport under those conditions. The airplane's POH has some easy to use graphs that show you what performance to expect out of the airplane at various density altitudes. Pilots who fly from high-elevation airports in the west are more keenly aware of density altitude than are pilots in other parts of the country. But even at lower elevations, air temperature makes a great deal of difference in the length of the ground run needed to take off and the ability of the airplane to climb once it has become airborne.

Because pilots from the flatlands aren't accustomed to density altitude making the difference between whether their airplanes will fly or just run off of the end of the runway, far too many of them come to grief when they fly in the mountainous areas or in the high desert regions. Pay attention to density altitude anywhere that you fly. Here in the midwest, where airport elevations usually run around 1,000 feet above sea level, give or take a little, a hot July afternoon, with temperatures in the 90s, can result in a density altitude several thousand feet high.

At any given gross weight an airplane will always require the same quantity of air molecules flowing across the wings to generate the lift necessary to support that weight. Airflow is the magic ingredient of lift. This means that when the air is thinner, more airspeed is required to produce the same airflow than in denser air. Therefore more *true airspeed* is needed to fly in higher-density altitudes than in lower ones. Let's understand the difference between true airspeed and *indicated airspeed*. Indicated airspeed is what you actually see in front of you, displayed on the airspeed indicator. The indicator works by sensing the amount of air being rammed into the opening in the pitot tube. When the air is thinner, containing fewer molecules in a given volume, the amount of air coming into the pitot tube is less; therefore the indicator senses less airflow and displays a slower reading.

True airspeed is the actual speed of the airplane through the air. When you get into high-density altitude or high absolute altitude conditions, there is a difference between indicated and true airspeeds. This phenomenon works to our benefit. Because the wings need the same amount of air flowing over them at all times to support a constant weight, you can still rely on the airspeed indicator to fly because it too will sense this diminished airflow in high-density altitude operations.

If the stalling speed of your airplane is 55 knots, assuming unaccelerated flight, it will always stall at 55 knots indicated airspeed. Even though you'll be going faster than 55 knots, in terms of true airspeed when the stall occurs at higher-density altitudes, the reading on the airspeed indicator will be 55 knots at any density altitude. The only thing that matters to your wings, engine, and propeller is the quantity of air molecules that is available for them to use to perform their respective tasks.

# Takeoffs, Climbs, and Descents

To take off, the wings of the airplane obviously have to have enough air flowing over them to produce enough lift to overcome the airplane's weight and fly. After the effects of density altitude are considered, the major determinant of the length of ground run before flight is possible is the surface wind at the airport. If you can take off into the wind, this headwind during the takeoff run allows the needed airflow around the wings to develop at a slower ground speed than in conditions when no wind is present. If you need 60 knots to take off and if the wind is blowing at 10 knots, if you can take off directly into this wind, the airspeed indicator will show 60 knots when the airplane is only going 50 knots across the ground because 10 knots of airflow is already present when the airplane was at a standstill.

We do our best to avoid a takeoff with any tailwind component. If we tried to take off with a 10-knot direct tailwind, our airplane would have to be running down the runway at 70 knots ground speed before there would be 60 knots of airflow around the wings. The difference involved in thundering down the runway to build that extra 20 knots of ground speed can result in a tremendous increase in the length of the run. For that reason, we always take off into the wind. There are a few airports, but not many, where takeoffs and landings have to be made in a certain direction because of obstructions very near the end of one of the runways. However, this isn't encountered very often, and operations from these airports should never be attempted by student or newly licensed pilots.

If your airplane needs 50 knots of airflow around the wings to fly, which is very close to the requirement of our Cessna 150, a takeoff into a headwind of only 5 knots (which is 10 percent of the takeoff speed) will reduce the length of the takeoff run by approximately 19 percent. A headwind of 25 knots (50 percent of the takeoff speed) will reduce the ground run by 75 percent. Conversely, a tailwind of only 5 knots will increase the run by about 21 percent. Many airports serving general aviation lightplanes have only one runway. Naturally, it is seldom possible to take off directly into the wind at these fields because the wind will be blowing across the runway at some angle or another most of the time. Even so, we take off in the direction that provides some headwind component from the existing wind.

Your airplane's POH will contain tables and graphs that will enable you to fairly accurately determine the takeoff distance under most conditions. The following factors influence the ground run's distance and are covered in the modern lightplane POH:

- Density altitude, figured by adjusting for airport elevation, atmospheric pressure, and temperature

- Actual gross weight of the airplane for this takeoff, which has a large effect on the length of the ground run
- Runway slope and condition, the effects of any incline in the runway, and the retarding effects of snow, high grass, loose dirt, or similar conditions
- Wind speed and direction, which will have a major impact on takeoff distance

As you can see, the most adverse takeoff conditions are present when you are faced with a combination of a heavily loaded airplane taking off from an airport at a high elevation above sea level with a runway of sod or similar retarding configuration, on a hot day, with an unfavorable wind. In the western United States and Canada, these factors operate together during many months of the year. There are situations when a normally aspirated lightplane just cannot take off from some airports. But even at lower elevations unfavorable conditions of weight, wind, and temperature can be deadly if you try a takeoff that your airplane just cannot perform. Use your POH, and believe what it says about airplane performance.

Quite early in your training, you'll be exposed to the various manners in which your airplane will climb. In lightplanes equipped with fixed-pitch propellers, as is our Cessna 150, climbs are always made at full throttle, with the desired climb airspeed being obtained by controlling pitch. Remember that pitch controls the angle of attack. There are two angles of attack that produce the two different climbs used in flying light airplanes. *Best rate of climb* is a climb that results in the most altitude gain in a given amount of time. *Best angle of climb* is the climb that gives us the most altitude gain in a given distance over the ground. Best-angle climbs are seldom used in the real world of everyday flying. The airspeed for a best-angle climb is slower than for best-rate, which means that when climbing at the best angle, the nose attitude is quite high. Your visibility over the nose is compromised, and the high attitude combined with the slower forward speed can overheat the engine. Best-angle climbs will be practiced in training, but you probably won't use them unless there is an obstacle near the end of the runway that you need to clear right after takeoff.

The best rate of climb will be flown at an airspeed faster than the best-angle speed, the nose attitude will be more comfortable, and the engine will cool better. If you do need to get over an obstacle after takeoff, limit your climbing at the best-angle speed. As soon as that obstacle is cleared, allow the airspeed to build to the best-rate value. Don't abuse the engine or sacrifice forward visibility any more than you have to.

Military fighters and airliners have angle of attack indicators in their cockpits that enable the pilots of these sophisticated airplanes to very precisely control the angle of attack in all situations. But, due to cost and complexity, virtually no lightplanes have such indicators, so we are left with determining our angle of attack by using airspeed. The airspeed indicator is not as precise a display of angle of attack, but it is certainly good enough for lightplane flying. So, we learn what the speeds are, as called out in the POH, for best rate and best angle of climb and use them accordingly to derive the needed performance from our airplanes.

At full throttle and at the same indicated airspeed, no two airplanes of the same type ever produce exactly the same rates or angles of climb, due to inherent, minor variations in manufacture and rigging from one airplane to the next. Similarly, even the very same airplane won't duplicate its performance from one flight to the next because there will always be at least some small variation in load and density altitude. So, even though the POH quotes values for best rate and best angle of climb, and the expected rates and climb angles derived from using them, be aware that there is inherent and inescapable variation in performance. If the POH figures show you that a certain takeoff will be critical in any given situation, amend the situation. Lighten the load if you can, or do something else to get into a more favorable condition. Many times, especially in flying out west in the summer, you can't take off in the heat of the day. You either do it in the early morning or later in the evening, after the temperature has cooled some.

As with other maneuvers, climbs should be made using both instrument and outside visual references to control the airplane. The POH often gives a cruise climb speed, which is the manufacturer's determination of the best climbing airspeed that will produce a reasonable rate of climb and at the same time be faster than the best rate of climb airspeed. When you use the cruise climb speed, your visibility over the nose will be better still, and the engine will cool adequately during protracted climbs because there is much better airflow through the engine compartment.

While climbing, you will notice the effects of P-factor. Remember that at higher angles of attack, the airplane has a tendency to turn to the left because of the asymmetrical thrust being produced by the propeller. To correct for this, add a little right rudder pressure. When you have the wings level, not banked, during a climb, sneak a look at the ball in the turn-and-slip indicator. To keep the ball centered, you'll need that little constant nudge on the right rudder pedal. You will occasionally see a sloppy pilot who climbs with the right wing banked down a little. That pilot either doesn't know better or is too lazy to do it right by holding a little right rudder pressure during climbs. In larger airplanes, you'll probably encounter a trim control for the rudder. If you're climbing several thousand feet, you can move the rudder trim over to the right a small amount and give your right leg a rest. We don't have a rudder trim in the Cessna 150, to reduce complexity and cost, and also because this airplane's little 100-horsepower engine and small propeller don't produce that much P-factor.

Elevator trim is also important during climbs. When the power and airspeed have been established to produce the desired climb, trim away the pressure that would otherwise have to be held on the control wheel to keep the nose attitude where you want it to be. Part of relaxing and enjoying the flying experience comes with using the trim to remove the necessity of holding control pressures, needlessly, for extended periods of time. Also, your climb will be more efficient when the airplane is properly trimmed because you won't have the variations in nose attitude that will result if you try to hold pressure constantly to attempt to keep the attitude at a given point.

In summary, you establish a climb by adding full power, then applying back pressure on the wheel to raise the nose, and adjusting the airspeed to the value that will produce the desired climb. As this is done, add right rudder pressure to compensate for the P-factor, and then trim away the pressure on the control wheel once the climb is stable. Like all of the other training maneuvers, in a short while you'll do all of this without really thinking about the steps involved, and it will become a smooth and coordinated transition from level flight to climbing.

When the time comes to level off from the climb at the desired altitude, the process actually begins about 50 feet before reaching that height. Lower the nose gradually, and while the nose is coming down to the level flight attitude, the airplane will climb that last little bit. Keep the power up at full throttle until the airspeed builds to cruising speed and reduce the rpm to cruise power. As the nose comes down, and the airspeed increases, remove the pressure on the right rudder that was applied during the climb to overcome the P-factor. Again, when you're stable in cruising flight, finish the job by rotating the trim control wheel forward a little to remove the forward pressure that it takes to hold the nose level. That's all there is to it.

If your climb has taken you high enough, after you're stable in cruise, it's time to start thinking about leaning the mixture for engine efficiency. In the past, we used to ignore leaning of the mixture, in normally aspirated engines, below 5,000 feet. In those good old days (that maybe never were) avgas cost far less than $1 per gallon. As fuel prices rose in the 1970s, much of the conventional wisdom about powerplant management underwent some critical reexamination. Today, most engine manufacturers approve of leaning the mixture of normally aspirated engines at any altitude, as long as the power setting is below 75 percent, and the engine doesn't run rough when leaned. Read what your POH has to say about leaning practices, and consult your instructor.

Leaning the mixture has several benefits. First, fuel consumption is reduced. The engine runs best at a proper mixture, and when you climb high and don't lean, the mixture becomes too rich because of the thin air at high altitude, which can foul spark plugs. When the mixture is too rich, the engine can't produce the power that it can at the right mixture setting. When you're cruising much above 5,000 feet, you need to have the engine producing the proper amount of power to give good, efficient cruise performance and airspeed.

Descents can be made in a power-off glide or more commonly by reducing the power from the cruise setting, but not all of the way back to idle. Glides with the power at idle need to be learned and are seldom used outside of the traffic pattern, during the landing approach. Power-off glides are not an efficient way to come down from cruising altitudes because glides are done at a relatively slow airspeed, and therefore, you don't cover much ground while gliding.

A long power-off glide from higher altitudes can damage the engine. While cruising, you've probably run the engine somewhere between 65 and 75 percent of its rated power output. At those power settings, the engine is producing quite a bit of heat, which is being dissipated through the normal airflow through the engine compartment. When the power is suddenly reduced to idle, and left there for an extended period of time, the engine can cool too fast because at idle power it won't produce anywhere near the amount of heat that it did at cruise. This phenomenon is called *shock cooling*. The name implies what happens. The engine cools at such a fast rate that it is shocked, and the shock can result in warped or cracked cylinder barrels or cylinder heads. Shock cooling refers to the rate at which the engine cools down, not the absolute amount of temperature difference between cruise and idle power. To avoid shock cooling, if you must do a power-off glide, like you will in the traffic pattern, the key to avoiding damage to the engine is to reduce power in a few steps to allow the engine to cool more slowly rather than all at once. A good pilot always learns how to take care of an airplane, regardless of who owns it.

Power-off glides are the first phase of learning how to descend. After you learn how to glide, your instructor will teach you how to descend with reduced power, but not at idle. Many aspects of learning to fly involve the building-block approach to teaching, and this is only one of those examples.

To perform a power-off glide, first look in the POH and find the manufacturer's recommended gliding speed. Usually it is very close to the airspeed used to obtain the best rate of climb. There are two gliding speeds that you should learn, and unfortunately, only one of them is usually shown in the POH. The POH gliding speed is what is known as the *maximum lift over drag speed,* which is abbreviated as *best L/D.* This is the speed, when gliding, at which the wings are producing the maximum amount of lift at the minimum amount of drag. Gliding at best L/D results in the most distance covered over the ground.

The other glide speed, not usually disclosed in the POH, is the *minimum sink* speed. This glide speed allows the airplane to sink at the minimum possible rate, expressed in fpm. Minimum sink speed is very important to glider pilots because using it allows them to remain aloft for the longest time, while searching for thermals that will allow the glider to climb if one is found. But there is a potential danger to airplane pilots in using minimum sink speed because minimum sink speed is very close to the stalling speed, often only 5 to 10 percent above stall. Gliding at an airspeed this slow demands excellent pilot technique, especially in maintaining a constant airspeed and being aware of how the stall speed automatically increases any time that the wings are banked or when any other acceleration is put on the wings.

Minimum sink speed does not provide much coverage over the ground while gliding because the airplane is moving so slowly. Using the best L/D speed results in traveling the farthest during a glide. There are a few times when it would be valuable to glide at minimum sink speed, and we'll talk about those situations later in this chapter. For now, when we speak of gliding, assume that we'll use the best L/D speed, as shown in the POH. Let's get back to how to enter a glide.

When in cruising flight, gradually pull the throttle all of the way back to idle. You'll need to apply back pressure on the control wheel to hold the nose level, or very slightly below level, until the airspeed bleeds off and reaches gliding speed. Then, just release a little of the back pressure and allow the nose to fall a little bit. You will then need to either raise or lower the nose to maintain the glide speed. If you're gliding too fast, raise the nose some; if you're below the target glide speed, lower it a little. Then, when the airspeed is stable, and you've nailed down the nose attitude needed to keep the speed where you want it, use the trim control to trim away the control pressure. You're now gliding.

The recovery from a glide—to resume a normal cruise configuration and speed—is also a fairly simple transition. About 100 to 150 feet before you reach the target altitude, smoothly add power all the way to full throttle and raise the nose to the level flight attitude. Let the airspeed build to cruising speed and then pull the throttle back to cruise rpm. Then make whatever minor adjustments are necessary in both nose attitude and rpm to establish stable cruising flight. Retrim to relieve the control wheel pressure that it takes to hold the nose level, and you're back in cruise from the glide.

# Turns

As previously mentioned, turns are accomplished by banking the wings down in the direction of the desired turn and simultaneously applying rudder pedal pressure in the same direction. The banking action causes the airplane to turn because the force of lift, generated by the wings, always remains perpendicular to the wings and consequently pulls the airplane around in the turn. The correct amount of rudder pressure keeps the turn coordinated so that the airplane is not skidding toward the outside of the turn or slipping into it. Some instructors tell their students to think of the rudder as the control that trims the turn, and that is not a bad way to view its use. Just remember that, unlike a boat, an airplane doesn't turn by rudder action; it turns by banking. The rudder is not needed to cause the turn, just to keep it coordinated.

The rudder is also being used, as we enter the turn, to counter *adverse yaw*. Adverse yaw is the natural tendency of the airplane's nose to swing in the direction opposite to that of the turn. This occurs primarily because of the way the ailerons create forces upon the airplane as the wings are banked. If we turn the control wheel to the left, the left aileron goes up, which forces the left wing down. At the same time, the right aileron deflects down, and the relative wind acting upon it forces the right wing up. The amount of drag that each moving aileron creates is not the same; the aileron going down, which is the right one in our example of a left bank, creates more drag than does the one on the inside of the turn, here the left one. This excess drag on the outside wing tends to pull that wing and causes the nose to swing to the outside of the turn.

Another factor in the creation of adverse yaw is that the outside wing has to move farther in the arc of the circle of the turn and therefore is moving faster through the air than is the wing on the inside of the turn. When the wing goes faster, it naturally creates more drag, which also has a pulling force on that outside wing, which in turn pulls the nose to the outside as well. If we use rudder pressure in the proper amount as the airplane is banked with the control wheel, the nose isn't allowed to swing to the opposite direction. It remains right there on the straight and level heading for a split second and then starts to move in the direction of the turn, as the banking of the wings actually starts the turning movement of the entire airplane.

Turns are normally divided into three classes, all related to the angle of bank: *shallow, medium,* and *steep.* Shallow turns are those in which the bank angle is less than about 20°. They require that some control wheel pressure actually be held into the turn to counter the airplane's inherent design stability that wants to keep the wings level. This stability is achieved by what is known as *dihedral.* When you stand in front of the airplane, looking right at the hub of the propeller, about 20 feet or more from the nose, you'll notice that the wings are attached to the fuselage in such a manner that they each appear to be bent upward toward the tips. They aren't really bent but are built so that the wing tip is slightly higher than the root of the wing, which is the fuselage end. By the use of dihedral, the design engineers have created a natural tendency of the airplane to level itself from minor excursions from wings-level flight. When one wing goes down a little, it creates more lift than its counterpart on the other side because the wing that has gone down ever so slightly is now level. More lift means that the lowered wing wants to rise. In this way, the force of lift produced by each wing is always working to remain in concert with the lift generated by the opposite wing and fly in a wings-level attitude.

Medium turns are those resulting from bank angles of approximately 20 to 45°. At these angles of bank, the aerodynamic forces designed into the airplane are such that there is, in smooth air, no requirement to hold pressure on the control wheel to keep the airplane banked. For that reason, medium turns are the easiest to perform correctly, and flight instructors introduce students first to medium turns. You'll see that about 30° of bank results in an easy, relaxed turn.

Steep turns are those in which the bank angle exceeds 45°. At these steep bank angles, the airplane will have a tendency to "overbank," which means that the bank angle will tend to increase unless opposite aileron pressure is used to overcome it and prevent the airplane from rolling on over. Steep turns also require more of the total lift of the wings to be used to turn the airplane, and less of it is available to overcome gravity. Hence, during a steep turn, the angle of attack has to be increased substantially to add the lift needed to maintain a constant altitude, and that requires a hefty pull back on the control wheel.

As the steepness of the turn increases, so must the back pressure on the wheel. If the turn is very steep, much over 45° of bank angle, you'll need to add some power to maintain a constant altitude. As the bank increases from wings level, so does the airplane's stalling speed. This increase in stalling speed is not in a linear relationship with the bank increase, but rather, the stalling speed starts going up dramatically after about 45° of bank. If you perform a turn at 60° of bank, you have little margin between the cruise airspeed in the turn and stalling speed at that bank angle.

When you're in a steep turn, it's very easy to not apply enough back pressure to keep the nose level and thereby allow the nose to fall. Once this happens, the airspeed can build rapidly, depending, of course, on just how far you've let the nose fall below the level attitude. Then, the airplane is in what is known as a *spiral dive,* with a high bank angle, nose low and losing altitude, and the airspeed increasing. This condition can get dangerous if not recognized early and if corrective action isn't taken. Your natural tendency will be to pull back on the wheel because you see the airspeed getting into the danger zone, but that's the exact wrong thing to do. At very steep bank angles, pulling back on the wheel, while the wings are still rolled over in a steep bank, just tightens the turn and exacerbates your problem.

To recover from a spiral dive, you must first lessen the bank angle by using the control wheel to apply the opposite aileron, and roll out some of the bank. Then, as the bank is shallowing, you should reduce the power (which will help keep the airspeed from increasing even more) and then use back pressure on the wheel to gradually pull out of the ensuing dive. If you don't lessen the bank first, excessive back pressure on the wheel, in an ill-fated attempt to reduce airspeed, can cause a stall. A stall in a steep turn, with high power and high airspeed, can be a very violent maneuver and should only be done in airplanes that are certified by the FAA for aerobatics and only by a competent aerobatic pilot. Although it seldom happens, there is a worse risk yet. If things have really gone to pot on you, and the airspeed is screaming, the bank is very steep, and you haul back on the control wheel, it is possible to so overload the structure of the airplane with high G loads that the structure fails, and something breaks, usually the tail first, followed quickly by wing separation. Don't be scared by this recitation of the possibilities. Your instructor will never let things get dangerous, and you won't either, once you're trained.

Now let's get back to reality and examine a medium banked turn in detail. Before starting any turn, always look carefully in the direction of turn, and be sure that there isn't any other traffic where you're going to turn. Then start the turn by gradually and simultaneously applying both aileron pressure with the control wheel and rudder pressure in the direction of the desired turn. The rate at which the airplane rolls into the turn is governed by both the rapidity and amount of control pressures added, so be smooth and gradual.

As the airplane rolls into the turn, you'll add a little back pressure on the wheel. In all turns, some of the total lift is now devoted to the task of turning the airplane, instead of all of it being singularly working to overcome gravity. You need to increase the angle of attack a little to increase the total lift so that you remain at a constant altitude. In a medium turn, the amount of needed back pressure isn't very much, so be smooth and gradual here too.

As soon as the airplane rolls from the level attitude into the bank, the nose should start to move along the horizon in the direction of the desired turn. The rate at which the nose moves will increase as the bank increases. Any variation in the coupled action of nose movement with angle of bank indicates that a control is not being used properly and that the turn is not coordinated, as follows:

- If the nose starts to move before the bank begins, the rudder pressure is being applied too soon.

- If the bank starts before the nose starts turning, or if the nose swings in the opposite direction, due to adverse yaw, the rudder pressure is either applied too late or an insufficient amount of rudder is being applied.

- If the nose moves up or down when entering the bank, excessive or insufficient back pressure is being applied to the control wheel.

When the desired angle of bank is reached, relax the pressure on the ailerons and rudder, taking out the rolling movement of the control wheel and the pressure on the rudder pedal. This allows the ailerons and rudder to streamline themselves in their neutral positions. The back pressure on the wheel should not be released, but rather it needs to be held constant, with minor adjustments in the nose attitude applied to maintain a constant altitude.

Throughout the turn, check your visual references on the horizon and occasionally glance at the altimeter to determine whether your pitch (nose) attitude is correct. Learn now that a pilot never gets all of the information needed from only one source, which we call a *reference*. In this case, the view outside of the windshield is the primary reference because it tells you how steep the bank is, how fast you're turning, and where the nose attitude is. Flying is an art of absorbing the information from more than one reference, primary and secondary, and then using this information to decide how to manipulate the controls to achieve a desired result. The altimeter is the secondary reference for determining if the nose attitude is correct.

You should also determine what you need to know about the bank angle from looking outside; but it will be a while in your flying career before you can tell if a turn is coordinated without looking at the turn coordinator. Glance at it; don't stare at it. Don't become mesmerized by any flight instrument. Using the instruments properly involves learning to scan them, see what they're saying to you, and doing what is needed to get back to the flight condition that you want. Scanning ability takes a while to develop, but start the process now. Scanning also means that your primary references are outside of the airplane's windshield and windows, not inside of the cockpit.

When you look at the turn coordinator, you want to see where the ball is inside of the fluid-filled tube. It should be in the center. If it's not, which side is it on? The old adage "Step on the ball" will get your turn coordinated. If the ball is on the inside of the turn, the airplane is slipping around and needs a little rudder pressure in the direction of the turn. If the ball is on the outside part of the tube, relax some of your rudder pressure in the direction of the turn, and the ball will slide back into the center. When the ball is on the high side of the turn, the airplane is skidding and that needs to be corrected also. Now, you've got a coordinated turn going.

Turn coordination will eventually become automatic and you'll rarely need to look much at the ball to see how you're doing in this regard, so long as you can see outside. But when you advance into instrument flying, you'll find that your senses will play tricks on you when you're deprived of the ability to see outside of the airplane. In instrument flying, the ball is an important reference. The human senses of balance and eyesight work together. When deprived of our ability to see whether we're upright, the sensory organs in our inner ears can send confusing signals to the brain. We think we're turning when flying straight and level or vice versa.

Viewing the airplane's nose attitude through the windshield is the primary reference for correct attitude, but it doesn't necessarily tell you the whole story. That nose attitude that you see may not be the correct one for maintaining a constant altitude. Steal a glance, as part of your instrument scan, at the altimeter and the vertical speed indicator. In combination, these two instruments will tell you the altitude and any associated trends in whether you're climbing or descending and how quickly any change is occurring.

Remember that the VSI has a significant lag (several seconds) in its response to changes in altitude and the indications that it gives. So, don't chase the VSI in an attempt to hold altitude. When you see that you are high or low or are climbing or descending, make a small correction with elevator pressure, pulling back or pushing forward slightly on the wheel to put the nose on a new reference point on the horizon. Wait a few seconds for the dynamics of the situation to settle down, and look again at the instruments to see if more or a different correction is needed. Don't stare at any one spot on either the instrument panel or outside of the airplane. Scan the instruments, and scan your eyes around the outside world. Then you can assimilate the information available from all of your references to make whatever control adjustments are necessary. The sooner you develop the habit of adequately scanning both the panel and outside, the sooner your control of the airplane will improve and become second nature.

During all of your turn, use both the ailerons and rudder to correct minor variations, just as you do in straight and level flight. Soon your turns will be stable and your corrections will be so smooth and slight that they will be almost imperceptible.

The recovery from a turn is begun just a few degrees before you reach the desired new heading, usually about 10° or so. Scan the DG while you are in the turn to check its progress and to know when to start the recovery to straight and level flight. The DG has no lag, and you can depend upon it to let you know just how far a turn has progressed. Also, you should know from looking outside how the turn is going and when you're near to the new direction in which you want to fly. Apply aileron and rudder pressures together in the direction opposite to that of the turn. As the angle of bank decreases, smoothly release the back elevator pressure that you've been holding throughout the turn; the back pressure isn't needed now that the wings are becoming level again.

It's important to coordinate and combine the release of the back pressure with the roll out of the bank; otherwise the nose will pop up at the end of the turn, and you'll gain some unwanted altitude. When the turn is completed, scan all of the outside and instrument references as you return to straight and level flight. Check the nose and wing tip positions on the outside horizon and then quickly look at the turn coordinator to make sure that you're not still unwittingly holding some aileron or rudder pressure. Finally, scan the altimeter and VSI to see if you need any correction to the nose attitude to hold a constant altitude.

# Climbing and Descending Turns

Climbing turns have more factors at play than do turns while maintaining a given altitude. First, a turn while climbing results in some loss of rate of climb. Because some of the total lift from the wings must be diverted toward the task of turning the airplane, there is less lift available to climb. All climbs in our Cessna 150 are made at full power, so you can't increase the power any more to offset the loss of climb rate inherent in performing a climbing turn. You have to settle for a minor degradation in climb rate during the turn.

If you turn at a bank angle that is either too shallow or too steep while climbing, that results in decreased efficiency, too. Too steep a bank results in too little lift remaining available to keep climbing, and in an airplane like our 150, which doesn't have a plethora of excess power, the climb rate will suffer dramatically. If you bank at too shallow an angle, the turn is difficult to control and maintain because of the airplane's dihedral, which wants to keep the wings level.

We want to strive for a medium banked turn as the best compromise and keep a constant angle of bank and rate of turn. It takes practice to do this well. Diverting your attention and dividing it from looking just at the airplane's nose into using all of the visual and instrument references available gives you a total picture of the maneuver.

There are three ways to begin a climbing turn. You can first enter a climb and then turn, first enter the turn and then pitch up and add power to start the climb, or do the climb and turn entries together. The thing that makes climbing turns difficult initially is that you are using and coordinating all of the flight controls together. You're pitching, rolling, and yawing (turning) all at the same time. The easiest of the three ways to enter a climbing turn is to start the climb first and then when you've got a stable climb under control, begin turning. As your skills rapidly develop, which they will, you'll progress to doing it all together and simultaneously entering both the turn and the climb.

Climbing turns have one important difference from turns conducted from straight and level flight and that relates to the use of rudder pressure. During a straight ahead climb, we have to hold right rudder to compensate for the P-factor, which wants to turn the airplane to the left. So, when making a climbing turn to the left, you'll find that, to enter the turn, you'll actually release right rudder pressure more than you'll add left rudder. When making a climbing turn to the right, you'll add far more right rudder pressure than you would to turn to the right in straight and level flight because it already takes some right rudder in a climb just to prevent the airplane from turning to the left. Don't be concerned because it takes you longer to learn to naturally coordinate climbing turns. Use the turn coordinator—that's why it's in the airplane.

When you start learning to make descending turns, you'll see that the rate of descent goes up while turning, especially if you are making your descent by using a power-off glide. The laws of physics don't change; whenever a turn is performed, some of the total lift is channeled into turning the airplane and that portion of the lift is no longer available to overcome gravity. To maintain your proper gliding airspeed while turning, you'll need to drop the nose attitude a little below what it would be for a straight ahead glide.

Maintaining good control coordination is important in all maneuvers, but it is vital in a gliding turn. During every flight, you'll be using gliding turns while in the traffic pattern to land. That phase of flight is, by necessity, conducted close to the ground, where you don't have the comfort and safety net of altitude to negate errors. During a glide, you'll already have some left rudder pressure applied, because of P-factor. Just as P-factor wants to turn the airplane to the left during a climb, it has the opposite effect during a glide, when the natural tendency of the airplane is to turn to the right. So, a left gliding turn takes more left rudder pressure than during straight and level flight, and a right gliding turn involves releasing the left rudder pressure that is already there, more than it does applying right rudder.

Most of the accidents that happen as a result of control mishandling occur in the traffic pattern, close to the ground. The majority of these involve a stall, followed very shortly by a spin. The turn from the base leg to the final approach is a particularly vulnerable place and time for this misfortune to occur. Often the turn is not timed properly, and the pilot senses a need to hurry the rate of turn, to avoid having the final approach off to the side of the centerline of the runway. Then, our hapless pilot shoves in the rudder to speed up the turn and yanks back on the control wheel at the same time. Presto, the yank causes a stall, and the heavy amount of rudder pressure, which caused a very uncoordinated turn, results in the nose snapping over into a spin. At this point, things will unravel so fast that the pilot will never know what just happened. When you're only a few hundred feet above the ground and a spin starts, it's all over.

There are two fast and rigid rules to live by, and this will never happen to you. First, never make steep turns in the pattern, and keep your medium ones coordinated. Second, any time that an approach, or any other part of the traffic pattern goes south, push the throttle in, get out of there, go around, and try again. If you obey these rules, you can't become the victim of a stall/spin accident.

Your instructor will teach you what are known as *cross-controlled stalls,* where the airplane is purposefully put in an uncoordinated turn and then stalled. This maneuver is taught up high, and demonstrated on your flight test when you get a license. Done high, it's totally safe and should make you aware of the risk in violating the two above-mentioned rules about flying in the traffic pattern to land.

# Ground Reference Maneuvers

The descriptive term *ground reference maneuvers* is applied to certain training maneuvers that are performed to teach you to control what the airplane is doing by paying attention to the relationship between the airplane's flight path and a track on the ground. These maneuvers consist of the *rectangular course, S-turns across a road,* and *turns about a point.*

These exercises teach the effect that the wind has on the airplane's course over the ground. You will learn how to recognize and anticipate these effects. The maneuvers show you how to control a plane so that it goes where you want it to go and is where you want it to be in relation to either a specific point on the ground or a path over the ground. About the only place that one of these training maneuvers is used in everyday flying is in the traffic pattern, which is a rectangular course. Turns about a point may be used if you are trying to get a good look at some point on the ground. S-turns over a road are almost never a practical part of a flight, but all three reinforce talents that you have to develop and that you will show to the examiner during your flight test.

An airplane flies through and is supported by the air mass in which it finds itself. Except on rare occasions, that air mass will be moving, and we call that movement of the air wind. In flight, the wind doesn't blow against or in relation to the airplane; the airplane is moving straight through the air mass that is supporting it. If you're a boater, you're already familiar with this concept, except that you've known it as current in the water. Visualize a simple example of what we mean. See yourself in a large room, like a ballroom, walking in a straight line across the floor, except that you're walking on a huge throw rug that covers most of the floor. You have a friend at one side of the room, holding onto the edge of the throw rug, who begins to pull the rug toward the edge of the room, at a right angle (90°) to your line of walking.

The result is that your path over the floor, below the rug, will be at an angle across the room. Even though you're walking in a straight line across the rug, the rug is moving, causing your direction of walk across the floor of the room to be different than your direction across only the rug. You will end up toward one side or the other of the room, depending on the side to which your friend is pulling the rug. That's exactly how wind affects the path of an airplane over the ground.

An airplane in flight cannot feel the wind because it is contained within that moving mass of air, just like you were contained on the moving rug. Some student pilots grasp this concept quickly, and others have trouble understanding it. Ground reference maneuvers are a tremendous aid in seeing, firsthand, how the effects of wind operate in flight.

# Rectangular Course

The rectangular course (FIG. 7-1) is a practice maneuver in which the ground track of the airplane is directly over all four sides of a selected rectangle on the ground. The central United States was originally surveyed, in the days of the pioneers, into mile-long sections, and the fences and tree lines that define these sections still exist in almost all of the rural areas. Country roads also generally follow these section lines. Pilots flying in other parts of the country may not have these convenient section lines, but they can easily find large farms, parallel roads, or other surface features that will work just as well.

One objective of these exercises is to develop your ability to pay attention to your flight path, the ground references, and a periodic instrument scan while controlling the airplane and watching out for other traffic in the vicinity. Another of the objectives is to gain a recognition of the drift of your flight path, caused by the wind, toward or away from your intended ground track.

Select a square or rectangular field, with sides approximately 1 mile in length. This maneuver is flown at a constant airspeed

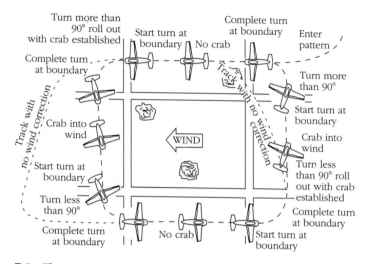

**7-1** *The rectangular course maneuver teaches proper compensation for wind in a traffic pattern.*

and altitude; about 600 to 1,000 feet above the ground will work the best. If your field has sides of only about a mile, you'll fly the course about ¹/₄ to ¹/₂ mile outside of the box. If your field has longer sides, where you can keep a good view of the boundaries over the nose, without the nose obscuring that view, you can fly right over the sides. Most of the time you'll be paralleling the sides, and your distance from each side should be the same and remain constant.

All of the turns in the pattern should be made when the airplane is abeam the corners of the course, and the bank angle should normally not exceed 45°. On a very windy day, steeper banks may be needed, but as a student pilot, you won't be flying on days when the winds are high. As your training and skills progress, your instructor will expose you to higher winds, but not for a while.

Refer to FIG. 7-1. Let's begin the pattern where shown, at the upper right corner of the figure, which is at the start of the downwind leg. We call it downwind because the wind is at your back, in line with your desired track over the ground. While you're flying down this leg, your ground speed will be the sum of your airspeed and the speed of the wind.

The first turn will occur at the end of this leg. Notice two things. First, you're going fairly fast over the ground, and there is a consequence of that high speed, which is that your turn will have to be made at a fairly steep bank angle. You need a steep bank to produce a rate of turn that is fast enough to get you turned parallel to the next leg and not get blown out away from it. Look at the dashed line that depicts a ground track that would be obtained if you didn't turn steeply. You want to stay within the desired distance from the next leg, not wander all over. Second, to be able to parallel the next road, you'll have to actually point the nose of the airplane into the wind, so the wind doesn't cause you to be blown farther away from the road than you want to be.

So, you'll have to make this first turn more than just 90° to end up pointed into the wind. Start the turn with coordinated control pressures to result in a fairly steep bank, maybe as much as 45°. Roll out of the turn smoothly but smartly, after the turn has gone beyond 90°. Just how much you need to turn beyond 90° is a function of how strong the wind is. It's a matter of judgment, and that's why you're learning this maneuver—to gain the experience that you need to develop that judgment.

Once you've completed the first turn, you're flying along one of the two *crosswind legs* of the rectangular course. The term *crosswind* implies that the wind is blowing across your track over the ground and not either from behind you or into your face. The feat along this leg is to have the airplane pointed into the wind just enough to parallel the desired course over the ground, without flying in over the road or getting blown out away from it. This angle between the heading of the airplane, which is the direction in which the nose is pointed, and the direction of your path over the ground is called the *crab angle*. As you fly down this first crosswind leg, you undoubtedly will need to adjust the heading of the airplane to maintain the desired track over the ground. Do so with small coordinated turns so that you don't overcorrect and head off into the opposite direction.

At the end of the first crosswind leg, you'll next make a turn onto the upwind leg. The upwind leg is parallel to the wind, flying directly into it. During the time that you're flying the upwind leg, your ground speed will be less than the airspeed, by whatever the velocity of the wind happens to be.

Note in FIG. 7-1 that although you were going down the first crosswind leg, the crab angle resulted in the airplane's already being pointed somewhat toward the direction of the upwind leg. Therefore, the turn from this first crosswind leg to the upwind leg requires that the airplane be turned less than 90°. The angle of bank necessary to accomplish this turn and end up at the correct position is about the normal angle for a medium turn, probably about 30° of bank. If the wind is really strong, you'll need less bank, the opposite of the steeper bank that you need at the end of the downwind leg on blustery days. Flying the upwind leg requires no crab angle because the wind is not trying to blow you from your desired ground track. The only effect that the wind has upon the airplane during the upwind leg is a reduction in the ground speed.

Now we're ready to turn from the upwind leg into the second of the crosswind legs. Look again at FIG. 7-1, and you'll see that this turn also needs to be less than a full 90° because you want to end up on the second crosswind leg with the necessary crab angle built into your heading that will keep you from being blown in, over the road. Plan this turn ahead of time, just like you did when you turned from the first crosswind leg onto the upwind leg. Make this turn onto the second crosswind leg a little shallower, in terms of bank angle, than the previous turn, and roll out of it before you've turned a full 90°. Then carefully observe your track over the ground and make whatever adjustments are needed to fly parallel to the road, again by making small, coordinated turns to finely tune your heading.

The last turn, which will complete your first circuit of the rectangular course, comes at the end of this second crosswind leg and is a turn onto the downwind. This turn needs to be more than 90°, just like the first turn you made from the downwind onto the first crosswind leg. At the same time that you're turning from the second crosswind onto the downwind leg, realize that the wind will be blowing you into the downwind, and your ground speed will start to increase.

This last turn is made with a fairly steep bank because you need to turn more than 90° fairly quickly. If you bank only slightly, the ensuing rate of turn will cause the turn to take too long to complete, and your ground track will suffer because you'll be blown into the rectangle.

After going around the course once, your instructor will probably have you do a few more laps. Nothing this complicated is learned, let alone mastered, on the first attempt. Also keep in mind that an illustration in a book can assume a perfect world, where a rectangular course has wind blowing perfectly parallel to two of the sides. In practice, this seldom happens. In real-world flying, chances are that your course over the ground will require some degree of crab angle on all four sides of the rectangle.

Two rules of thumb will help, whatever the wind is:

- When the wind is behind you, the turn must be steeper and faster.
- When the wind is head-on, the turn must be shallower and slower.

The rectangular course can be understood sooner if you can pick out a course that has longer legs. I've had students find a course that has had legs as long as 2 miles each. Then, you get a chance to relax for a bit between turns and adjust the needed crab angle because each leg takes $1\frac{1}{2}$ or 2 minutes to fly. If you pick out a short-legged course, you'll be whipping around it so fast that you won't have time to either think about what to do next or contemplate and absorb what just happened on the leg or turn that you're leaving.

The turns are the keys to this maneuver, and they require most of your effort, planning, and judgment. The rectangular course prepares you to fly the traffic pattern at the airport, and everything that you learn about turns and crab angles is applicable in the landing pattern. Remember what we said earlier about the turns from downwind onto crosswind and the turn from crosswind onto final approach in the traffic pattern. These turns are performed at low altitude, and the turn from downwind onto crosswind is steeper and faster than a normal medium turn. It's not difficult to get either of these turns uncoordinated, especially if you try to hurry them along with excessive rudder application. The result is that if you stall the airplane, the stall can be accompanied by yawing, which can cause the airplane to snap into a spin.

The solution is to learn the rectangular course maneuver, but first and foremost, never allow yourself to be so devoted to maintaining a track over the ground that you fail to fly the airplane. If you're in the landing pattern, you can always abandon the approach, add full power, and climb out to try the whole operation again. The same thing goes if you're doing a rectangular course and feel uncomfortable about any phase of it, including a safe outcome. Every wise pilot executes a safe go-around more than a few times in his flying career. Only the unwise and unsafe pilot remains so determined to make every approach conclude in a landing that she never executes a go-around. Flying airplanes is not an activity in which to engage in blind determination, except for the determination to be safe.

# S-Turns across a Road

S-turns across a road are a series of 180° turns that cross a road between each semicircular turn. Imagine a dollar sign ($) in your mind. The vertical line through the dollar sign is the road, and the S is the depiction of the 180° turns. The ground track that is flown won't stop with just two turns, each in the opposite direction, but the maneuver should continue for several turns so that the path over the ground looks like two or three dollar signs stacked on top of each other. Each S is equal in size and uniformly proportioned when the maneuver is done correctly. This maneuver promotes your ability to compensate for the effects of the wind and also enhances the habit of employing a scan that divides your attention between inside and outside references.

Choose a straight stretch of road, a least a mile long, preferably longer, with the wind blowing directly across it at a 90° angle. For our explanation here, assume that the wind is blowing from the right toward the left in relation to the desired dollar sign. We'll begin the exercise by flying at an altitude between 600 and 1,000 feet above the ground and by flying directly toward the road, at the top of the S, with the wind directly behind the airplane's heading.

When you are exactly over the road, start the first turn, to the left, immediately. Because the airplane is headed downwind, the ground speed is the greatest at this point, and the rate at which we're leaving the road is rapid. Therefore, roll into a steep bank so that the rate of turn is fast to minimize the drift away from the road.

As you near the halfway point in this first 180° turn to the left, the airplane's heading is changing from downwind to a crosswind heading, so the ground speed decreases. Begin to shallow out the bank, noting that your crab angle is toward the road and is the greatest due to the effect of the crosswind's trying to blow you away from the road.

After completing the first half of the first turn, your heading becomes more and more an upwind heading as the turn progresses, and your ground speed slows even more. Continue to gradually reduce the bank throughout the second half of the first turn. By doing this, your crab angle is completely gone, and the wings are once again level as you cross the road at the conclusion of the first 180° turn. When an S-turn is done correctly, the wings level just as the road passes beneath the cockpit.

There is no time to waste. As you cross the road, start a right turn. You are now flying directly into the headwind, so the turn needs to be made with a shallow bank and resulting slow rate of turn, at first. After this turn is halfway completed, it progresses from a crosswind to a downwind heading. Then, the bank angle and rate of turn both need to increase to keep the turn properly proportioned. Then the bank increase will be steady, and not all at once, because the crosswind component is being removed gradually as you complete the second half of the right turn. The goal is to once again roll the wings level as you cross over the road at a right angle to it.

You should maintain a given altitude throughout this maneuver, just as you did when flying the rectangular course. The bank angle and rate of turn will be constantly changing to achieve a truly symmetrical semicircle over the ground on each side of the road. The bank angle and turn rates are changing because the objective in these ground reference maneuvers is to fly a precise, predetermined track over the ground. When you are flying in normal cruising flight, and turn the airplane to a new heading, you aren't worried about the actual track over the ground. The minor variations that wind makes in ground track is of no concern up high, in cruise. But down in the traffic pattern, a precise ground track is the goal.

## Turns about a Point

Turns around a point involve flying a perfectly circular path over the ground, circling around a reference point that is in the center of the circle. The point of this maneuver is to have the radius of your circle around the point remain constant at all times.

Flying a turn around a point is very similar to an S-turn across a road. First, find a good reference point, such as a large tree in the middle of an otherwise empty field, a large silo, or a prominent intersection of two roads. Begin the maneuver in the same way as you did the S-turn, by flying exactly downwind with the wind directly behind you. Students tend to prefer to do turns around a point with the reference point off to their left because they can see it more easily out of the left cabin window as they sit in the pilot's seat. But after you learn to do it to the left, you need to also practice turns around a point to the right also because the examiner can ask you to do it either way, or both ways, during your flight test.

As you come abeam the reference point, start your turn with a coordinated application of aileron and rudder pressures. As the turn progresses around the first quarter of the circle, you are coming to the place where you'll be flying into a direct crosswind. The combination of your increased ground speed because the wind is behind you and the fact that you'll be flying into a direct crosswind means that you roll into the turn using a fairly steep bank, continue to steepen it, and obtain a faster rate of turn during this first quarter of the way around the circle. When you get a quarter of the way around, you need to be crabbed into the wind, which means that the nose of the airplane has to be pointed slightly toward the point on the ground.

During the next quarter of the turn, two things are happening. Your ground speed lessens as you fly into the wind and end up flying directly into the wind as the halfway point in the circle is reached. Also, the crosswind component is decreasing as you turn into the wind. Therefore, during this second quarter of the turn, you bank angle needs to be shallowed some from the steep bank that you had during the first quarter.

For the third quarter, your bank will constantly be shallowed because the wind has slowed your ground speed and it will be trying to blow you in toward the reference point as soon as you turn away from the heading that was directly into the wind. From this point until past the three-quarters position, your bank will be the shallowest of the entire maneuver. During this third quarter, you won't actually make 90° of turn because the airplane needs to be crabbed into the crosswind that you're now encountering again.

When you get to the three-quarters point in the turn, the effects of the wind change again. Now the crosswind starts lessening because you're turning away from the wind, toward the downwind portion of the turn. Your ground speed starts to pick up due to the tailwind. So, leaving the three-quarters point, you need to begin to steepen the bank again to compensate for the increased ground speed and the elimination of the crosswind.

Turns about a point end when you're once more abeam of the reference point, flying directly downwind, where you began. These turns, combined with S-turns across a road, teach you how to control your airplane's ground track in all wind conditions. S-turns are almost never an end in themselves, but turns around a point can be. There will probably come a time in your flying career when you will want to have a look at something on the ground (from a safe altitude). We fly turns around a point at the same 600 to 1,000 feet above the ground as we do most of the other ground reference maneuvers. After you get a license, obey the FARs and common sense, and don't fly around an object of interest any lower than that. The only way to examine an object on the ground is by flying circles around it. Good pilots fly circles; poor ones will end up flying an oval because they don't know how to compensate for the effects of the wind.

There are other ground reference maneuvers that include figure eights on pylons and around pylons, figure eights across a road, and power-off descending spirals around a point. All of them accomplish the same goal—honing your ability to fly the airplane in constantly changing wind conditions and paying attention to the ground reference point(s), the track over the ground, the instruments in the cockpit, watching for other traffic, and flying the airplane with good control coordination. The pilot who masters these maneuvers is also a master of the airplane.

## Not-So-Normal Landings

At the end of your first few lessons, you will make a normal landing with either calm wind or a wind right down the runway, relatively smooth air, and a nice, long paved runway that had no serious obstacles to the approach. If you face more challenging circumstances early on in your training, your instructor will probably make the landing so as not to overload you with more than you can handle.

In reality, particularly in cross-country flying, such landings are not the norm. As a pilot, you have to be able to deal with uncooperative winds, turbulent air, soggy sod runways, and short fields that are surrounded by factories, power lines, and broadcast antenna towers. Let's discuss a few techniques for dealing with the real world in which pilots fly.

## Crosswind Landings

Crosswind landings are actually more normal than are landings when the wind is directly down a runway. If you fly from a single-runway airport, as most airports are, you have only two directions in which to put the airplane on the ground. Seldom will the wind be right down the runway from either direction. You'll be making most of your landings with at least some degree of crosswind. Even if you fly from an airport with multiple runways, you can't avoid crosswinds. The chance of having to battle a 90° crosswind may be less, but you'll still often have some crosswind component. In World War II, when most airport runways were still sod, the British had the right idea. Airports in the United Kingdom were large circular fields, with no "runways" per se. Rather, pilots just observed the wind and took off and landed directly into it. With the advent of paved runways, we lost that advantage and now have to cope with crosswinds.

There are two methods of doing a crosswind approach and landing: the *crab* method and the *wing-low* method. Your instructor will teach you one or the other as a primary way of approaching and landing in a crosswind, depending upon her preference. Regardless of which way becomes primary for you, you should also learn the other.

The wing-low method is the easier of the two to perform because, when you are set up for the approach, the dynamics of the crosswind correction don't change much throughout the remainder of the approach and landing. To do it, you fly a normal traffic pattern (correcting for the wind on the various legs like you did in the rectangular course) and roll out of the turn from base to final, aligned with the centerline of the runway if possible. Then you lower the wing that is on the upwind side (the side from which the wind is blowing). Next, you apply as much *opposite* rudder pressure as is needed to keep the airplane from turning. You make only minor adjustments in the bank angle and opposite rudder pressure as needed, all of the way down final, to keep the airplane lined up with the runway. You hold the wing down and opposite rudder control condition all of the way to touchdown.

During the final, and just before the wheels touch the ground, the airplane is *slipping* into the wind. The wing-down condition pulls the airplane into the wind, keeping it aligned with the runway. The opposite rudder keeps the nose, and hence the entire airplane, from turning. The ball in the turn coordinator is near the end of the tube on the upwind, wing-low, side. Slipping is a bad technique when making normal turns in flight, when you want the ball in the center. But here, the slip is intentional.

Be aware that the rate and angle of descent increase when slipping because some of the wings' lift is devoted to pulling the airplane into the wind, just as some of the lift is not used to overcome gravity whenever the wings are banked. Slipping is a very good technique to correct for a crosswind, and it has other uses as well. In airplanes that don't have wing flaps, like many of the older classic ships, slipping is the only way to increase the angle of descent during final approach, once the airplane is already in a power-off glide. Modern airplanes, equipped with wing flaps, allow us to use those flaps to modulate our descent. Some airplanes are placarded against slips when the wing flaps are extended. If yours is, extend the flaps only to the limit permitted when slipping; otherwise, you can't use the wing-low method on crosswind landings. Most of the time you won't be using full flaps in crosswinds anyhow because full flap deployment makes the airplane a bit more difficult to control in the crosswind; their full extension provides more surface area for the wind to act on, and the increased drag associated with full flaps can make it take longer for a power application to take effect, if you need power to shallow the glide or to go around.

It is probable that most pilots do not like to use the wing-low method of crosswind correction because of the necessarily long period of slipping all of the way down the final approach. A slip feels awkward until you really get used to it. Passengers are sometimes uncomfortable with the airplane in this attitude, particularly if the crosswind is strong and the resultant bank angle is steep to stay in line with the runway.

When the wind is so strong that the bank angle gets so steep that even full opposite rudder will no longer keep the airplane from turning, you have exceeded the *maximum crosswind component* for your airplane. You've reached the limits of controllability, and you just can't land on this runway with this wind. This happens rarely, but if it does, recognize that you can't change the laws of physics and the design of the airplane. You've got to either use another runway at the airport or go to another airport that has a runway more favorably aligned with the prevailing wind.

Low-wing airplanes and those that have long wings have another problem with the wing-low method. They can get into a situation where the bank angle would result in the wing tip striking the ground before the landing gear touched down. For this reason, you'll seldom see an airliner, with its long wings, perform a wing-low crosswind approach and landing.

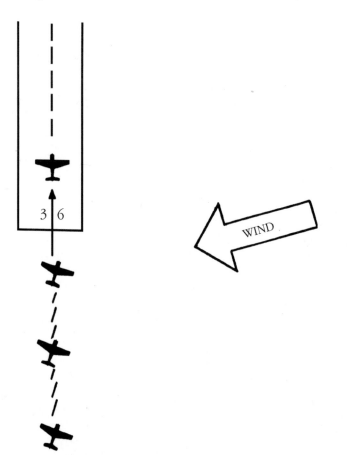

**7-2** *The crab method of crosswind correction. Be sure to straighten the airplane in line with the runway before flare and landing.*

The other method of coping with a crosswind is called the crab method because the airplane is crabbed into the wind, with the wings level, during the final approach (FIG. 7-2). The airplane is crabbed into the wind to keep the final approach path aligned with the centerline of the runway. Again, you now see the relevance of learning the ground reference maneuvers discussed earlier, especially the rectangular course.

This crab angle is held, and adjusted as necessary with slight coordinated turns, until just before the moment of touchdown, when the upwind wing is lowered, and the nose must be kept aligned with the centerline of the runway by applying opposite rudder pressure. You absolutely must not allow the airplane to contact the ground while still crabbed because the landing gear is not designed to absorb the strong sideload that would result. The gear legs will break if the crab angle and resulting sideloads are great enough. At best, you'll skip the airplane on the runway, risk what is called a ground loop, and quickly explore the weeds off to the side of the runway.

The crab method is more difficult to learn and use with consistently good results because at the last minute significant control inputs have to occur and equally significant attitude changes have to be made to get the wing down, align the nose with the centerline, and complete the landing. Everything happens at once.

Perhaps the best method on crosswind approaches is to compromise between the two methods. You can crab the airplane most of the way down the final approach, shifting to the wing-low configuration several moments before landing. This way, you make everyone comfortable for most of the approach, rather than having a protracted period of slipping, yet you eliminate all of the gyrations with the controls at the last instant. This is the way that I fly most crosswind approaches. Being "born and bred" in lighter airplanes, and having learned to fly in my youth in a classic tailwheel airplane that had no flaps, I learned to slip early on and still fly all of the way down final in a slip when the crosswind is strong. To me, slipping is fun, and I'll often use a slip to modulate my descent angle on final, even if I'm landing into a direct headwind or on a day when the wind is calm.

The *flare,* or *roundout* as it is sometimes called, still has to be made before you touch down. Only naval aviators land without flaring because that's the way carrier landings are done. Their airplanes are designed and built with landing gear that are strong as a bridge girder, and they can take the pounding. Your airplane isn't and can't. When we flare for a crosswind landing, we still have to carry the crosswind correction (now wing-low regardless of how you flew the final approach; FIG. 7-3). As you flare, two things happen. First, your airspeed decreases, so the control surfaces lose some effectiveness, and you may have to increase the control pressures on the ailerons and rudder to keep everything straight and aligned with the runway. Second, the velocity of the wind often lessens very near to the ground, so maybe some of the correction for the wind that you experienced while on final needs to be removed.

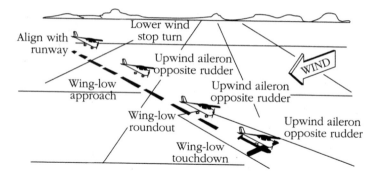

**7-3**  *The wing-low method of crosswind approach and landing.*

Wind speeds usually are less within the last 50 to 100 feet of the approach due to *surface friction,* which is the friction that the moving air encounters as it blows across the actual surface of the earth. Friction tends to slow the movement of the air across the ground, and hence the absolute wind speed drops.

During the flare for a crosswind landing, do not level the wings; keep the upwind wing down all of the way throughout the flare and contact with the runway. You'll intentionally touch down on one main landing gear, which is the upwind wheel, and the nose wheel should still be off of the ground when the main gear touches down. Don't try to lower the other main, but use the ailerons to keep the upwind wing down, and the other main wheel up, off of the ground. As your forward momentum decreases, and as the wings lose their last vestige of lift, the downwind main wheel will settle to the runway even though you've been trying to keep it up with aileron control and may well have the ailerons fully deflected.

When we make a landing in an appreciable crosswind, we vary one other aspect of normal landings. If the wind is very strong, you don't need to worry about holding the airplane off of the runway until it stalls. Allow it to contact the ground just a few knots above stall, but still in a good, flared attitude (FIG. 7-4). When the wings stall, we cannot control the airplane with ailerons as well as we can while the wing is still flying. During crosswind landings, we want to preserve control authority so that we can keep the upwind wing down and the nose aligned with the centerline with the rudder. But, don't forget to still use a pronounced flare; the last thing that you ever want to have happen is for the airplane to contact the runway, during any conceivable landing, on the nose wheel first.

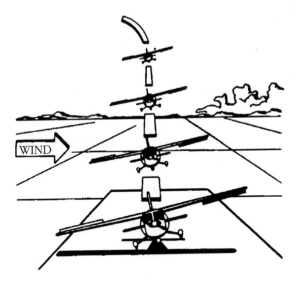

**7-4** *Crosswind flare and touchdown.*

Now comes another important distinction. Recall the comment earlier that the Cessna's nose wheel steering is deactivated in flight, when the nose strut is fully extended as weight is removed form it? When the nose strut fully extends as the airplane takes off, the rudder pedal steering to the nose wheel is mechanically disconnected. When the nose wheel of the Cessna does touch down upon landing, it is streamlined straight ahead, in line with the longitudinal axis of the airplane. Our Cessna 150 will roll straight ahead, even if you're a little behind the eight ball in straightening the rudder pedals to neutral. Obviously, if you do touch down with the opposite rudder input still applied, as the nose strut depresses and the weight of the nose comes to bear on it, and if you continue to hold that rudder pressure, it will start to steer, and off you go into the weeds again.

In most Pipers, and some other makes, nose wheel steering is never deactivated. The nose wheel turns in flight every time that a rudder pedal is depressed. You need to know which system your airplane has because if yours doesn't disconnect the ground steering as soon as the nose wheel lifts off, it is imperative that you kick the rudder pedals to neutral the split second before the nose gear touches. If you don't, it'll be cocked over to one side, and the sideloads that you put upon it will probably bend or break the nose wheel structure.

During the landing roll out, you need to keep the aileron correction applied, increasing the amount of control wheel pressure and aileron deflection as you slow down because the control surfaces become less effective as the speed drops. By the time your roll out is finished, you should have the control wheel fully deflected toward the wind, if you haven't done so already.

As you slow down during the roll out, the effects of the crosswind become more pronounced. All airplanes have more vertical surface area behind the main gear than in front of it. The sides of the fuselage, vertical stabilizer, and rudder contain a lot of square footage. When the crosswind blows against them on the ground, it pushes against them and tries to turn the airplane into the wind. This effect is called *weathervaning* and is familiar to any boater who has tried to dock a boat in a crosswind. You have to keep the upwind wing "down" by turning the control wheel toward the direction from which the wind is coming and use the rudder pedals to steer as you roll out and taxi. Weathervaning is an even more pronounced problem for tailwheel airplanes because their main gear is farther forward along the fuselage than in a tricycle gear arrangement, thereby exposing more of the fuselage to the turning effect of the crosswind because more of the fuselage is aft of the main landing gear.

Also remember FIG. 6-6, the taxiing diagram. Wind is always affecting an airplane that is still in contact with the ground, and you have to compensate for its effects.

# Landing in Turbulent Air

When the air is rough or it's windy, it's best to use power-on approaches and leave power-off glides to calmer days. When the airplane is being bounced around by rough air, which usually accompanies stronger winds, we will also want to fly the final approach with some extra airspeed. We'll need the extra speed to keep the effectiveness of the flight controls up where we can compensate for the rocking and rolling induced by the rough air. Remember that control surfaces lose effectiveness as airspeed decreases, and their effectiveness, called *control authority,* gets better at higher airspeeds.

If the wind is gusting, which it usually is when it's rough, we need to determine how much to increase the airspeed on the final approach. We do this by finding out what the *gust factor* is. The gust factor is the strength of the wind, during gusts, over what the steady-state wind is. For instance, if the control tower reports that the wind is 15 knots, gusting to 25, the gust factor is 10. Then figure on adding one-half of the gust factor to the normal approach speed. In this case, we'll add 5 knots. If the POH for your airplane recommends anything different, by all means follow the dictates of the POH, as you should do in all circumstances.

Because you are carrying extra airspeed on the final approach, you could make very minor attitude adjustments with the control wheel, varying pitch. But don't get carried away; make sure that you don't pitch the nose up enough to bleed off your extra speed. Such trade-offs are limited, and a coordinated combination of pitch and power corrections is preferred.

Partial flap deployment may be helpful, but full flap extension would be detrimental because of the large amount of drag created by full flaps. In rough air, you want to be able to add power if needed, to either arrest a sink rate that develops or to recover lost airspeed. If you have the flaps hanging all of the way out, you compromise your ability to do that quickly. When you are using partial flaps during final approach, the nose attitude will be higher and flatter than it would be with full flaps, especially if you're carrying very much power during the approach. Therefore, the flare will not be as pronounced as usual because the nose is already higher, and less pitch change has to occur to get into the landing attitude. Just as we did in the crosswind landing, let the airplane land just a few knots above stalling speed to preserve control authority. Just don't let the nose wheel touch first. Touching down on the nose wheel will probably result in a condition euphemistically called *wheelbarrowing,* which is what happens when the airplane is rolling on its nose wheel alone. This predicament will require some artful control handling, together with a larger measure of luck, to extricate yourself without seriously bending the airplane.

In moderate to severe turbulence, landings should be made from power-on approaches with the airplane as nearly level as possible with the nose up at touchdown and avoiding all possibility of wheelbarrowing. When the wind is howling, and the air is like a washboard, you need good, positive control authority all of the way to touchdown. The throttle is not fully retarded until the airplane is firmly planted on the runway and rolling on all three wheels. This extra power is used to provide an extra margin of control; if things start looking haywire, or if the airplane starts bouncing or feeling like it's going to wheelbarrow, the only out is to immediately apply full takeoff power and get the airplane airborne again. Then you can go around for another try.

As a student, you won't be flying solo in this kind of weather. Unfortunately, some pilots encounter real turbulence and wind only after they've left the instructor's nest and are on their own. Sometime late in your training, your instructor should take you out on a rough, windy day so you can see what it's like before you experience these conditions by yourself for the first time. If you don't get a chance to fly in winds or rough air before you get your license, grab an instructor and fly afterward when the opportunity presents itself. Once you get your license, you aren't finished taking instruction when needed, or prudent, to enhance your flying skills.

# Landing on Soft Fields

Originally all airports were sod fields. Today, few actually are, but you need to know how to operate from them because you'll deprive yourself of some of the utility of a personal airplane if you always shy away from grass fields. If the surface is firm and smooth, there is no practical difference between using a sod or a paved runway, except that even neatly mowed grass is not as friction free as is pavement, so your takeoff runs will be a little longer, and your landing rolls will be shorter. If the grass hasn't been mowed lately, these effects can become marked, so watch out when trying a take off from a sod runway where the grass is long and the runway length is short.

The most common difference between grass and pavement occurs when the field is soggy or soft. In the spring, a grass field is often soft before the winter moisture has thoroughly dried out from the ground and from the spring rains. During the winter, in many parts of the country we see rain rather than snow, which can keep a grass runway soft for months on end. Many of the same effects on airplanes result from a snow-covered runway, regardless of whether the surface underneath of the snow is pavement or sod.

When you land on a soft field, you have to judge, before the landing is attempted, just how soft the field is. Airplanes with tricycle landing gear, certainly the norm today, can easily get stuck. Nose tires are often smaller than main gear tires, and they support a lot of weight, with the engine and propeller right above the nose gear. Small nose tires can act like a knife, slicing down through the soft surface deeply enough that the airplane is quickly rendered immobile. Remember that the nose gear structure is the weakest of the three, and if it digs into the surface, it'll probably bend or break if you keep trying to blast the power in an attempt to keep the airplane moving. One of the keys to operating in soft conditions is to keep moving and not let the airplane stop before you want it to. If you keep moving, while holding the control wheel all of the way back, you can generally, but not always, lighten the nose gear's load enough to prevent it from digging into the mud or snow. You'll need a lot more power to taxi because the soft surface is hindering the progress of the main gear too. This extra propeller blast acts on the elevators, and if you've got the wheel all of the way back, the tail will tend to ride lower, keeping the nose wheel light.

If the nose wheel does start sinking into the soft surface, be careful. The last thing that you want to have happen is to dig the propeller into the ground. Any propeller strike, no matter how slight, requires an immediate shutdown of the engine and a thorough inspection by a qualified maintenance technician before it is started again. If the propeller strike results in stoppage of the engine from the propeller strike itself, most engine manufacturers require that the engine be disassembled and inspected for internal damage. For all of these reasons, tail-wheel airplanes operate much better from soft fields.

If all of your landings are full-stall landings, as they should be unless the wind conditions dictate otherwise, there isn't much difference between the actual landing on a soft field and a normal landing. When performing a soft field landing, the secret is to keep the wings supporting the airplane's weight as long as possible and to touch down at the slowest possible speed. The approach to a soft field is the same as for a hard one, except that after the flare is begun, you don't want to let the airplane touch early. Keep the flare going, and hold the main gear off of the ground for as long as you can. It's absolutely imperative that the nose gear be off of the runway when the main gear touches down.

Be ready to need power to keep the airplane moving. If the field is truly soft, you won't have much roll after landing, and you can get bogged down very quickly. Keep the wheel all of the way back after touchdown, which you should be doing anyhow, and stay off of the brakes. Be prepared to push the throttle in so you don't get stuck. If you do get stuck in the mud or snow, accept it and don't blast the power to try to get moving again. If you're stuck, you probably haven't damaged anything yet; if you try to get unstuck by using engine power, you probably will. Shut the airplane down, get out, walk to the FBO, and get a tow bar and tug to move the airplane. Then, the only damaged part will be your pride.

## Landing on Short Fields

On occasion, you'll be faced with the need to land on runways that aren't much longer than the minimum distance required to stop your airplane. Short-field landings are achieved by making a precise approach, where the final is usually flown at 1.3 times the airplane's power-off stalling speed, in landing configuration. In our Cessna 150, landing configuration means having the flaps fully extended. Our landing gear is firmly welded in place, so we don't worry about having it retracted or extended. In airplanes with retractable gear, landing configuration implies that the gear will be down. On your flight test, you will be asked to demonstrate a short-field landing, assuming that there is an obstacle, 50 feet high, right at the approach end of the runway. In real-world flying, most short fields have fairly clear approaches; otherwise, flying into and out of them might be impossible for many airplanes during many months of the year (remember density altitude). But you do need to know how to clear an obstacle and then get the airplane down and stopped in the minimum distance.

The techniques used to accomplish a short-field landing are quite a bit different from those used to make a normal arrival. Remember what we said earlier about a good landing requiring a good approach? It could not be any truer than when making a short-field landing. A stable, slow approach is imperative; you want to concentrate on getting the airplane down as soon as possible and then stopped before running out of runway. With this concern, you can't be still trying to stabilize the approach only moments from touchdown. If the approach isn't as perfect as you can make it, go around early and set up for another try.

Flying down the final leg, adjust the angle of descent to clear the obstacle without any excess altitude, yet be safe. You don't want to be 100 feet over the obstacle when you pass it, but you don't want to scrape the tires on it either. As you clear the obstacle, smoothly reduce the power to idle, if you've carried any power on final. Don't chop it all at once because at this slow approach speed, a high sink rate may result from a sudden reduction of power, and you might not have enough airspeed to arrest that sink rate during the flare.

When you flare, be ready for the airplane to land sooner than it does with a faster approach speed. Because you've got less airspeed to bleed off in the flare, it happens quickly. Let the airplane touch on the main gear, as always. Achieving minimum landing roll requires heavy braking. On an ordinary roll out after a normal landing, you let the aerodynamic drag of the airplane do the slowing and use brakes sparingly, if at all. In tricycle-gear airplanes like our 150, aerodynamic drag really declines once we're rolling at a speed below about 60 to 70 percent of the touchdown speed, so it won't help much when you've got to get stopped *now*.

We want to get the airplane on the ground as soon as possible. Land with the nose wheel off of the ground but then let it settle sooner than you normally would because we can't safely apply the brakes until the nose wheel is down. The minute the nose wheel touches, get on the brakes and start retracting the flaps, which have been fully down. Raising the flaps robs you of some of the aerodynamic drag, but getting them up helps much more by getting rid of whatever lift is still left in the wings. This transfers the weight of the airplane to the landing gear sooner and dramatically increases the effectiveness of the brakes. While braking, make sure that you're holding the wheel all of the way back to transfer as much of the weight as possible to the main gear; there is no brake on the nose wheel.

Applying heavy braking while the wings are still supporting an appreciable amount of the airplane's weight can result in your locking the brakes and skidding the tires. Skidding actually increases the stopping distance and also compromises your ability to steer, causing a loss of directional control. That's why antilock brakes are becoming so popular on cars, but they were first invented for large airplanes, as were disc brakes.

Many general aviation accidents happen during the landing roll because pilots get complacent and lose directional control. The same thing is even more likely to occur during heavy braking because airplanes are not designed to be ground vehicles; they are flying machines. The ground-handling characteristics of all airplanes are terrible compared to the driving stability of a car. The landing gear is a weak structure, the brakes aren't nearly as effective as modern auto brakes, and the tricycle arrangement is much less stable than the four wheels, or more, of a ground vehicle. Always remember that you're flying an airplane until it's parked and the engine is shut down.

# Emergency Landings

Chances are very great that you will never be faced with the prospect of making an emergency landing away from an airport. Modern airplanes and their engines, properly maintained, are probably about the most reliable machines of their complexity ever developed. There are three general categories of emergency landings, two of which are precautionary and one of which has to be made immediately.

The one that requires an immediate landing is when the engine fails completely. Most total engine failures occur because the pilot has mismanaged the fuel supply. You might forget to change tanks (more than one airplane has landed in a farmer's field with an entire tank full of gas), might not have properly preflighted the airplane and therefore didn't discover water or some other contaminant in the fuel supply, or more inexcusably, just plain run it out of gas. Sudden engine failures due to actual mechanical failure are very rare if you take care of your airplane and perform the scheduled maintenance.

The two types of precautionary landings away from airports aren't the result of a sudden and total power loss. If some sort of mechanical failure occurs in the engine, as has happened to me, seldom does the engine quit without warning. In my case, a cylinder fractured, and the rpm dropped to around 2,000, but I was able to fly the airplane, albeit at a slower speed, for the few minutes that it took to get back from the practice area to our airport. If the airport hadn't been so close, I would have selected a good field and made a landing there.

The second type of precautionary emergency landing doesn't imply a current engine failure. This type of off-airport landing can occur because the pilot has the good sense to land while the engine is still running, but the fuel supply is critically low. Better to accept the inevitable and land in a nice field, under full control while you still have the services of the engine than to blindly fly on until fuel exhaustion occurs. Other reasons for precautionary landings can be approaching bad weather (many accidents also happen because VFR pilots bore on into IFR weather without the training or the airplane equipment to handle it), approaching darkness in an airplane not equipped for night flight, or becoming so totally lost, in inhospitable terrain, that you need to land when a decent place is found.

If you do a precautionary landing, you'll probably have some explaining to do to the FAA, the insurance company, and maybe to the airplane owner. I would much rather compose such letters or have such phone conversations from the comfort of my office chair rather than from a hospital bed if I were to blunder ahead and have a serious accident.

The National Transportation Safety Board (NTSB) investigates all fatal aviation accidents and many nonfatal ones as well. The NTSB has found that several factors operate to interfere with a pilot's ability to act promptly and properly when faced with an emergency. Many of the aviation safety organizations have come to similar conclusions, which are, in no particular order of causation:

- *Reluctance to accept an emergency situation as it develops.* A pilot who allows her mind to become paralyzed at the thought that the airplane will shortly be on the ground, regardless of what is done, is severely handicapped in the handling of the situation. An unconscious desire to delay this dreaded moment might lead to such errors as failure to maintain flying speed and unintentionally stalling the airplane, delay in the selection of a suitable landing area within gliding distance, and general indecision.

- *Desire to save the airplane.* In an off-airport landing, some damage to the aircraft is likely. The other truth is that if a lightplane comes to earth, under control, and with the wings level at touchdown, serious injury to the occupants is very unlikely, unless, of course, the airplane hits a building or something similar while still traveling fairly fast. The landing speeds of lightplanes are slow in the first place, and if they are landed in a field where even some braking can occur before they hit something, the impact speed will be very slow indeed. But metal is never as important as flesh and bones. The moral is: Don't worry about the airplane; protect yourself. There are even situations when sacrificing the airplane will protect those inside of it.

- *Undue concern about getting injured.* Fear is a vital part of a person's natural self-preservation instinct. But panic is one of our biggest enemies. No one can handle pressure if panic sets in. One of my airline captain friends said it best: "If emergency procedures are practiced to the point that they just become additional procedures, they cease to be emergencies." Don't panic and you'll come through about anything that an airplane can dish out to you.

When you are flying cross-country, don't get too complacent and develop some good habits. Watch along the way for suitable fields in which to land if the engine quits or starts to fail. It's a very good idea to always know that wind direction on the surface. It can easily be determined from smokestacks, trees, ripples on ponds of lakes, or a myriad of other sources. If the time comes that you do have to set up for a forced landing, you'll be way ahead of the game if you don't sacrifice precious time and altitude in the glide, trying to figure out the wind conditions before you can start to plan a landing approach.

The best emergency landing spot is an airport. Don't laugh; in most parts of the country an airport of some kind is seldom more than a few minutes flying time away from your present position. The keys here are good navigational skills, knowing where you are at all times, and reading your chart (map) often enough to know what's around you. Even if you don't fly into sod fields often, or maybe you never have, practice finding them. Go out and make a flight to locate small, sod fields that you've never seen before. This isn't very easy the first few times that you try it, but being able to find a farmer's private landing strip may be just the ticket someday to an uneventful landing when you need to get down.

Next to an airport, the best site for landing is a good, long, hard, smooth field without obstacles. Be alert for power lines; they can be invisible until it's too late to avoid them. Major transmission lines are marked on your chart, so know where they are as your flight progresses. Assume that any road has normal electrical and phone wires running along it, so if you have to cross a road on final approach to your landing site, plan to be at least 100 feet high as you cross it, to avoid the wires that are almost certainly there.

If you have any agricultural background and can pick out a field of wheat, oats, rye, or other grass crops, great. It's likely to be relatively smooth, and the crop won't hurt the airplane as

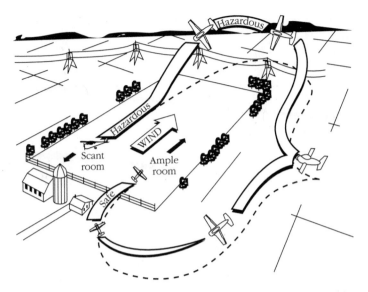

**7-5** *In an emergency, a downwind landing might be safer. Notice the obstacles in the path of a normal upwind landing.*

you land. But don't shy away from a plowed field if it is otherwise the best field in which to land. If possible, and if the wind conditions allow, land parallel to the furrows.

Landing downwind will result in your contacting the ground with more forward speed than if you can land upwind. But if the wind isn't strong, that might be acceptable if landing downwind results in an approach with few obstacles or with less maneuvering at low altitude (FIG. 7-5). It's much more likely that if anything goes wrong, and a serious accident ensues, it will be a result of the pilot forgetting to always fly the airplane first and keep it under control with adequate airspeed. Maneuvering at low altitude, with the stress of a forced landing already playing on the pilot's mind, has led to many a loss of control and low-altitude stall, when the result should have been an acceptable landing and a walk to the farmer's house to ask to use the phone to get a ride home.

Another of aviation's time-honored cliches is that the sky above you is of no use. This applies to practicing stalls and other maneuvers at a safely high altitude, but it also has something to say about cross-country flying. The more altitude you have if an emergency develops, the more flexibility and options you have in dealing with it. I am not suggesting that every flight has to be made at 10,000 feet above the ground, but why fly cross-country so low that your options are seriously compromised?

Excess altitude can always be shed, but if the engine quits, you can't climb. If you pick a good field while still quite high, and circle above it as you glide down, you can give it an even closer look for wires, ditches, livestock, and other hazards to a safe landing. If you're high enough, you might just be able to find a better site. But again, use common sense. Except in the most dire of circumstances, don't change fields at the last minute, You're now flying a glider, and a good landing must be preceded by a good approach. If you abandon your chosen field for another, don't make that choice when you're so low that you can't set up a good approach for the landing, or you won't make a decent landing.

If the engine ever stops, or begins to fail, immediately go through the engine-out checklist and drill, found in the emergency procedures section of your POH. First and foremost, establish the proper gliding speed for your airplane, and maintain it. Then, check the fuel selector, and if possible in your airplane, switch tanks. The rest of the checklist items will vary somewhat from one airplane to another, but look at FIG. 7-6 for an idea of what is contained in most engine-out drills. Although you can't totally commit the engine-out section of your airplane's POH to memory, you should be familiar with

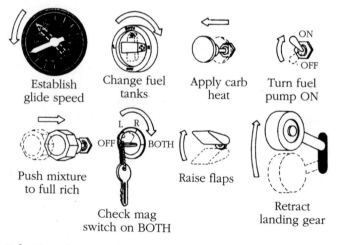

**7-6** *Typical engine-failure checklist.*

it. Know where the checklist is, be able to find it quickly, and use it.

The most critical time for a total engine failure is within the first 100 to 1,000 feet after takeoff. The natural urge is to turn back to the runway from which you just departed. As a student or newly minted private pilot, *don't* even think about it. When an engine fails in the departure climb, the first thing to do is to quickly get the nose down to the gliding attitude. The high-nose attitude that is normal in a full-power climb will result in a very fast depletion of airspeed if the engine quits producing power. You're climbing at an airspeed than is fairly close to the glide speed, and if you don't lower the nose right now when an engine failure happens, you suffer a very high risk of stalling. Get the nose down immediately.

Before you even think about turning back to the runway, take some time now, in the quiet time of reading this book, to consider several of the factors that dictate otherwise. First, you would need a steep turn and have to turn more than 180° just to get aimed at the runway. During that steep turn, you will have a very high rate of descent and lose lots of altitude, as is always the case in a steeply banked gliding turn. Next, remember that you have already flown some distance from the runway and that same ground must be traversed again if you're to make it back to the pavement. The chances are very slim that you would make it, after the altitude loss that is inevitable from the steeply banked gliding turn. Then, you wouldn't actually be lined up with the runway's centerline, and therefore some low-altitude maneuvering would be required to get lined up, and that's always potentially lethal. Even if you make it through the turn, still have enough altitude left to maneuver and get lined up with the runway, you're then facing a downwind landing. If you don't have sufficient altitude, and land short, your ground speed will be fast (because you're going downwind), and the risk of injury goes up exponentially with an increase in ground speed at touchdown.

So, the only real choice if faced with an engine failure right after takeoff is to put the nose down and land relatively straight ahead. Of course, some maneuvering to find the best landing site is OK. The acceptable amount of turning depends on how high you are when the total failure occurs. Maybe as much as a 90° turn would be allowable, maybe less if you're fairly low already.

Glider pilots get different training. A glider has no engine, so its pilot doesn't worry about engine failure. But there is an analogy.

In the United States, most gliders are launched by being towed aloft by a powered airplane. In Europe, many more glider launches occur by using a winch, with a long cable that pulls the glider up and launches it. Glider pilots are trained to deal with a break in the tow rope or an engine failure of the tow plane. Gliders perform so much better than airplanes do when an airplane is gliding that a glider pilot can turn back to the runway if a tow rope breaks on takeoff. Conventionally in the United States, glider pilots are taught how to turn back at or above 200 feet above the ground if the tow rope breaks or if the tow plane has a problem.

As an airplane pilot, you can't do that. As you gain experience and develop the judgment that it can bring, you can decide when a turn back may work. If you're at 2,000 feet after departing from a 2-mile-long runway at a major airport, you might have enough height and room to turn around and land. But if a total engine failure happens right after taking off from a typical general aviation airport, it's suicidal to attempt to go back to the runway. A wise pilot thinks about every flight and plans necessary alternative courses of action. When you are on the runway for takeoff, glance around and see what is off of the end of it. Know where the obstacles are that a minor amount of turning would avoid. At your home airport, where most of your takeoffs will occur, you should know the environs of every runway as well as you know the layout of your home. If the rare engine failure does occur, you know where to go almost without thinking about it. Just as is the case for dealing with most of life's anomalies, preparedness and a cool head are the answers.

Before we leave this subject for more enjoyable discussions, take a moment to again emphasize in your own mind that the most important thing to do in any emergency, including but not limited to engine failure, is to keep the airplane under positive control, and that means maintaining adequate airspeed. Pilots have landed in woods, forests, on hillsides, and even in the water and walked or swam away completely uninjured. If you land almost anywhere, under control, with the wings level and perform a stall landing before you let the airplane touch down, the most likely outcome will be a hike to the nearest house to use the phone or to the nearest road to bum a ride.

## Flight Plans

A *flight plan* is a form that you'll fill out prior to takeoff for any cross-country flight (FIG. 7-7). Most of the time, you'll tele-

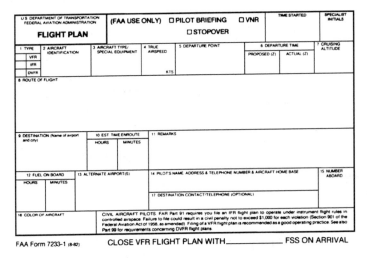

| U.S. DEPARTMENT OF TRANSPORTATION FEDERAL AVIATION ADMINISTRATION **FLIGHT PLAN** | | (FAA USE ONLY) | ☐ PILOT BRIEFING ☐ STOPOVER | ☐ VNR | TIME STARTED | SPECIALIST INITIALS |
|---|---|---|---|---|---|---|
| 1 TYPE VFR IFR DVFR | 2 AIRCRAFT IDENTIFICATION | 3 AIRCRAFT TYPE/ SPECIAL EQUIPMENT | 4 TRUE AIRSPEED KTS | 5 DEPARTURE POINT | 6 DEPARTURE TIME PROPOSED (Z) / ACTUAL (Z) | 7 CRUISING ALTITUDE |
| 8 ROUTE OF FLIGHT | | | | | | |
| 9 DESTINATION (Name of airport and city) | | 10 EST TIME ENROUTE HOURS / MINUTES | 11 REMARKS | | | |
| 12 FUEL ON BOARD HOURS / MINUTES | 13 ALTERNATE AIRPORT(S) | | 14 PILOT'S NAME, ADDRESS & TELEPHONE NUMBER & AIRCRAFT HOME BASE | | | 15 NUMBER ABOARD |
| | | | 17 DESTINATION CONTACT/TELEPHONE (OPTIONAL) | | | |
| 16 COLOR OF AIRCRAFT | | CIVIL AIRCRAFT PILOTS. FAR Part 91 requires you file an IFR flight plan to operate under instrument flight rules in controlled airspace. Failure to file could result in a civil penalty not to exceed $1,000 for each violation (Section 901 of the Federal Aviation Act of 1958, as amended). Filing of a VFR flight plan is recommended as a good operating practice. See also Part 99 for requirements concerning DVFR flight plans. | | | |

FAA Form 7233-1 (8-82)     CLOSE VFR FLIGHT PLAN WITH_____ FSS ON ARRIVAL

**7-7**   *The FAA flight plan form.*

phone the nearest FAA FSS and give the data to the briefer there. The form lists your aircraft identification, route of flight, destination, fuel on board, number of people on board, estimated time en route, and other pertinent information about the flight that you will undertake.

Flight plans aren't required by the FARs for VFR flights. While you're still a student pilot, your instructor will insist upon your filing one for every dual instructional and solo cross-country flight. After you gain your private pilot certificate, you should still use them. If you are taking a cross-country flight very far from your local area or at night, or if the trip will take you over sparsely populated areas, water, rough terrain, deserts, or swamps, a flight plan should always be filed.

If you are ever forced down and are on a flight plan, the Civil Air Patrol (CAP) search and rescue procedures begin automatically 30 minutes after your scheduled arrival time at your destination if the flight plan hasn't been closed by the pilot of the flight. So, when you arrive at your destination, be sure to always close your flight plan with the nearest FSS. If you encounter any delays en route, call the nearest FSS either by radio or by phone and modify your flight plan to show a new arrival time. I've served in the CAP since the 1960s, as a search and rescue pilot and squadron and group commander. It's no fun to be awakened at 3 a.m. to get your troops out to start a search mission, only to be looking for somebody whose airplane is safely in a hanger and who, himself, is snugly in bed at home, and who didn't close his flight plan.

# Emergency Locator Transmitters

The FARs require that airplanes used for cross-country flying be equipped with a device called an *emergency locator transmitter* (ELT). The ELT is a radio transmitter that is mounted in the airplane. It is battery operated and is automatically activated by the G forces that occur during a crash. When it is subjected to these forces, it emits a distinctive "whoop-whoop" audio signal tone on both of the international emergency frequencies, 121.5 and 243.0 MHz. ELTs are designed to continuously transmit for at least 48 hours over a wide spectrum of temperature ranges.

Both the United States and Russia have earth satellites in orbit that continually listen for ELT signals. Again, from my own CAP experience, I can tell you that very few ELT signals go unheard by at least one of these satellites. Both countries cooperate, immediately sharing the location of any signal that one of the satellites hears in the boundaries of the other nation, as well as anywhere else on earth. As a further safety measure, the FAA encourages pilots, while flying cross-country, to tune their communications radios to 121.5 MHz and listen for an ELT signal. You won't be able to monitor 243.0 MHz; that is the military emergency frequency, and your civilian radios don't tune for it.

If you hear an ELT, there won't be any doubt as to what it is. Mark on your chart the position of your airplane when you first heard it and where you where when the signal faded away. In the meantime, immediately contact the nearest FAA ATC facility, and let them know what you're hearing, your location, and route of flight. Knowing these details will enable the CAP search planes to better "box" a search area. CAP planes are equipped with a direction finder that enables them to home in on the ELT signal and fly to the aircraft in distress. Your alertness might save a life.

# Emergency Instrument Procedures

It should never happen to any pilot who has done proper flight planning, but it is possible that sometime you might find yourself smack in the middle of instrument weather conditions. Weather

**7-8** *Never allow "get-there-itis" to rule your judgment. About 40 percent of all lightplane accidents are weather related.*

forecasting is surely not an exact science, but human nature is the greatest cause of inadvertent IFR encounters. Let's see how a typical example of this misfortune might unfold (FIG. 7-8).

A private pilot has a critical sales presentation to make in a city 300 miles away from her home, and the meeting is scheduled for 2 p.m. At 7 a.m. that morning, our aviator calls the FSS for her weather briefing, starting the process of planning her flight. She learns that the weather is excellent VFR at both the departure and destination airports. However, there is a warm front lying between the two cities that contains a 50-mile-wide area of low clouds and freezing rain. But, the conditions are expected to improve as the day goes on, according to the weather mavens.

So, our pilot drives to the airport, gets some coffee, and kills a little time chatting with the folks at the FBO. At 9 a.m. she checks with the FSS again and learns that the area of poor weather has improved a little, but that it's still strictly IFR. So, back to the coffee machine she goes.

Now at 10 a.m. she's getting antsy. It's only 4 hours until the time that she's got to see the customer who will make her sales quota for the year. She checks weather again, and the FSS briefer is still dispensing doubt about whether this flight can be made VFR. After hanging up the phone and realizing that there now isn't enough time to catch an airline flight or drive, she makes her decision. The bad stuff is lifting, just like the forecast said it would, but not quite as quickly as forecast. It's got to be at least minimal VFR by the time she gets to the frontal area, and it's only 50 miles wide anyhow, so there won't be much of a problem. Sure, she's not instrument rated, but she has been flying for 2 years now and has almost 300 hours of flying time. Plus, what will this sophisticated, quota-busting customer think of doing business with someone who can't travel only 300 miles to make an appointment that has been on the calendar for over a month?

But, the quota never gets met or exceeded; our pilot never gets there. CAP search crews, who themselves waited until evening to start searching, so the weather could go by, find the wreckage just before dark. The hometown newspaper carries the story the next day, and a depressing story it is. Remember this scenario because without a doubt it'll happen more than a dozen times each year. Those who are ignorant of general aviation will reinforce their feelings that little airplanes are dangerous—just look what happened to their smart, ambitious, and career-climbing friend.

Acting upon the proven theory that people are human and will, on occasion, make dumb decisions in the face of their better judgment, the FAA has attempted to cut the accident rate of non-instrument-rated pilots "pushing the weather" by requiring that, as a part of the private pilot flight test, each applicant must demonstrate an ability to control the airplane by reference to flight instruments alone. Also, you must be able to show the examiner that you can fly well enough on instruments to save your life by turning around, climbing, or descending if necessary and flying back to the good weather that you left behind you.

This doesn't mean that you have to have an instrument rating or that such advanced skills are necessary, desirable, or even practical for everyone. But a few hours of dual instruction in instrument flying could keep you alive on the day that your judgment falters, and it is therefore required by the FARs before you take the private pilot practical exam, which we often call the flight test. This elementary training is a far cry from that needed to qualify for an instrument rating; it is intended only to provide you with the minimum skill needed to get you out of trouble if you stumble into IFR weather. Think of it as a lifeboat.

In most cases when a pilot is accidentally caught in instrument conditions, VFR weather is behind him, from where he just came. Therefore, by being able to keep the airplane under control, turn around, and fly on a constant heading for a few minutes, most hapless pilots can extricate themselves and return to VFR weather. It's not hard to do, but it's not as easy as it sounds.

When you lose visual contact with the ground, your senses of balance and direction go haywire. Nonfliers find this hard to believe, but it is absolutely true. Your sense of equilibrium is gone. Although the brain gets a part of its balance information from the inner ear, that data is incomplete and must be supplemented with visual cues. You will find yourself leaning to one side, straining against a bank that isn't there. If you're turning in a coordinated turn, it feels like you aren't turning at all.

The instruments know better and don't lie. But it takes a while for most of us to place our trust, and our lives, in the hands of little gyroscopes, needles, and gauges. There is one important rule about instrument flying: *Always believe the instruments*. If the turn needle says that you're turning, disregard whatever you feel is happening and *believe the turn needle*.

This is the central theme to be learned in controlling your airplane without visual reference to the ground. Your body and its senses will lie to you. Don't ever forget that unfortunate but infallible fact. Believe only the inhuman instruments.

Most non-instrument-rated pilots get into serious trouble within a minute of two after flying into clouds. A wing drops slightly, the airplane starts a gentle turn, and next, the nose drops a little to increase airspeed in order to make up for the loss of lift resulting form the bank. Then the bank continues to increase and the nose keeps slowly falling, trying to compensate for less lift.

Finally, the pilot notices—and probably hears—the increased airspeed from the falling of the nose. Doing what he thinks is right, he pulls back on the wheel, which begins a now fatal sequence of events. Pulling back on the wheel while the airplane is in a steep bank accomplishes only one thing—the banks steepens more. He will never realize that he is in a spiral and that he cannot pull the nose up until he first levels the wings.

Then, one of two things happens next. He either continues spiraling and pulling back on the wheel until he has overloaded the structure of the airplane with G forces and the airframe fails, or he just spirals, ever faster in airspeed and turn rate, until he hits the ground. Either way, the rest of us read about it in the accident statistics. To avoid this scenario and to save your neck, you have to realize the importance of the turn needle (turn coordinator) any time you stumble into a condition where you lose visual reference with the surface.

While on the subject of loss of visual reference, be aware that clouds aren't the only cause of that loss. At night, without moonlight, it can be very difficult to keep visual reference if the area over which you're flying is sparsely populated. With no city lights or extensive road systems to provide visual cues, you're an island in a sea of air, totally without visual reference points to keep your senses working properly.

Two other ordinary conditions can lead to a loss of visual reference. One is dense haze, such as the kind that besets the eastern part of the United States in the summer, and its cousin, smog. With the visibility at the 1-mile minimum for VFR flight in certain areas of airspace, or even at 3 miles as is required in other airspace, especially if flying into the sun, ground contact can easily be lost, even if there's not a cloud in the sky. If you have to fly in marginal visibility, keep your altitude as low as reasonable for the terrain and obstacles. The disabling effects of haze on visual reference increase with altitude.

The other situation is present when flying over water. Unless the visibility is very good and there is a distinct horizon, it's very easy to become disoriented and lose visual reference over large bodies of water, where you're at some considerable distance from the shoreline. This can happen to any pilot who flies along the coasts or the Great Lakes. Night flying over water should only be attempted by an instrument-rated pilot. It's virtually impossible to keep adequate visual references to control an airplane over water after dark, regardless of how good the weather is. The Caribbean nations don't allow VFR flights at night for this very reason.

If you keep the needle centered, you won't be turning, and without a turn, the *graveyard spiral* can't develop. Under these instrument conditions, you can pretty much ignore the ball in the tube, unless it gets ridiculously out of center. The best way to fly the needle under these circumstances is to use your feet to keep the needle centered. If you see the needle showing a left turn, kick in a little right rudder. Don't cross-control with the wheel and prevent the airplane from banking, just initiate the correction with your feet. You're not interested in precisely coordinated flight; you're interested in keeping the airplane upright and not turning and in keeping yourself alive in the process.

Your airplane will also almost certainly be equipped with an attitude indicator, commonly called an artificial horizon. Use it as a reference also. It can't tell you if the airplane is turning, but it does let you know if the wings are level or banked and what the nose attitude is. So, use the turn coordinator and attitude indicator together to keep out of a turn and to keep the wings and nose basically level. Now you've learned rule 2, which is *stay out of turns—keep the wings level.*

That takes care of directional control; now let's work on keeping the nose level. The attitude indicator is the primary instrument to use for this task. We use the attitude indicator as the primary reference because it has no lag between airplane attitude changes and its indications and is one of the easiest instruments in the panel to interpret. The secondary information about the nose attitude will come from the airspeed indicator. Unless you alter the power setting, which you shouldn't do in this emergency situation unless things get really out of whack, the airspeed will change as the nose attitude does.

Don't chase minor deviations in either the airspeed or the attitude indicator. Overcontrolling is something you definitely want to avoid, so relax and look for trends that need altering, and don't try to eliminate every little blurp in attitude deviation. Using the airspeed indicator to control the nose attitude is more difficult because it requires far more interpretation than does the attitude indicator. Also, there is some lag between a change in nose attitude and the resultant change in airspeed. It is very easy to overcontrol if you try to chase the airspeed indications. What we're looking for is a trend that needs correction.

If you notice, for instance, that the airspeed is lower than cruise speed, look for a moment to see if it's continuing to decrease or if it's stable. If the airspeed is continuing to go down, the nose attitude is probably quite high and needs to be lowered. The faster the trend is developing, the greater the deviation in the nose attitude from level. Likewise, if the airspeed is increasing, the nose is below level. If the buildup in speed is occurring rapidly, you're in a dive; if the speed is slowly increasing, the nose is only slightly below level.

The altimeter can also be used to cross-check the nose attitude. Remember the interchangeability of altitude and airspeed? When the nose goes up or down, some altitude change will also occur, assuming a constant power setting. This information is not as reliable an indicator of nose attitude as is that gleaned from the attitude indicator and airspeed because eventually the effects of a *zoom climb* or *dive* will play themselves out. But the altimeter is useful as a cross-check.

As long as the attitude indicator shows the little airplane symbol as being close to level, and if the airspeed is constant, the airplane's nose is level.

Whenever you're flying, you know to use light, relaxed control pressures on the wheel and rudder pedals. This is even more important in instrument flying. Overcontrolling will get you into trouble a lot faster than will too little pressure, as long as you're doing something to correct for attitude deviations.

# Back to Better Weather

Now that you've stabilized the airplane and have it under positive control, the next goal is to get turned around and fly out of the bad weather, toward the good conditions that are probably close behind. You only need to turn about 180° to solve your predicament. We're going to turn a little bit differently than we do under VFR conditions because the goal here is to keep the airplane under control and not lose it; we're not concerned about the best coordination of rudder and aileron pressures.

We need to talk a little more about the turn indicator. In some airplanes, the indicator is made so that it is very easy to establish a controllable rate of turn. This indicator has two little marks at the top, one mark on either side of the center. These marks are commonly referred to as the *doghouses,* after their distinctive shape. When the turn needle is deflected so that the top of the needle lies directly under a doghouse, the airplane is turning in the direction of the needle deflection at a rate of turn of 3° per second, known as a *standard rate turn.* There is also a type of turn indicator that does not have the doghouses. If your airplane is equipped with this type, a standard rate turn of 3° per second is achieved by deflecting the turn needle just outside of the center mark, without covering any of it. This is called a *one needle width turn.* These indicators are not typically installed in modern airplanes or in an airplane that has an updated instrument panel.

The more common instrument, which you're far more likely to encounter, is the turn coordinator with a little airplane symbol in place of the outdated vertical turn needle. The turn coordinator is also calibrated to allow a pilot to make a standard

**7-9** *Read the turn coordinator as you would the needle in the older style turn-and-slip indicator. Remember that the turn coordinator does not indicate pitch.*

rate turn. Look at FIG. 7-9, which shows a turn coordinator instead of a turn needle. See the little marks with L and R directly below them? When the little airplane symbol is deflected so that the wings of the symbol line up with these marks, you're in a standard rate turn.

The third rule is *a standard rate turn continued for 1 minute will result in a 180° change of direction.*

Now, before starting the turn around to get out of the IFR weather, you need to know what direction to fly to accomplish that. You need to know the *reciprocal heading* of the heading that you were flying when the conditions deteriorated. The best rule of thumb to quickly figure reciprocals is to add or subtract 200 from the present heading and then do the reverse with the number 20. Here's how it works: If you're flying along on a heading of 120° (southeast), add 200 in your head, which gives you 320 and then quickly subtract 20, which results in the reciprocal of 120, which is 300°. Some folks can directly add or subtract 180 with mental math, but most of us can't, especially when under stress.

If your original heading is 290°, you can't accomplish anything by adding 200, because there are only 360° in a circle. So, subtract 200, resulting in 90, then add 20, resulting in 110°, which is the reciprocal of 290°. Practice these mental gymnastics a few times while flying in normal conditions and it'll become very easy.

Look again at FIG. 7-9. In this picture, you'll see a DG immediately to the right of the turn coordinator. This is the newer type of DG, which you'll probably see in your trainer. If you have this newer type, notice how it shows the full 360° circle of headings. With this type of DG, it's possible to read a reciprocal right from the face of the instrument. If your airplane has the older, drum-style DG, you have to resort to the mental math to determine your reciprocal.

To begin the turn, only use the rudder. You are flying the turn coordinator, and it is crucial that you establish and maintain the standard rate, 3° per second turn. Do it with your feet because you can be much more precise that way. Allow the airplane to bank during the turn, and keep it under control with the ailerons. Don't fight the airplane's tendency to bank, but don't let the bank get steep, say beyond about 30° at the most. You are turning in this unconventional way, which results in somewhat uncoordinated flight, simply because it's easier to keep things upright and keep the turn at standard rate.

As you start the turn, notice the time. Almost every airplane has a clock in the instrument panel, but many of them don't last very long in the high-vibration environment of an airplane instrument panel. I usually fly with a wrist watch that has a sweep second hand and sometimes I wear my digital athletic watch. Either will do, so long as you can time 1 minute on something. Continue the standard rate turn for 1 minute; then, using smart pressure on the opposite rudder pedal, roll out of the turn. Don't overdo the roll out pressure—you're not stomping grapes into wine. You want to roll out quickly but without overcontrolling. Look at the DG and check your heading, and cross-check it against what the magnetic compass is saying. If you need some minor corrections to get onto that reciprocal heading, do them with the rudder pedals.

Don't get lazy and depend on the DG—time the turn. DGs can fail too, and you shouldn't depend on it for everything you need to know. During the turn, it's OK to monitor the progress by glancing at the DG, but don't get transfixed on it and forget to maintain control of the nose attitude. Remember that during a turn, you're vulnerable to losing control much more so than during straight and level flight.

Then, when you're established on the reciprocal heading, you only have two things to do: First, prevent turning by keeping the turn coordinator centered; second, keep the nose level by using the attitude indicator and the airspeed indicator. Repeat these two things over and over again in your mind to maintain the reciprocal heading until you are in VFR conditions again. Time will seem to creep by, so don't get excited if it seems to take forever to fly out of the weather. As long as you're going toward the good weather that you were in before this entire problem occurred, you will get there eventually.

The chief value of this method lies in its simplicity. Don't change the trim because doing so will cause the non-instrument-rated pilot far more trouble than benefit. Anything that diverts your attention from the turn coordinator or needle, attitude indicator, and airspeed indicator must be regarded as extraneous and ignored until you are out of the soup. Nor should it be necessary to adjust the throttle setting more than once, unless you lose control and end up either stalling or in a high-speed spiral.

As soon as you find yourself in instrument conditions, it may be helpful to set the power about 10 percent below normal cruise, especially in an airplane that is faster than our Cessna 150. This slowdown will ease the loadings on the wings if there is turbulence. Also, less power will help slow any airspeed increases that result from getting the nose low and will help prevent the graveyard spiral. It also helps ease any tendency you might otherwise have to overcontrol the nose attitude.

One way to make this power change is to pull out the carb heat, without touching the throttle; then you don't have to monitor the tachometer while reducing throttle, which would divert your attention from the flight instruments. If the outside air temperature is below approximately 75°, there is a good possibility of carburetor ice forming when flying in visible moisture or in clouds. Applying carb heat as soon as you get into those conditions can act to remove that possibility from the list of your potential problems.

As long as you keep the airplane under positive control, chances are extremely good that this adventure will be something that you'll talk about, and help others learn from, for years to come. Just remember that your goal is control, not finesse. For a non-instrument-rated pilot to try to be extremely precise in the clouds will almost undoubtedly lead to serious overcontrolling and eventual loss of control. Keep your wits about you, don't let panic set in, and you'll do fine.

But because you're a careful person to start with, you're learning to fly from a competent instructor, and you have the desire to learn as much as you can, which is evidenced by your reading material like this book, you won't blunder into IFR weather in the first place, will you?

# 8

# Weather

Airplanes fly in a sea of air that supports them. The condition of the atmosphere at the low altitudes where we fly is constantly changing, and we use the word *weather* when we talk about the state in which we find the lower levels of the earth's blanket of gases. Weather can be the biggest benefactor in making for an extremely pleasant flight, and it can also be a demon at times, tossing an airplane about, restricting a pilot's visibility outside of the cockpit to nil, and occasionally making it nigh impossible for us to fly. Next to knowing how to physically manipulate the controls of an airplane, every pilot needs a working knowledge of the elementary principles of meteorology and its terms and jargon.

Airplanes became reliable machines, from a mechanical point of view, long before World War II. Since then, pilots have been able to depend, with ever-increasing confidence, on the aircraft itself to maintain flight. But humans will never control the weather. It is the one variable with which we must deal as impotent bystanders. Although we can equip larger airplanes with radar sets to see precipitation associated with thunderstorms, deicing gear to enable them to fly in conditions that generate inflight icing, and similar modern electronic aids, we still can't change the basic fact that the weather will be what it will be.

Weather is the cause of most accidents in lightplanes. To put that statement more correctly, the cause of these accidents is pilots' inability to handle certain types of weather conditions, their ignorance of them, or both. Machines don't make mistakes, people do. Rarely, a maintenance technician might err, or a design engineer might let something get past all of the design processes and reviews. The greatest number of mistakes that influence aviation safety are made by pilots. You need to know which weather conditions present hazards to flight in small airplanes, how to discern where those conditions are, how to avoid them, and what to do if you inadvertently encounter them.

To enable us to know what the weather is around the country, and beyond its borders in many instances, the FAA maintains a network of regional automated FSSs to serve the weather and flight planning needs of pilots. These stations are relatively new, having replaced a nationwide system of smaller FSSs that were far more numerous and in the past linked to each other by teletype. The newer stations still have human personnel working at them 24 hours a day, and you may personally go to the FSS for a weather briefing if you live near one. This is done less now because the number of FSSs has been drastically reduced, but the newer stations are far larger and more capable in their primary role of disseminating weather information.

A few years ago, in-person weather briefings were quite common, and there was an unmatched comfort in being able to see all of the weather maps yourself, instead of just hearing a description of the conditions affecting your planned flight from a briefer, over the telephone. But the price of progress and keeping these government services free to pilots has been closing most of the smaller FSSs and consolidating them into regional operations. The FAA provides a toll-free telephone number for pilots' use. If you dial 1-800-WX-BRIEF, you will automatically be connected to the FSS that serves the geographical area from which you are placing the call.

If you are a licensed pilot and have a personal computer with a modem, you can access the FAA's weather briefing data by use of the *direct user access terminal* (DUAT) system. This service has been free to pilots since its inception, by use of another 800 telephone number to call it up from your computer. As this edition is being written, the FAA is once again going through some belt-tightening, and who knows what the future of DUAT will be. It may change to a toll number or have some other mechanism for charging the user for the service.

You can access most of the data over the Internet if you know how to use the World Wide Web (WWW). Just connect to the WWW, and use a search engine to look for "aviation weather." You'll be greeted with more sites than you can imagine. Do some surfing, and bookmark the sites that you find the most easily usable.

Several private sector companies offer weather briefing services by computer, too, naturally for a fee. Some pilots prefer the commercial services, claiming that the output is more logically organized and easier to interpret than the government products. As you advance in your aviation career, try them all, and decide what's best for your needs.

Home television can also be a source of weather data. Most cable systems carry The Weather Channel, which gives great real-time views of weather radar returns throughout the entire country. But this source of data provides only general weather pictures, outlooks, and trends. The information is not presented with an orientation to aviation needs. Although you should always get as much weather wisdom as possible from a multitude of sources, The Weather Channel and similar television products are never a substitute for an FSS or DUAT briefing.

FSSs can be contacted while you are in flight, using standard radio frequencies. If you need to update your briefing while airborne, want to report weather conditions that are different from what was forecast, or need any other FSS service, don't hesitate to use your radio and give them a call. Just be courteous, and don't use the radio, instead of the phone, for an initial, detailed briefing. Although the briefer at the FSS will accommodate you if you do that, it ties up the frequency for an extended period of time, when no one else can call. The same goes for filing your flight plan. If you depart from a remote airport where there is no pay phone, you can file over the radio. Otherwise, drop a coin in a pay phone and call the 800 number. A VFR flight plan must be opened and then closed by the pilot, and using the radio to call an FSS to perform that short task is a good example of the proper use of radio communications with FSSs.

# Preflight Weather Briefings

The FARs require that you familiarize yourself with the weather forecasts and conditions along your route of flight and that it be done before the flight begins. If you are going out for a local flight, around the area of the airport, a call to the FSS asking for the current conditions might suffice, satisfying both the legal requirement and the common sense one. But if you're planning to leave the local area, you need to obtain a preflight briefing, either from an FSS or by using DUAT. Let's assume that we are planning a cross-country trip, away from the local airport.

Three preflight weather briefings are available through the FSS: standard, abbreviated, and outlook. Tell the specialist at the FSS which briefing you want, including some background information that is necessary for the specialist to conduct the briefing for your needs: aircraft type, route of flight, proposed departure time, and aircraft identification number or the pilot's name. While you are still a student pilot, tell the briefer so; you'll find these people are very helpful, and most will go more slowly and anticipate your level of understanding if they know in advance that you are a student. All FSS contacts are recorded for everyone's protection in case a dispute arises later about whether the pilot even received a briefing; this information could be used for accident investigation purposes and in any civil lawsuits that may arise as a result of an accident. The contents of the briefing are also recorded for the same reasons.

During your briefing, you'll find it much more productive if you don't interrupt the briefer with questions. Save them until the end, and then ask as many as you need to fully understand the briefing. Even though there is an established protocol for each of the types of briefings, some briefers are more complete than are others. Don't hesitate to ask and, if necessary, insist upon getting the information that you need.

## Standard briefing

You should request a standard briefing for any planned flight when you have not received any previous briefing for this trip at this time. The specialist will automatically go through a list and provide the following information applicable to your proposed flight:

- *Adverse conditions.* Significant meteorological and aeronautical information that might cause you to alter your proposed flight plan. These items include hazardous weather, runway or airport closures, navigational aid outages, and the like.

- *VFR flight not recommended.* When a VFR flight is proposed (that is one of the things that you should tell the briefer as a part of the opening comments that you make about the background information) and sky conditions or visibilities are present or forecast at the surface or aloft that, in the specialist's judgment, would make the successful outcome of the flight doubtful under

VFR, the specialist will describe the conditions, the affected locations, and use the phrase, "VFR flight is not recommended." This caution is advisory in nature because the pilot is the final authority for all aspects of the flight, including whether it should be commenced or continued.

- *Synopsis.* This is a brief statement that describes, in general terms, the type, location, and movement of weather systems or air masses that might affect your route of flight.

- *Current conditions.* In this section of the briefing, the briefer will give you the exact reports of the weather, current as of the most recent hourly report, at the airports of departure and arrival. In addition, you'll be told about the current weather at selected locations along your planned route.

- *En route forecast.* You'll be told what the aviation weather forecast is at your destination airport. The specialist might also give you the forecast at your departure airport if it looks like departure airport weather might be a factor, as well as the forecasts at selected airports along your route.

- *Destination forecast.* If not given as a part of the en route forecast, you'll be given the forecast at the destination airport.

- *Winds aloft.* Next, the briefer will tell you the forecast winds aloft. These are not current data, but forecasts that tell you what to expect in terms of wind directions and velocities aloft. They are given in 3,000-foot increments and also include the predicted temperatures at the various altitudes.

- *Notices to airmen* (*NOTAMs*). These are reports of such things as runway closures, inoperative navigational aids, construction cranes operating near an airport, and similar information that you need to know, either along your route or at the airports of departure or destination.

- *ATC delays.* These are reports of IFR flight delays in the air traffic control system and are usually not important to the VFR pilot, unless you are heading into a major airline airport.

- *Other information.* Normally the "other information" section of the standard briefing is optional on the part of the briefer and is used upon the pilot's request. Most briefers will tell you other important information without your requesting it, but don't assume that they will. Other information includes such items as activity along military training routes and in military operations areas (MOAs), approximate density altitudes at various airports, procedures for dealing with the U.S. Customs Service, and the like.

## Abbreviated briefing

You should request an abbreviated briefing only when you have already had a previous standard briefing for this flight at the proposed time. The abbreviated briefing is used to supplement the data that you already have. When you talk to the briefer, be sure to tell her what information you do have and when you received it. If your data is obsolete, your abbreviated briefing may be converted to a standard one.

## Outlook briefing

An outlook briefing is used when your proposed departure time is more than 6 hours from the time that you call the FSS. The outlook briefing is for planning purposes only, such as when you what to know whether a VFR flight is very likely possible. A standard briefing should and must be obtained before takeoff. The closer in time that you can get your standard briefing before your proposed departure time, the more reliable the information will be.

## In-flight briefing

In-flight briefings should only be used when you can't get a briefing in person or over the telephone. Using the radio for an in-flight briefing ties up that radio frequency for an extended period of time and is discourteous to other pilots. Someone else may need the channel for a quick but important inquiry, and someone else's "hogging" the frequency could prevent the dissemination of important information to another pilot. But, if you have to, use the radio, because you don't want to ever conduct a cross-country flight with no briefing at all.

# En Route Flight Advisory Service

This service, provided by the FAA through selected FSSs, is known as *flight watch*. It is designed to give pilots who are en route timely and meaningful updated weather advisories pertinent to the flight, route, altitude, and type of aircraft being flown.

Flight watch is not intended to be used for obtaining complete weather briefings or for the opening or closing of flight plans. It mainly serves as a clearinghouse for weather conditions that have been reported by other pilots. As your trip progress, and you encounter any significant weather, especially conditions either much better or worse than forecast, get on the radio and contact flight watch at the nearest FSS. Let them know what the conditions are that prompted your call. Pilot reports such as these are perhaps the most meaningful weather information that we can get. Forecasts are nice, current reported surface conditions are better, and knowing what another pilot actually encountered is best.

These flight watch services are provided by specially trained personnel at selected FSSs throughout the country. To contact one, use the radio frequency 122.0 MHz. Begin your call by saying the name of the flight watch facility you're calling, followed by your aircraft type and identification, and then the name of the very-high-frequency omnidirectional radio (VOR) nearest to your position. For example, "Cleveland Flight watch, Comanche 81 Lima Lima (the call sign for 81LL in phonetics), over Mansfield VOR."

# In-Flight Weather Advisories

The National Weather Service issues three types of in-flight weather advisories that are designated as *convective SIGMETs, SIGMETs,* and *AIRMETs*.

The term *SIGMET* is derived from the words *significant meteorological*. When you hear an ATC facility or an FSS say that there is a SIGMET issued, pay close attention. You're about to hear something that has significance to all aircraft, whether to you in a Cessna 150 or the captain of an airliner. A convective SIGMET is issued to warn all pilots of dangerous conditions caused by convection, such as tornados, lines of thunderstorms, thunderstorms embedded in other clouds, and areas with 40 percent or more thunderstorm coverage. All of this is bad stuff, and you don't want to stumble into any of it.

A SIGMET is issued for other very dangerous conditions, such as severe and extreme turbulence, severe icing, and widespread dust storms. These are dangers that would affect any aircraft, regardless of how sophisticated or well equipped it is.

AIRMETs warn of weather conditions that are potentially dangerous to light aircraft but don't pose a threat to larger, better-equipped airplanes such as airliners or corporate jets. An AIRMET is issued for moderate icing, moderate turbulence, sustained winds of 30 knots or more at the surface, widespread areas with ceilings below 1,000 feet or visibilities less than 3 miles, and extensive areas where mountains will be obscured by clouds or other restrictions to visibility.

Both SIGMETs and AIRMETs have a phonetic letter designator followed by a number, for instance, SIGMET Bravo 1. Succeeding advisories will retain the same alphabetic designator for so long as that particular weather condition exists, but the number changes as new advisories are sent out, to let you know how recent each report is. Alpha (for A) through November (for N) are used for SIGMETs, and the designators Oscar (for O) through Zulu (for Z) are attached to AIRMETs. SIGMETs and AIRMETs are automatically announced, as soon as they are issued, by radio from FSSs and are also distributed throughout the weather reporting system to all FSSs.

As you can see, the government has gone to considerable effort and expense to create a weather reporting system and in maintaining it, just to keep pilots informed of the conditions and to keep us out of trouble. To understand what you're being told by this system, you are required to learn enough about weather basics in your training that the information is meaningful to you. Let's spend some time with the basics.

# Air Pressure

As we stand upon the earth's surface, we are surrounded by an ocean of air around and above us. At sea level, that air weighs about $1\frac{1}{4}$ ounces per cubic foot, which means that it presses down and around us with a pressure of about 14.7 pounds per square inch. By international convention, it was decided that when the air pressure is such that it causes a column of mercury, contained within a vacuum tube to rise 29.92 inches, we will call that *standard barometric pressure*. There is nothing really standard about this particular barometer reading; it's just an arbitrary point that was chosen as a starting point for measuring deviations in air pressure.

Our concern with air pressure is not limited to the fact that several of our most important flight instruments operate by sensing air pressure. For weather purposes, we need to understand that variations in air pressure are linked with and are harbingers of variations in the weather.

If the earth had a constant temperature over its entire surface, there wouldn't be any variations in air pressure nor would there be any significant difference in the weather from the equator to the poles. But, of course, the temperature isn't the same everywhere. The sun heats the earth's surface unequally. Different kinds of terrain absorb different amounts of heat, even in the same season of the year.

For example, a certain portion of the surface, such as the paved areas of a city, will absorb much more heat than will the surrounding farm fields. The air above the city becomes warmer than the air around the city. As air warms, it expands, and as it expands, it becomes lighter as a product of that expansion. Because this warmer air is now lighter than the cooler air around it, the warmer air rises. This rising column of air is called a *thermal* or *convection current*. A thermal will usually continue to rise until it reaches an altitude at which it cools to the point that whatever water vapor is in the air condenses and forms a cumulus cloud. These thermals are the rising currents that glider pilots search for, and when good ones are found, they can sustain a glider in flight for hours.

Meanwhile, the rising and expanding thermal has created a small area of low air pressure at its base, and the relatively cooler air of higher pressure surrounding the thermal wants to rush in and equalize the pressure. Presto, a wind is born. This same process, on a vastly bigger scale, creates the huge areas of low air pressure that move across the earth's surface, "making" our weather patterns.

Areas of high atmospheric pressure exist for just the opposite reason. Cool air is heavier and denser, is often clear of extensive cloud cover, and is said to be stable. To a meteorologist, stable air is air in which the cumulus clouds will not build up into thunderheads. Student pilots sometimes assume that bumpy air is "unstable," although the exact opposite is often true. For example, the cool air behind a cold front might be bumpy, as it usually is, but it is stable because it contains relatively little water vapor and doesn't form thunderheads. This is why, as a flier, you will normally associate highs with good weather and suspect lows of harboring or generating poor flying conditions.

When we speak of "warm" and "cool" air in this context, the terms aren't used in an absolute sense, but rather, they are relative. If the temperature at a given place is 90°F, and that location is surrounded with 85°F air, the 85°F air is referred to as "cool."

In the northern hemisphere, the winds around a low-pressure area are counterclockwise, and a high has air flow rotating clockwise around its center. The air from a high is always flowing toward a low because the atmosphere is always trying to equalize the variations in pressure, but it never accomplishes it. This exchange of air from highs toward lows is deflected to one side by the earth's rotation from east to west. In the southern hemisphere, the rotations around highs and lows are reversed from what we're used to north of the equator.

# Fronts and Air Masses

There are two basic classifications of air masses, *tropical* and *polar*. These labels come from the parts of the world in which the particular air mass forms, which is in a tropical region or in a colder area. When that air mass starts moving, it has to travel over a route that is predominantly over oceans or land. If it travels over open water before reaching us, it is further classified as *maritime,* and when its route takes the air mass over land, it is referred to as *continental*. Then, the last step in deciding upon the final nomenclature to attach to an air mass is to classify it according to its temperature, relative to the other air surrounding it. You might have already surmised that these last two classes are *cold* or *warm*. So, the complete classification of an air mass might be polar continental cold or tropical maritime warm.

The route that an air mass takes when it starts moving on its trek across the globe is important to a meteorologist because the route will define many of the future characteristics of that mass. The air mass that travels over water is going to pick up far more moisture than one that has journeyed over land.

Once an air mass starts in motion over the surface of the earth, it will overtake or displace other air that is in its line of travel. The boundary line between the two masses is called a *front*. When one air mass is overtaking another, there is surprisingly little mixture of the two at the frontal boundary, and it will often take thousands of miles of travel on the part of the overtaking air mass before the front between the two dissipates.

A *cold front* is the transition and boundary area between a cooler air mass and the warmer air that it is overtaking. Again,

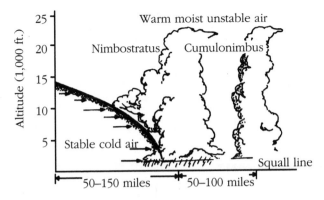

**8-1** *A cold front usually travels about 300 to 400 miles per day in summer, about 500 miles per day in winter.*

the term *cold* is relative and only implies that the invading air mass is cooler than the air being displaced.

When you view a cold front in cross section (FIG. 8-1), it appears to be wedge shaped at its leading edge because the heavier, cooler air overtakes the warmer air in its path by sinking under it. The warmer air is forced upward as it rises, the water vapor contained in the warmer air condenses, and clouds form. The atmosphere is always colder, on a grand scale, as you go up in altitude because the sun heats the surface of the earth and the air is warmed from contact with the ground. Very little warming of the air occurs as the sun's rays pass through on their way toward the ground. Because the frontal zone of a cold front is fairly narrow, the warm air rises quickly as it is pushed up rapidly by the oncoming cold air. This causes the condensation of the water vapor in that warm air to also occur quickly, resulting in cumulus clouds that can rise very high, even into the stratosphere, generating thunderstorms, sometimes of monumental proportions.

A cold front is usually a fast-moving phenomenon, and the cold air behind it is stable, heavy, and clean, generally resulting in good flight visibility. Because they move so fast, cold fronts normally come and go often within 24 hours. As a by-product of their speed, the weather associated with cold fronts can be violent. Long and well-developed lines of thunderstorms, called *squall lines,* are a frequent occurrence along the boundary, or frontal zone. Most tornados that occur in the midwest are another by-product of cold fronts. Generally, the greater the temperature differential between the oncoming cold air and the warm air being pushed up and out of the way, the more violent the weather in and near the frontal zone.

Be especially careful for granddaddy thunderstorms accompanying cold fronts in the spring and early summer. In these seasons of the year, the polar air masses coming down from the arctic are moving very fast. The arctic hasn't yet warmed, and the temperature of the arctic air can be very cold, relative to the air already over the midwest, which has enjoyed warmer temperatures. These vast temperature differentials are so great that cold fronts in these times of the year have the potential to generate large thunderstorms and tornados. The storms alone, even without associated tornados, can be lethal to any airplane in their paths, as well as also to people and structures on the ground. Some of the worst tornado outbreaks in U.S. history have occurred along springtime cold fronts.

The prime determining factors for the strength of the weather produced by a cold front are the speed of its movement across the surface, the temperature differential between the two air masses, and the moisture content of the warm air that is being forced upward as the invading cold air mass rushes in to displace it. For pilots, the saving grace in cold fronts is their speed. Because they generally do move so fast, the adverse affects that accompany them come and go quickly. If you have a cold front coming that dictates delaying a flight, you generally only have to wait a day, and the front will be gone. Many pilots have landed at an airport during a long trip and sat in the FBO's office for a few hours, allowing the frontal zone to pass, and then resumed their cross-country flights.

A *warm front* is the transition area between an advancing mass of warm air and the cold air mass that the warm air is overtaking (FIG. 8-2). The leading edge of the advancing warm air rides up and over the cooler air. Warm fronts move more slowly than do cold fronts and the weather changes that they produce are also different.

Because of their slower speed over the ground, the frontal zone of a warm front is much more spread out and less distinct than is the frontal zone of a cold front. Warm fronts also cover a much larger area. Warm fronts cause changes in the sky condition that consist of a gradual deterioration from the good flying weather in the cold air to the low clouds, poor visibility, and, usually, precipitation, all of which are contained within the oncoming warm air mass.

Warm air is inherently unstable and generally contains more moisture than does cold air. The poor aviation weather associated

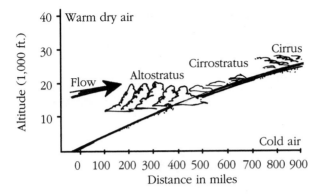

**8-2** *Warm fronts are normally less violent than cold fronts and affect a much wider area. Improvement in the weather after they pass is much slower than after a cold front.*

with a warm front can last for quite some time. Occasionally, a warm front will really slow down and become a *stationary front.* A stationary front's presence is usually the cause of the days-long onset of misty, low-ceiling, and poor-visibility weather that is seen in many parts of the country, especially in the winter. But the weather that is associated with a warm front is seldom violent, and the air within it is seldom turbulent. Most instrument-rated pilots would far rather fly in a warm or stationary front than deal with the conditions found in a cold front.

But for the VFR pilot who is not rated to fly instruments, warm fronts can pose lethal risks. Because their effects cover large areas, sometimes hundreds of miles, if you fly into one, your only course of action is to retreat to the rear. Don't expect the weather in a warm or stationary front to improve anytime soon, because it won't. If you're on a cross-country trip and failed to get an accurate picture of the weather that would affect the route of the flight, and if you encounter a warm front, you may get to spend more than one night in a hotel along the way, waiting for the front to slowly work its way across the landscape. If the front becomes stationary, you might be riding an airliner home and then have to go back and get your airplane a few days later.

On the contrary, a cold front moves fast, and the weather in it deteriorates and subsequently improves quickly. It is sometimes possible to successfully and safely fly VFR through a cold front. Sometimes the ceilings in a cold front are high enough to permit VFR flight through the frontal zone. But don't try it if the front is producing thunderstorms; if it is, they had better be widely scattered and not forming squall lines. If there aren't any more than widely scattered thunderstorms, and the ceiling is high, you can circumnavigate them. This decision is a difficult one to make, and the wise pilot always errs on the side of conservatism. I can't even tally the number of times that I've driven or taken an airliner all the way to my destination and back, thinking after I saw the weather first-hand that I could have flown the trip in a VFR airplane. But, I completed each of those trips successfully, and some who have chosen to fly in dubious weather are now statistics.

# Dewpoint

There is always some water vapor in every air mass. When water vapor cools enough, the water condenses. Therefore, there is always a temperature at which the present moisture in the air condenses into visible water that becomes either clouds or fog. Fog isn't really different from a cloud; it's a cloud that has no separation between its bottom and the ground. In other words, fog is a cloud that goes right down to the surface. The temperature at which the condensation occurs is called the *dewpoint*. Depending upon how much water vapor there already is in an air mass, the air may have to cool only a very few degrees, sometimes even one or two, before the water vapor condenses. Sometimes the amount of cooling will be quite significant, such as 20 degrees or more, before there will be condensation.

Pilots need to know the dewpoint of the air mass in which they're flying, as well as the present surface temperature. When you know these two numbers, you can predict the likelihood that some form of visible water will pose a hazard to your flight. If the spread between the present temperature on the ground and the dewpoint (which is also measured at ground level) is less than about 4°F, look out. Rain, fog, low clouds, snow, or some kind of visible moisture or precipitation is likely, if not then, in the near future.

# Lapse Rates

Under normal conditions, the temperature of the atmosphere cools as you rise in altitude. The sun heats the surface of the earth, and that heat then radiates from the ground upward into the air. The normal decrease in air temperature with increasing altitude is 3.5°F per 1,000 feet. This is known as the *normal lapse rate.* Remember this number; it will come in handy from time to time.

When the sun's heat and the radiation from the ground set up a thermal, the air within this ascending column of air cools at a different rate, which is 5.5° per 1,000 feet. The air within the thermal will continue to rise, and cool, until that air cools to its dewpoint. Then, clouds will form at whatever altitude the air is when it reaches the dewpoint. This rate of cooling inside of a thermal is called the *dry adiabatic lapse rate.* While the air in our thermal is rising, the dewpoint of that rising air is also declining along with the ambient temperature. The dewpoint in the column of air that makes up the thermal is decreasing at the rate of 1°F per 1,000 feet.

By performing some simple subtraction, you can see that the thermal is approaching the dewpoint at the rate of 4.5°F per 1,000 feet. Now that we have this number, we can easily determine the approximate height of the base of cumulus clouds. Take the ground temperature, subtract the dewpoint, and divide the result by 4.5. Then, you'll have a fairly close approximation of the height, above the ground, of the cloud bases. For example, let's assume that the temperature at our airport is 87°F on the ground, and the dewpoint is 68°F. The difference between these two numbers is 19. When you divide 19 by 4.5, the result is 4.2. This tells us that the cloud bases will be about 4,200 feet above the ground.

This method of determining cloud heights is valid only for cumulus clouds. It is a very good general rule that pilots who are not instrument rated should not fly above cloud layers, even if the clouds are only of the scattered variety. A scattered layer of clouds can become a broken layer, then become an overcast. If you get caught on top of an overcast, and don't have an instrument rating, this is as much an emergency as is an engine failure, maybe even a worse one.

But there will be times when the cumulus clouds are very scattered and it will be safe for you to fly above their tops, as long as they aren't continuing to build vertically. When cumulus clouds are present, vertical thermals are too, and it's this vertical rising of the air within the thermals that produces what pilots call *low-level turbulence.* Again, if the clouds are extremely few and very scattered and aren't still building vertically, you can climb above the clouds and escape the low-level turbulence that exists below them. You'll usually find smooth air above the altitude that the thermal reaches its dewpoint. When you do elect to fly above such a scattered layer, be very alert for any thickening of the cloud cover. If more clouds start to appear, descend right now and get below their bases. Whatever you do, don't risk getting trapped on top of a solid layer of clouds.

# Cloud Types

There are two primary types of clouds, called *cumulus* and *stratus,* that concern pilots. A third type of cloud, called *cirrus,* is not important to fliers of lightplanes. Cirrus clouds are frozen ice crystals and occur above 20,000 feet. Many subspecies of clouds result from the altitudes where the clouds form and from combinations of the primary kinds. As far as aviators are concerned, the classifications that are noted in the chart and discussion below are the easiest to understand because they are determined by altitude.

Cirrus (Ci)
Cirostratus (Cs)          High clouds
Cirrocumulus (Cc)          20,000 feet and above

Altostratus (As)          Medium clouds
Altocumulus (Ac)          8,000 to 20,000 feet

Stratocumulus (Sc)
Nimbostratus (Ns)          Low clouds
Cumulus (Cu)              Below 8,000 feet
Stratus (St)
Cumulonimbus (Cb)

*Cumulonimbus* are cumulus clouds that are producing precipitation, usually rain. The word *nimbus* signifies rain, and when nimbus is used in conjunction with a class of cloud, it means that the cloud is producing rain, snow, sleet, or a mixture of precipitation. Cumulonimbus clouds are referred to as Cb's by the meteorologist and by other people as thunderheads. Cb's are formed from the ordinary and quite innocent little cumulus clouds when the air is unstable. In unstable air, the fluffy little cumulus cloud simply begins to build vertically, and its top can rise well above 30,000 feet, from its relatively low base. Every thunderstorm that you have ever seen had it genesis in a little puffball cumulus cloud.

The towering, castlelike cumulonimbus is full of turbulence generated by violent vertical winds within the massive cloud, and it also likely contains lightning, hail, and drenching rain. These clouds are killers to all aircraft regardless of the size or type and whether they are in flight or on the ground. Fighter pilots, who fly the strongest airplanes, avoid them; lightplane pilots should take the cue and do the same. The ride through some storms will be unsurvivable, literally tearing the airplane apart. In the early 1970s, I got caught in the edge of a thunderstorm. I was flying IFR, in a layer of clouds, talking to a controller as I was nearing the destination airport. The airplane had no radar, and the type of storm detector that senses lightning hadn't yet been developed. Because I was in the clouds, I didn't see what was coming. For a few seconds, the world got totally black, but the air was still smooth. Then, the hammers of hell let loose, and the twin-engine Piper Aztec was all over the sky. Only the fact that I had had aerobatic training probably saved the day because I was able to right the airplane from being nearly inverted. When I got out of the storm, I asked the approach controller if he had seen the storm on his radar (ATC radar, in those days, was much more able to "see" the precipitation associated with thunderstorms than it is today). He allowed as how he had seen the storm and told me that if I were to make the instrument approach to the airport, I would have to go through the edge of it. I promptly informed him that there was no approach that I had to make that urgently and then went about 20 miles away to another airport. So much for relying on others to keep you out of thunderstorms. That night, back at home, the evening newspaper reported a tornado that hit about 5 miles from where I estimated I was when I penetrated the storm cloud.

A thunderhead is classified as a "low cloud" because the base of the cloudy area is low. You'll never be able to climb over one in a lightplane or, for that matter, in most airliners. Even if you could get over the top, the hail spewing out of a thunderstorm could still get you. Never try to fly underneath a thunderstorm either, because the violent vertical winds inside the cloud are accompanied by terrific updrafts and downdrafts from below. If you're caught in these vertical currents, you can't outclimb the downdrafts or dive through the updrafts without tearing the airplane apart—they're that strong.

*Cumulus* we've already discussed. Cumulus is the Latin word for *heap,* and that's a good description of the fair-weather cloud that is white and fluffy and forms at the top of a thermal. Glider pilots look for cumulus clouds as a primary marker of where they can find a thermal that will provide the upward current of air to keep a sailplane aloft, sometimes for hours.

*Stratus* is an even layer of clouds with a uniform base that is usually widespread. Fog that does not touch the ground is a good example of a stratus layer. Often, when there is one stratus layer that you can see, there are additional layers above it that you can't see from the ground. Sometimes these multiple layers of stratus clouds will extend as high as 20,000 feet.

*Nimbostratus* is a low, dense, and dark stratus layer producing precipitation, which is usually in the form of steady rain, sleet, or snow. Its base is often ragged in appearance and in most cases, a layer of altostratus, from which it has formed and settled, lies above the nimbostratus.

*Stratocumulus* is a layer of cumulus clouds that forms when the cumulus clouds are so numerous that they combine to form a solid layer. It forms in waves and rolls because the cumulus clouds are not uniform. Stratocumulus is low and potentially dangerous to the lightplane pilot because it presents a hazard of icing if the temperature in the clouds is near freezing. The vertical currents inherent in cumulus clouds are still there, with their associated turbulence. Usually stratocumulus doesn't produce steady rain, but mist and drizzle are possibilities.

*Altocumulus* is a layer of cumulus clouds that has formed at the medium altitudes and is somewhat like cirrocumulus in appearance. However, the globules or ripples in altocumulus are more pronounced than they are in cirrostratus (FIG. 8-3). It is often called a "mackerel sky" and its presence indicates brewing storm conditions.

*Altostratus* is a dense, grayish sheet, similar to cirrostratus, but it is heavier and occurs at the middle altitudes. It is ordinarily followed by rain, sleet, or snow.

*Cirrocumulus* is a small, high-altitude cumulus cloud with a fine grain or ripple pattern. As with altocumulus, these clouds predict stormy weather to come (FIG. 8-4).

*Cirrostratus* is a layer that gives the sky a milky look. The thin, high haze is made up of ice crystals that often cause a ring to form around the sun or moon. These clouds usually indicate the approach of bad weather within the next 24 to 36 hours.

*Cirrus* is the general classification of all of the high-altitude clouds, which are composed of ice crystals. Commonly called "mare's tails" or "feathers," cirrus clouds are carried by very

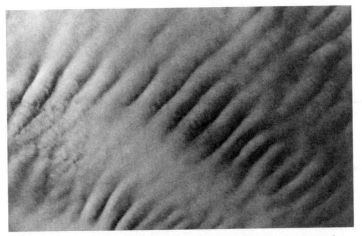

**8-3** *Altocumulus generally form between about 8,000 and 18,000 feet. These clouds often precede a progressively lower ceiling and some form of precipitation.*

**8-4** *Cirrocumulus form at about 20,000 feet and are composed of ice crystals or supercooled water droplets.*

strong upper winds. Often they originate from the anvil-shaped tops of distant thunderheads. When that happens, the high-altitude winds are so strong that the wind, which can exceed 100 mph in velocity, has actually ripped the top away from a thunder-head. Scattered cirrus are fair-weather clouds and indicate good weather for at least a day to come. When they get more dense and widespread, they become cirrostratus.

# The Weather Map

The weather map can give you a tremendous amount of information after you have learned the basics of reading it. Few pilots are meteorologists, but there will be many times in your flying that you will be able to tell quite a bit about the weather from looking at the weather map, which is particularly useful when there is no professional meteorologist around to assist. You are not required to read a weather map of this sort to pass the knowledge test for a private pilot certificate, but like many other subjects, knowing more than the bare minimum to pass the test will serve you well.

The heavy, curvy lines on the typical surface weather map are lines connecting points of equal barometric pressure and are called *isobars*. Usually, they are drawn 4 *millibars* apart. A millibar is the unit of atmospheric pressure used by meteorologists instead of inches of mercury because the millibar is an international measurement. Standard sea level pressure of 29.92 inches Hg is equal to 1013.2 millibars. Recall that wind is caused by the differences in air pressure; the atmosphere is always trying to equalize pressure. Isobars that are close together on the weather map indicate that the differences in air pressure are close together, which in turn means that the wind velocities will be stronger.

Around areas of low pressure, the wind rotates counterclockwise in the northern hemisphere and, due to the friction of the wind's passing over the ground, the wind blows inward across isobars at about a 30° angle, up to an altitude of 2,000 above ground level (AGL). Above that, the winds will shift to being more parallel to the isobars. Around high-pressure areas, the winds blow clockwise and outward at the same angles down low, and parallel to the isobars above 2,000 feet AGL.

Cold fronts are displayed on the map as a heavy line with a saw-toothed edge, The points of the saw teeth point in the direction toward which the front is moving. A cold front generally travels about 300 to 400 miles per day in summer and upwards of 500 miles per day in the winter.

Warm fronts are depicted with semicircles along the side of the line. The semicircles point in the direction of the travel of the warm front, just like the saw teeth do for a cold front.

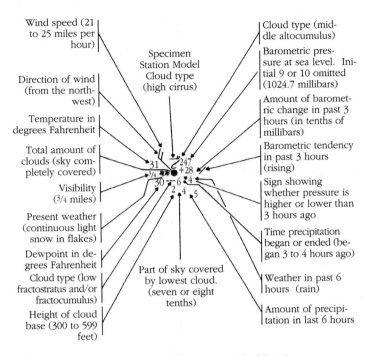

Wind speed (21 to 25 miles per hour)

Specimen Station Model Cloud type (high cirrus)

Direction of wind (from the northwest)

Temperature in degrees Fahrenheit

Total amount of clouds (sky completely covered)

Visibility (3/4 miles)

Present weather (continuous light snow in flakes)

Dewpoint in degrees Fahrenheit

Cloud type (low fractostratus and/or fractocumulus)

Height of cloud base (300 to 599 feet)

Part of sky covered by lowest cloud. (seven or eight tenths)

Cloud type (middle altocumulus)

Barometric pressure at sea level. Initial 9 or 10 omitted (1024.7 millibars)

Amount of barometric change in past 3 hours (in tenths of millibars)

Barometric tendency in past 3 hours (rising)

Sign showing whether pressure is higher or lower than 3 hours ago

Time precipitation began or ended (began 3 to 4 hours ago)

Weather in past 6 hours (rain)

Amount of precipitation in last 6 hours

**8-5** *Weather reporting stations seldom report all of this data on a weather map.*

Due to the general wind circulation patterns around the world, the United States has prevailing winds that blow from the west, toward the east. We refer to these as "westerly" winds because, when referring to wind direction, you label it as the direction *from* which the wind is coming. More often than not, especially in the summer, you can get a fairly good prediction of tomorrow's weather by noting what the weather is about 400 miles west of you today.

Each weather reporting station in the United States is shown on the weather map by means of a coded *station model*. FIGURE 8-5 is an example of a typical station model. FIGURE 8-6 is a portion of a surface weather map that shows how these reporting stations appear.

## Mountain Effects

Mountains create conditions of both wind and weather that pilots trained in the flatlands are ill-equipped to face. No pilot

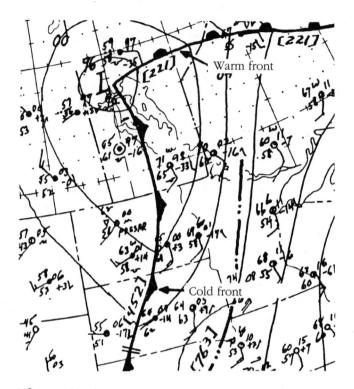

**8-6** *Typical surface weather map showing data from several reporting stations.*

should fly in mountainous terrain without first undergoing both ground and flight training in the art and peculiarities of mountain flying. This is especially so when there is any appreciable wind blowing. On the windward, or upwind side of a mountain, rapidly moving air dams up against the mountain because the mountain obstructs the normal air flow. This causes increased air pressure on the upwind side because the air slightly compresses as it is forced up against the side of the mountain. When you fly in this area of increased air pressure, your altimeter will sense, and display, an altitude *lower* than what would be correct.

As the wind blows up the side of the mountain, it creates an updraft. These updrafts can be very turbulent if it's a windy day. In an airplane like our Cessna 150, it's possible for the updraft to be so strong that you can't stay at a level altitude, even with the power at idle. Glider pilots, who are pros at what we called "flying the ridge," can intentionally get into this updraft and stay aloft from this "ridge lift" for hours. When mountains form chains, such as the Appalachians do, a sailplane can fly for hundreds of miles, right along the face of the mountain ridge. Don't try this in an airplane, and don't try it in a glider for that matter until you are very experienced and get the proper instruction first.

On the downwind (leeward) side of a mountain, the air is spilling over the top and increasing in velocity. Recall from our study of aerodynamics that when air velocity increases, the pressure of that parcel of air decreases. So, the increased velocity forms an area of low air pressure on the downwind side of the mountain. In this area, the airplane's altimeter will sense and show an indication that is *higher* than would be correct. This effect has killed more than one pilot who didn't know better and who flew into the terrain, thinking that the airplane was high enough to clear the rough terrain.

As the air goes over the top of a mountain, it naturally creates a downdraft. These downdrafts can be lethal on windy days. Most lightplanes can't outclimb the downdraft, particularly if the airplane is heavily loaded or if the density altitude is high, which it usually is in mountainous terrain.

The best rule is not to fly in mountains if the wind is blowing hard. Even on a reasonably still day, be at least 2,000 feet above the highest peak or ridge in the area. Only the foolhardy try to fly in the mountains in marginal weather; the peaks and ridges are easily obscured by the clouds or reduced visibility. Don't try to fly in the mountains in the winter in a lightplane. The chances are very high that the winds will be strong. If you were to be forced down, you'd probably not be found for months because the winter snows quickly blow in and cover all traces of people and airplanes within a very short time, far less time than it would take rescue crews to find you.

For summer flying, plan your flights in the mountains to end no later than noon, perhaps even a little earlier. By restricting your flying to the mornings, when the temperatures are cooler, you won't suffer the ravages of high-density altitudes as much as you would later in the day. Also, the surface winds tend to increase in the late mornings and continue until shortly before evening. With the early sunrise in the summer, if you get up and get going, you can obey this rule of thumb and still get several hours of flying in before it's time to park the airplane for the day.

# Icing in Flight

When we talk about icing, we mean the ice that can form, under certain weather conditions, on the airframe of the airplane. It can adhere to the wings, tail, struts, landing gear, radio antennas, propeller, and anything else that sticks out into the wind. Icing is likely to be encountered any time that an airplane is flying through wet snow or rain when the outside air temperature is near freezing or slightly above 32°F. You'll almost surely get severe icing if you fly in freezing rain. Ice can also be found in clouds when they are at temperatures near the freezing mark, but as a VFR private pilot, you shouldn't ever be in the clouds in the first place.

*Rime ice* resembles the flaky, milky stuff that gathers around the freezer unit of an inexpensive kitchen refrigerator. *Clear ice* is hard and translucent, like the surface of an ice skating rink. *Mixed icing* is a combination of both rime and clear ice. All of the three types of ice are dangerous, but clear ice is the worst because it is denser, heavier, and more difficult to remove quickly.

Ice has several effects, and none of them are pleasant. First, when ice forms on the wings, it alters their shape and deprives them of some of their ability to produce lift. When you are flying an airplane with ice on its wings, you are flying an unknown and constantly charging airfoil and are, therefore, truly an experimental test pilot. For sure, any ice on the wings increases the stalling speed, but nobody knows by how much.

Ice forming on the propeller causes it to lose efficiency in the same way, by changing its shape. You never know how much thrust the propeller can produce once it has ice, until it quits generating enough to keep you flying. Ice on the blades of the propeller causes an imbalance between or among the blades. Propellers are carefully balanced because at their high rotational speeds, imbalance can create vibration, often very large amounts of vibration, depending on the degree of imbalance. There have been cases of iced-up propellers causing enough vibration to literally tear an engine from its mounts.

Ice is very heavy. When it forms on the airframe, the wings must support that added weight. Now you have an airplane that quite easily is so heavy that it exceeds its maximum gross weight and must be kept in the air by wings that have already lost a part of their lift and by a propeller that isn't generating the proper amount of thrust. It's also quite probable that the ice will partially, or completely, block the engine's air intake; then the engine will only be able to produce partial power at best and will quit altogether at worst. Not a pretty scenario.

If you ever get into icing conditions, turn around and do it quickly, assuming that you just left an area where there was no ice. Perhaps you can climb into colder air where the moisture is already frozen and therefore won't adhere to the airplane. That's the preferred tactic for a pilot who is instrument rated but not for the VFR pilot. You can't enter clouds without an instrument rating, and because there are surely clouds above you, producing the wet snow or rain, climbing isn't much of an option.

For the VFR pilot, the best bet is to safely descend into warmer air below you while you are turning around. Best of all, always stay clear of ice and the conditions in which it is possibly found. If the weather has any potential for icing—usually determined by a combination of cloud cover, ceiling, precipitation, and temperature, watch out. The FSS briefer should caution you about it because it will be the subject of either an AIRMET or a SIGMET, depending upon the forecast severity. If you don't get such a warning, depending on the season of the year, ask for information about freezing levels and for pilot reports of icing along your proposed route.

## The Weather Decision

Now you should be able to easily identify the weather impediments to a safe flight. Remember that weather is the cause of more lightplane accidents than anything else. The weather problems to be aware of can be boiled down to three different hazards: reduced ceilings and visibility, winds and their resulting turbulence, and airframe icing. Avoid these dangers, and the weather won't get you. Separately or together in storms, these three conditions are the ones that threaten us if we fly in them. Every pilot must learn to accurately gauge the presence and extent of these dangers and understand the weather conditions and forces that produce them.

Most pilots have long depended upon the FSS network and its briefers to give complete weather briefings and help interpret the current and forecast conditions along the routes of planned cross-country flights. The best weather briefing has always had its limitations, and these limitations may increase in the future. The FAA has steadily reduced the availability of live briefings, conducted face to face with the FSS specialists, by consolidating the FSS network into a few regional automated stations. Most of us can now only talk to a briefer by telephone.

In the future, if not in the present, increased emphasis will be put on pilot self-briefing by DUAT or by contracting with one of the private weather information companies. Some day we may be left to our own devices to gather and interpret weather data. You can do it, as many pilots have done for years. Obviously, experience is a valuable teacher; until you gain it, just make sure that your interpretations and the decisions guided by them are on the conservative side. It is easier to begin this educational process if you understand the weather reporting system, its inherent weaknesses, and the limitations of weather forecasting. First of all, there are situations than cannot, even today, be predicted with acceptable accuracy. They are

- The time that freezing rain will begin
- Location and even the occurrence of severe turbulence
- Location and occurrence of icing
- Ceilings of 100 feet or less before they occur
- Thunderstorms before they have visibly begun to form
- Fog
- Hurricane movement more than 12 hours in advance

In short, the worse the weather may become, the less accurate the forecast is likely to be. This underscores two important points: Pilots have to make decisions on the spot, and they have to be conservative in those decisions. If professional meteorologists cannot precisely predict where a thunderstorm will form, certainly a pilot can't be expected to. Being conservative means being safe (FIG. 8-7).

Here are some very general rules of thumb applicable to various weather situations that usually can be usefully forecast:

- A forecast of good flying weather (ceiling of 3,000 feet or more and visibilities of 5 miles or greater) is usually dependable for about 12 hours in advance.
- A forecast of poor flying weather (ceiling below 1,500 feet and visibility of less than 3 miles) is much less accurate 12 hours in advance, but it is very accurate for a 3- to 4-hour period in the future.
- Ceiling and visibility forecasts should be highly suspect beyond the first 2 to 3 hours of the forecast period, especially if a significant change in either is predicted during the time span of that forecast period.
- Forecasts of poor flying conditions are most reliable when there is a distinct weather system involved, such

**8-7** *Again, your need to get someplace should never influence your assessment of the weather.*

as a low, a front, a trough, or the like. Be aware that there seems to be, from a pilot's perspective, a tendency among meteorologists to forecast these conditions on the optimistic side.

- The weather associated with fast-moving cold fronts, such as squall lines, severe thunderstorms, and tornados, is the most difficult to accurately foresee.

- Forecasts of surface visibilities are less reliable than predicted ceilings.

- The presence of snow in a forecast or in a station report makes any predictions about visibility pure guesswork.

You should take some useful guidelines from the above and apply the weather basics that you will learn in your training. Prepare for any cross-country flight by including the following in your analysis:

- Check the locations of areas of low pressure, fronts, and troughs. Cold fronts that are moving fast usually mean quickly developing violent weather, particularly if the air mass that they are displacing is warm and moist. They will be followed by quick clearing, with higher than normal surface winds and bumpy air. A slow-moving cold front can have much the same weather associated with it as does a warm front: wide frontal zones of clouds, poor visibility, precipitation, turbulence and icing above the freezing level. Not all cold fronts are severe; the determining factors are usually the speed of movement of the front and the amount of moisture present.

- Check the moisture content of the air masses and their stability along your planned route of flight. The temperature-dewpoint spread can be used to estimate the amount of moisture, which is greater the closer the dewpoint is to the actual surface temperature. Unstable air allows thunderstorm development.

- When thunderstorms are present, request the altitudes of the bases and tops during your weather briefing. You'll never be able to fly on top of a thunderstorm, but knowing how high they are gives you a hint about how violent they might be. Thunderstorms will continue to build throughout the midday and into early evening. Never fly closer than 10 miles to a thunderstorm because the turbulence extends well beyond the visible thunderhead. Never fly underneath a thunderstorm, even if you can see the ground on the other side because the vertical wind currents exist below the visible cloud as well as within it.

- The danger of structural icing exists in a moist air mass at temperatures within a few degrees either side of freezing, particularly within cumuliform clouds. Clear ice is most common in cumuliform clouds, and rime ice is common is stratiform clouds. But either type of ice can appear in any cloud.

- Carburetor ice can develop at temperatures as high as 75°F in moist air. Be aware of and watchful for the symptoms of carb ice. In an airplane equipped with a fixed-pitch propeller, the noticeable symptom will be a gradual reduction of rpm. Correct the problem quickly by always applying full carburetor heat to clear the ice. Unless you have a carburetor air temperature gauge, don't use partial heat.

- Approach mountain ranges at an angle whenever possible and make sure that you know the wind direction before getting close to them. If there are any clouds present, they will usually be on the downwind side. If there is any appreciable wind, be at least 2,000 feet above the ridge or peak before reaching it. Winds in excess of 50 knots at the top of the ridge or peak might create a *standing wave* over the downwind side of the mountain, and the turbulence from a standing wave might extend for miles downwind of the mountain. The presence of a flat but concave cloud, called a *lenticular cloud,* over or downwind of the mountain ridge or peak indicates the existence of standing waves. But this cloud won't form if the air mass is dry because it takes moisture to form clouds, even if there is a standing wave.

- Be aware of when *wind shear* might be present. Wind shear is the rapid change of velocity and direction of the wind within a very narrow altitude band. Wind shear can occur whenever there are high surface winds, high winds aloft at fairly low altitudes, thunderstorms in the vicinity, or a *temperature inversion.* A temperature inversion occurs when the air gets warmer as your altitude increases, not colder as is normal. Inversions are usually caused by a warm air mass overtaking a cold air mass that does not retreat as it normally would. Sometimes the cold air gets trapped by geographical features, such as in a valley.

- Most air traffic controllers feel that a clearance by ATC to change altitudes in flight, to approach and land, or to do anything at all, means only that the airplane that they are controlling won't conflict with other traffic under their control. They see their job as having the sole responsibility to separate aircraft from each other. Controllers are often of the opinion that they are not responsible to any degree for determining the safety of what you want to do—that decision is up to the pilot in command. Often controllers are in a dark room, maybe hundreds of miles from your location, and have no first-hand knowledge of the weather where you are flying. They have access to the same weather data as the pilot but often can't judge what's going on like the pilot can who is there. The courts have frequently held controllers responsible, at least to some degree, for some accidents. But think like they do — arguing about who's at fault after an accident is not nearly as productive as is preventing the accident.

The basic responsibility to determine all of the factors affecting the conduct and safety of each flight rests on the pilot in command. If you are ever given a clearance or a directive by a controller that, if executed, would put you in a precarious situation, don't do it. You have the regulatory right and sometimes the duty to request an amended clearance. You may be asked to explain your reasons, and if so, do it. Don't ever let someone else put you in a position of danger.

We've already said to always let controllers know that you are a student pilot during every call that you make to the controller at an ATC facility who is handling your flight. Even after you get your license, if you ever feel that you're getting into a pressure situation, let the controller know your problem. If you're approaching a large and busy airport for the first time, let ATC know that you are unfamiliar with the area; otherwise they may ask you to report passing certain landmarks on the ground and you will have no idea where they are. Often, especially at night, I'll tell a ground controller at a strange airport that I'm not familiar with the airport so that my taxi instructions will be more understandable. In my decades of flying, I can count on a very few fingers the times that I have encountered a controller who was not polite, helpful, and courteous. A good many of them are also pilots, and all of them are there to smoothly and safely expedite the flow of air traffic. They take their jobs seriously, and most are very good at it.

# 9

# VFR Navigation and Communications

In the United States, all aircraft fly under either VFR or IFR. Operating under IFR doesn't necessarily mean that the weather is poor; an IFR flight can be conducted in very good weather as well as in weather that requires IFR. The choice depends primarily upon weather conditions, aircraft equipment, pilot qualifications, and pilot preference. As a student pilot or newly certificated private pilot, you'll strictly be flying under VFR until you can gain the training and flight experience needed to qualify for an instrument rating.

## VFR Weather Minimums

VFR flight is permitted only when the weather conditions are at or above certain minimum ceiling and visibility values. In addition, there are requirements for VFR flight that you must maintain certain horizontal and vertical distances from clouds. These minimums vary according to the various classes of airspace in which an aircraft might be operating, whether it's day or night, and the flight altitude of the aircraft. We'll go into the subject of the classes of airspace later in this chapter.

The hardest part of determining whether you may legally fly VFR is the determination of your distance from clouds. In some instances, you're required to be at least 500 feet from a cloud; in others the mandate might be 1,000 or 2,000 feet. Often it's nearly impossible to decide how far you truly are from a cloud or layer of clouds. The key to regulatory compliance is conservatism. The keys to safety include that as well as common sense. Because IFR traffic can fly right through clouds, the idea is to stay far enough away from clouds, as a VFR pilot, so that when you see an IFR airplane pop out of a cloud, you have ample room to safely avoid a collision.

When the weather conditions are worse than the VFR minimums, you have no choice but to file an IFR flight plan, obtain an IFR clearance from ATC, and fly under their control. But you cannot do that until you receive an instrument rating. For quite a while, every new pilot must adhere to the VFR rules.

# Right-of-Way Rules

Because, operating under VFR, you won't be flying in the clouds or often operating in airspace where the air traffic control system has the responsibility to keep airplanes apart, it will be your responsibility to "see and avoid" other aircraft. Rules have been established in FAR 91.112 to prevent midair collisions. Just like when you're driving a car, there must be a system of right-of-way rules and adherence to it, or chaos would develop. You need to learn and remember these rules because the need to know them comes rapidly when you discover a potential conflict with another airplane. Then, you won't have time to fish the regulations out of your flight bag and study who has the right-of-way. The rules are as follows:

**FAR 91.113: Right-of-way rules; except water operations.**

(a) Inapplicability. This section does not apply to the operation of an aircraft on water.

(b) General. When weather conditions permit, regardless of whether an operation is conducted under instrument flight rules or visual flight rules, vigilance shall be maintained by each person operating an aircraft so as to see and avoid other aircraft. When a rule of this section gives another aircraft the right-of-way, the pilot shall give way to that aircraft and may not pass over, under, or ahead of it unless well clear.

(c) Distress. An aircraft in distress has the right-of-way over all other air traffic.

(d) Converging. When aircraft of the same category are converging at approximately the same altitude (except head-on or nearly so), the aircraft to the other's right has the right-of-way. If the aircraft are of different categories—

    (1) A balloon has the right-of-way over any other category of aircraft;

(2) A glider has the right-of-way over an airship, airplane, or rotorcraft; and

(3) An airship has the right-of-way over an airplane or rotorcraft. However, an aircraft towing or refueling other aircraft has the right-of-way over all other engine-driven aircraft.

(e) Approaching head-on. When aircraft are approaching each other head-on, or nearly so, each pilot shall alter course to the right.

(f) Overtaking. Each aircraft that is being overtaken has the right-of-way and each pilot of an overtaking aircraft shall alter course to the right and pass well clear.

(g) Landing. Aircraft, while on final approach to land or while landing, have the right-of-way over aircraft in flight or operating on the surface, except that they shall not take advantage of this rule to force an aircraft off the runway surface that has already landed and is attempting to make way for an aircraft on final approach. When two or more aircraft are approaching an airport for purpose of landing, the aircraft at the lower altitude has the right-of-way, but it shall not take advantage of this cut to cut in front of another aircraft that is on final approach or to overtake that aircraft.

As you can see, most of these rules are based on common sense and courtesy. From a practical point of view, never insist on your right-of-way if you have it in a particular situation. Presume that you are the only one to see another aircraft, and further presume that the pilot of any aircraft that you see doesn't see you. Whenever you are operating in the vicinity of military or airline aircraft, it's especially important to assume that they don't see you. They're almost always operating under IFR, regardless of how good the weather may be. Because of the speed differential between them and you, the high cockpit workloads they have, especially during takeoff and landing, and the limited visibility from some large airplane cockpits, operate under the assumption that they haven't seen you and be prepared to alter course accordingly.

# Navigation

Once you've learned how to physically handle an airplane and have a working knowledge of the regulations, flying your airplane cross-country, on an accurate course, is a relatively simple matter (FIG. 9-1). There is a network of radio navigational stations

**9-1** *Cross-country flight is an expression of the freedom of flying. Just be sure that you thoroughly plan every flight.*

that almost unfailingly lead you from anywhere to anywhere in the United States (and much of the rest of the world), and this together with the satellite-based navigation system has made air navigation so painless and simple that the average private pilot routinely completes flights that were, only a few decades ago, largely reserved for professional aviators.

This doesn't mean that you only have to learn to operate aircraft radios and satellite receivers, which are all lumped together in the term *avionics*. Aircraft electrical systems and radios fail, so you've still got to know how to navigate on your own, by looking at your chart, and the ground, the way it was done for a long time, before all of the electronic aids came into existence. The FAA has wisely seen fit to use the private pilot knowledge and flight tests as vehicles to ensure that you adequately demonstrate your ability to plan, plot, and fly a course without resort to electronic navigational aids.

It's significant that the FAA considers the multibillion dollar electronic system as an *aid* to air navigation; it's there simply to make flying easier, more efficient, and somewhat safer. These electronic aids do not relieve you of the responsibilities of *planning* and *thinking*.

The term *contact* navigation means navigation using references on the ground to navigate from one place to another. It is not hard to do, and even with all of the electronic aids turned on, I still like to navigate by looking out of the windows. The only things that you need for contact navigation are a ruler with a protractor attached, which is called a *plotter* (FIG. 9-2), the

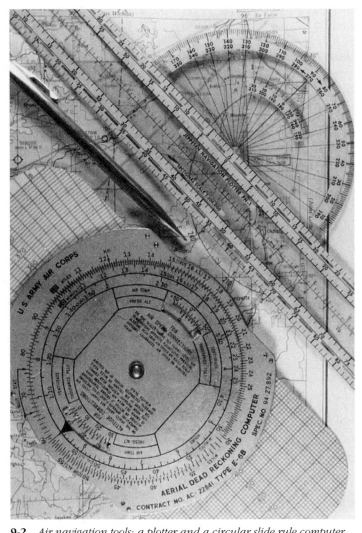

**9-2** *Air navigation tools: a plotter and a circular slide rule computer. This type computer is rapidly being supplanted by electronic pocket calculators that feature aviation functions.*

aeronautical chart for the area where you're flying, a pocket computer of either the circular slide rule or electronic type, the compass in the airplane, and a clock in the instrument panel or on your wrist.

# Aeronautical Charts

The maps that aviators use to navigate are called *charts,* and they come in several different types to serve the needs of various kinds of operations and aircraft performance levels. The ones that are used by almost all lightplane pilots for VFR navigation are *sectional aeronautical charts*. They are published by the National Oceanic and Atmospheric Administration, a part of the U.S. Department of Commerce.

Another chart format that can be used is the *world aeronautical chart,* commonly called a WAC. WACs are not used very often anymore because their scale is twice that of a sectional chart, and they do not have nearly as much surface detail as do sectionals. In the past, many high-performance airplanes used WACs, but today virtually all such airplanes fly their flights IFR, so they use instrument charts. WACs will probably be discontinued in the near future.

Sectional charts contain a truly amazing amount of information, and the reverse side of the face panel of the chart contains its legend. The legend can be daunting at first sight, but most of the symbols used make very good sense, once you study them (FIG. 9-3).

The sectional chart is drawn at a scale of 8 statute miles per inch, and the WAC chart is at 16 statute miles per inch. The sectional is much more detailed than is the WAC, and the WAC covers just about twice the geographical area as does a sectional. WACs can serve a valuable purpose for flight planning. The government does issue a wall planning chart, but it covers one-half of the United States on one side. The wall planning chart can be used to get a general idea of how far things are apart, where radio aids are located, and the like. But the WAC gives a much better view of the terrain and shows almost all of the airports. Because few lightplane flights are longer than 200 to 300 miles, WACs make great planning charts but aren't so useful for actual navigation as are sectionals.

A sectional is the chart of choice for private pilots. Even if you go on in your flight training and obtain an instrument rating and use IFR charts for en route navigation in the IFR system, you'll still need to have sectionals with you on every IFR

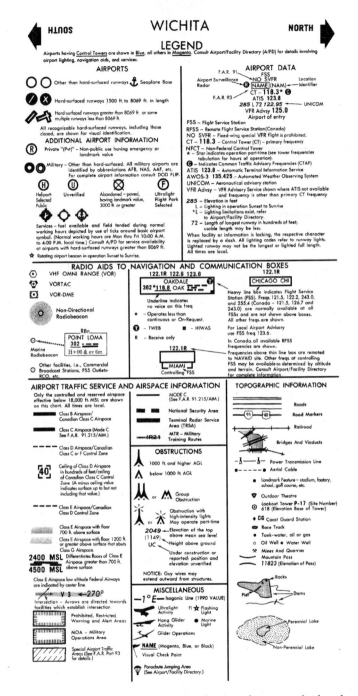

**9-3** *A sectional chart has a legend for the information displayed on it.*

flight. The IFR charts show almost no terrain features because the IFR system is set up to automatically give IFR airplanes the proper terrain clearance when they fly in the system. But an instrument pilot must rely on sectionals for all of the information displayed on them that is not shown on IFR charts. Each sectional covers an area of about 150 by 285 miles, so it's not an overwhelming task to have the few on board the airplane that you will need for a typical cross-country flight. Thirty-seven sectionals cover all of the area within the 48 states, not counting Hawaii and Alaska. Almost no one has them all because they are revised about every 6 months. Most pilots buy the one or two that cover their area of operations and then buy more for the few flights per year that go for hundreds of miles.

The sectional chart displays ground elevation above sea level with different background colors ranging from green at sea level through successively darker shades of tan and brown as terrain height increases. As you learn to use the charts, you can get a good idea of the terrain elevation in a particular area just by noticing the background color of the chart.

Your flight instructor will help you learn the various symbols used on sectional charts. Take a look at FIG. 9-3. The data at the very top shows the name of the chart, which is the name of a larger city somewhere within its coverage area, and then there are two arrows, pointing in opposite directions. These arrows, labeled "North" and "South," allow you to unfold the chart to the side that displays the northern or southern half of the coverage area.

Right below the name of the chart is the section of the legend that has all of the airport symbols on the left side. This system of airport symbols tells you if an airport has fuel sales, the number of paved runways and the length of the longest one, and whether the runways are paved or of some other surface type. A symbol will tell you whether the airport has a control tower and, if so, what the radio frequency is to call the tower. You will also be able to see if the airport has ground lights for night operations. To the right of the symbols is the box of printed data that accompanies each symbol, which gives even more detailed information about that airport.

Below that, the legend tells you how to identify the various radio aids to navigation and how to interpret the data shown about each one. Below that is the largest part of the legend, which explains all of the ground features that are shown on the chart and the symbol for each one.

There's so much information on a sectional that you will never digest it all. When you need to know about a certain local area or flight route, you'll study that portion in detail. All of the areas of restricted airspace are shown, as are the power lines, freeways, rivers, railroad racks, and unusual terrain features. All of this is depicted to enable you to know where you are and to guide your flight to its destination. Never fly with sectionals or any charts that are out of date. The FARs require that we have both appropriate and current charts, even for a local flight. Appropriate means that the chart covers the area of the flight. Current means that the edition of the chart that you're using is the latest revision. Radio frequencies get changed often, new radio towers get built, and airports open and close.

Even when flying locally, you can't possibly memorize all of the radio communications and navigational frequencies in your area. So, carry a current chart, even if you don't plan to leave the airport traffic pattern. An airplane might get disabled on your airport's runway, requiring you to go somewhere else to land and wait until your airport opens up again. There are many reasons that you might need to go to a different airport, and without a chart, you won't know its elevation or radio frequencies.

Your local FBO probably sells sectionals. If you are planning a flight in advance, get the chart as early as you can, so long as it will be current when the trip actually occurs. Because charts are revised about every 6 months, the date of the next revision is shown on a sectional. That way, you can tell when the one you have will expire. Don't wait until the last minute to get a chart for a cross-country trip; the FBO may be out of stock. Many pilots buy their charts from catalog sources; you can choose the method that suits you best.

# Meridians and Parallels

You are probably familiar with the imaginary lines that have been drawn around the globe to determine position and direction. This system hasn't changed for centuries, and it is still the basis for all modern concepts of where you are and how to get where you're going. Navigation doesn't take a degree in mathematics, or I could have never learned how to do it. What it does require is an elementary understanding of how circles and spheres are divided into degrees of position around a circle or on the surface of a sphere.

The earth has been crisscrossed with lines of *latitude* and *longitude*. The horizontal lines that start at the equator and circle the earth between the equator and the north and south poles are called *parallels* because they are parallel to each other; they never touch one another or converge. Parallels are used to express *latitude*, which is either north or south of the equator, and distance from the equator. That's all you get from a parallel, one line that goes all of the way around the globe and that is either north or south of the equator.

We obviously need to know more about our position than just how far north or south of the equator we are. To give us more data, the earth is further divided by vertical lines that run from the north pole to the south pole, and these are called *meridians*. Meridians offer the missing piece to the position puzzle. They all begin at one of the poles, run vertically across the equator, and then reconverge at the opposite pole. Because meridians all start at one pole and reconverge at the opposite pole, they are never parallel to each other.

Meridians tell us *longitude,* which is that missing piece of the problem if you tried to determine where you are using latitude alone. The meridian that runs through Greenwich, England, has been designated as the *prime* or *zero* meridian. This was decided by international agreement in the nineteenth century, when Britain ruled the waves and the worldwide navigation system was dedicated to marine navigation.

Meridians give us east-west orientation on the surface of our sphere called earth. That, combined with the knowledge of our north-south line of position, gathered from the parallel on which we're located, solves the puzzle. We can now express any position, anywhere on our planet, by using a simple combination of latitude and longitude because where a parallel crosses a meridian is a point of position. (Recall from your high school geometry that a point is created by the intersection of two lines. You never realized that you'd wait so long for that little ditty to become relevant to something that you'd really do.)

The prime meridian is the zero meridian, and all meridians west of it, around the globe to the halfway point, are expressed as west longitude. When you get exactly halfway around the world, you're on the 180th meridian. From the prime meridian east bound, which is called east longitude, you go halfway around again to the 180th meridian. The 180th meridian is also known as the *international date line.*

# Obtaining a Course

*True course* (TC) is the direction, measured in degrees, in which your destination lies from your point of departure, in relation to the north pole. From here on out, we're going to assume that you're doing your flying in the northern hemisphere. If you do ever fly south of the equator, all navigational references are to the south pole.

Imagine yourself standing in the center of a large circle, with your body facing due north. Your nose is then pointed at 0°, which can also be called 360° because they are the same. Your right shoulder is pointed due east, and that's referred to as 090°. Your posterior is looking due south, or 180°. Finally, your left shoulder is aligned to the west, or 270°. Remember that there are 360° in a circle.

In FIG. 9-4 we are measuring a true course, using the Dallas-Fort Worth Sectional. The first step in determining a true course is to use the ruler part of the plotter and lay the straight edge so that it bisects the airport symbols of both the departure and destination airports. Then, take your pencil and actually draw a line on the chart between the two airports. Don't be hesitant to draw on the chart; it's the only way to do it. Even if you fly frequently, you'll be getting a new chart about every 6 months, when the newest revision comes out. In our example, we're planning a flight from Childress, Texas, to Mangum, Oklahoma. The airport symbol for Mangum is a little hard to see, but it's at the upper right edge of the figure.

After drawing the course line between the two airports, you next have to determine its direction, from north. Find a meridian that is close to the halfway point along the route. That's easy in this case because this is a short trip, and there is only one on the chart between these two airports.

Then, place your plotter's straight edge along the course line with the protractor's zero hole on the point where it is directly over the meridian. Now, read the direction of the course line at the outer edge of the circular part of the protractor, where the meridian emerges from the zero hole up through the protractor. You see that the outer rim of the protractor is calibrated in degrees, with two sets of numbers, one set just below the other.

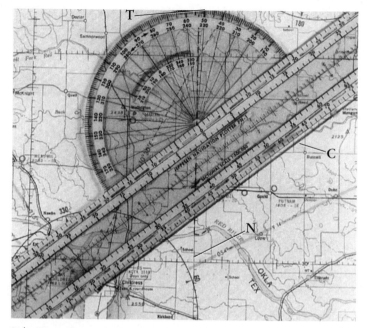

**9-4** *Measuring a true course: Position the plotter with the protractor's center hole on the midmeridian (N) and the straightedge along the course line (C). True course, 053°, is then read on the protractor's scale at the top.*

To measure your course line, you've got to use some common sense. From even the most cursory look at your course line, you see that flying from Childress to Mangum, you'll be going northeast. Because northeast is somewhere between north (0 or 360°), and east (90°), you see that the direction of your course line is 053°. When we fly from Mangum back to Childress, the course will be 233°. Be careful that you have not accidentally measured the reciprocal of your actual course line that you intend to fly by cross-checking yourself to see if the measurement that you've obtained makes sense.

## Cruising Altitudes

Before proceeding with further calculations, you need to determine your cruising altitude so that you can apply the winds aloft being forecast at or near that altitude to the rest of the navigational problem. The FARs dictate that, under VFR, if you want to cruise at more than 3,000 AGL, and below 18,000 feet MSL, you are limited to certain altitudes, based on your *magnetic course* (MC). Magnetic course is the TC corrected for magnetic variation, which is explained later in this chapter.

If your MC is eastbound, anywhere from 0 to 179°, you must fly at an *odd* thousand-foot altitude *plus* 500 feet (3,500, 5,500, 7,500, etc.).

If the MC is from 180° on around to 359°, or westbound, you are then required to fly at an *even* thousand-foot altitude *plus* 500 feet (4,500, 6,500, 8,500, etc.).

Airplanes flying under IFR fly cruising altitudes based on the same system, but they don't add the 500 feet to either the odd or even thousand-foot altitude. In this way, there is always 1,000 feet between VFR aircraft that might approach each other head-on, and 500 feet between a VFR aircraft and an IFR aircraft that are converging somewhat head-on. Obey this rule without fail and you'll go a long way toward preventing a midair collision.

There is a way to remember this rule that is, unfortunately, not very complimentary. An air force instructor once said that the memory device to use is to remember that "only odd people fly east." Because I'm located in the midwest, and fly eastbound quite a bit, I've never forgotten which way the rule works.

From the permitted altitudes that you have to chose, the specific altitude will be determined by several factors, including wind, terrain heights, obstructions along your course, airspace restrictions, cloud levels, distance of the trip, and freezing levels. You want an altitude that gives you the best tailwind, or the least headwind, whenever possible. But because this is a relatively short trip, you'd burn quite a bit of excess fuel by climbing to the higher altitudes; we would only be there a short time before it would be time to start down again. Regardless, on the flight from Childress to Mangum, we must choose an odd-thousand altitude plus 500 feet.

# Wind Correction Angle

You've already learned from the ground reference maneuvers discussed earlier that when an airplane is in flight, it is carried along in the same direction as the movement of the air mass that supports it. It will always fly *through* the air at its regular cruising speed, but at the same time, it will be carried *with* the air movement across the ground, just as a boat is carried with the current, independently of the speed of the boat through the water. Just as you must point a boat's bow to one side of its intended destination to compensate for sideways drift, so must you do the same with an airplane to correct for wind.

In your preflight weather briefing, you obtained the forecast of the winds aloft. Because the forecast predicts the wind speed and direction at 3,000-foot intervals, you might have to do a little interpolation to arrive at the values applicable for your chosen cruising altitude.

To figure the wind correction angle, we'll draw a wind vector, which is an exercise in trigonometry made simple. In this day and age of electronic navigation, pocket computers, and electronic calculators, some instructors don't even teach wind vectors anymore. But this problem and its graphic solution are both very valuable in giving a student pilot a keen sense of what the wind is doing to the airplane and how that effect alters a flight's path over the ground. Doing wind vectors gives a "picture" that is worth a thousand words. It also imparts a "feel" to what the wind is doing to the airplane so that when the day comes that you need to alter course in midflight, to go to an alternate airport or divert around weather, you can ad-lib a wind correction that might be pretty close to what you'd figure if you had the time to accurately determine it, or you can do so if the batteries fail in your electronic wonder calculator.

Let's go through the steps involved in drawing a wind vector:

1. Draw a vertical line on a blank piece of paper; this line will represent north-south. Mark the top of the line with an N. Place the zero hole of the protractor part of your plotter on this line and then rotate the entire plotter until 053° appears on the outer edge, lined up with the N-S line. Make sure that as you rotate the plotter, you keep the zero hole over the line. Then, reproduce your course line by drawing another line, outward from the N-S line with the straight edge of your plotter, as shown in FIG. 9-5. The length of this line is not important, but make it about 5 or 6 inches long. This line corresponds to your true course.

2. Now, let's enter the wind values. We need to know two things: the direction from which the wind is blowing and the speed of the wind. Assume that the winds aloft at your altitude are forecast to be from 330° at 30 knots. Line up the plotter with the zero hole at the point where the course line

**9-5**  *Wind vector. The first step is to reproduce the true-course line. The vertical line represents the midmeridian.*

intercepts the N-S line (our imaginary meridian). Use the point of your pencil, through the zero hole, and put a dot there. Now, just move your plotter vertically up the paper, keeping the N-S line right under the 330° mark on the protractor, until the bottom straight edge intersects the N-S line at the point that you've just made with your pencil (which is also the point where the course line intercepts the N-S line). Then, draw a line to represent the wind speed and direction. Draw this line along the bottom straight edge, and, using the mileage scale on the straight edge, draw a line 30 miles long. If your paper is small, you can halve the wind speed if you want, to keep the size of the diagram smaller, and therefore draw it only 15 miles long. We've done this on FIG. 9-6, due to the size of the page.

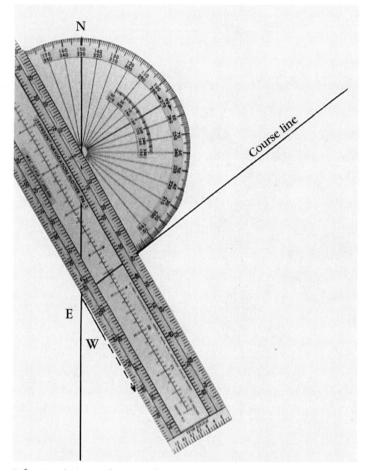

**9-6**  *Wind vector. The second step is to draw a line representing the wind direction and speed.*

3. The final step is to intercept the course line with a line drawn from the end point of the wind line that we drew in step 2. Make sure that you ascertain the very end of the 15-mile-long wind line that you drew. This measurement is important. This final line, from the end of the wind line to the course line, also has a definite length, and that is the cruising speed of the airplane, in true airspeed. Let's assume that our airplane will cruise at the chosen altitude at a speed of 115 knots. Because we halved the wind speed line, the airspeed line will be only 57 miles long, to keep the diagram in scale.

So, draw a line 57 miles long, again by using the scale at the bottom of the straight edge by rotating the plotter as necessary until the airspeed line is 57 miles long. Remove the plotter from the paper for a moment.

The completed wind vector diagram appears in FIG. 9-7. Measure the angle at P with your protractor; that's the amount of angular correction necessary to compensate for this wind. It

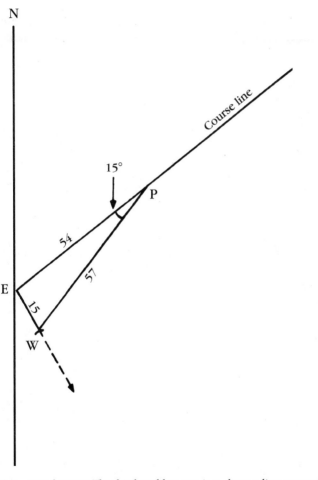

**9-7** *Wind vector. The third and last step is to draw a line connecting the end of the wind line (W) to the true course line (EP). The length of this line is the airspeed at which you'll fly. Then, the angle at P is the wind correction angle, 15°. Line EP, when measured, reveals the ground speed.*

is called the *wind correction angle* (WCA). Magically, the length of the line from points E to P will be your ground speed. When you measure the line E-P, the length is 54 miles. Because we halved all of the speed values, $54 \times 2 = 108$; so your ground speed is 108 knots. Measuring the angle at P, you discover that the WCA is 15°.

At this juncture, one note of caution is in order. Some older airplanes have airspeed indicators that are calibrated in miles per hour, not knots. Wind speeds are *always* given in knots. So, if you think in miles per hour for the true airspeed of your airplane, or if the airplane's manual speaks only in miles per hour, use your pocket computer to quickly convert those miles per hour into knots. A fairly accurate formula to do the conversion is miles per hour divided by 1.15 equals knots, in case you need to do it by hand, without your computer.

In our example, the vector diagram shows that the line E-W, representing the wind, is from your left as you fly up the true course line (E-P) in the direction of 053°. We now want to determine what our *true heading* is. We use the word heading to refer to the direction in which we'll point the nose of the airplane to compensate for the wind. The word *course* refers to our path over the ground. The rule for this correction is *subtract* for a wind from the left; *add* when the wind is from the right. There really isn't a catch phrase to use to remember this rule, other than to think of it as the fact that there are more right-handed people than there are left handers, so right is more. If you are mathematically inclined, you remember that the symbol $<$, pointing to the left, indicates less than, while $>$, pointing to the right, means greater than. In this case, we need to subtract a WCA of 15° from our true course of 053°, which results in a true heading of 038°.

# Variation and Deviation

Don't go away just yet; there are a couple more simple corrections to make before you arrive at the number that will actually appear on your compass as the heading that you will fly.

The first of these corrections comes from information that is displayed on the aeronautical chart. It's called *variation*. Unfortunately, the magnetic north pole and the true, geographic north pole are not in the same place. So, the lines of magnetic force that radiate from the magnetic pole aren't the same as the meridians of longitude that we use to measure courses on our charts.

The variation between true north and magnetic north changes as we go west and east of the line at which the two are the same. This line of 0 variation is in the eastern United States. Here, with our example being in the west, variation will be significant. The chart shows that the variation (the old-fashioned and more scientifically correct word is *declination*) along the route from Childress to Mangum is 8° east. These lines of variation are displayed on the chart by means of heavy, red, dashed lines running from the top of the chart to the bottom.

Here's your last navigational rule to remember: add west variation, subtract east. The rhyme that works to remember this one is "West is best, east is least." Because the magnetic variation along our route is 8° east, we'll subtract it from the true heading of 038°, and arrive at our *magnetic heading* (MH) of 030°.

Finally, you need to correct for *deviation*. Deviation is the error in the compass itself. This error, inherent in the installation of a compass in an airplane, is caused by ferrous metal in the airplane, by the magnetic interference from the radios and other electronic devices in our airplane, and because no instrument is exactly precise. The ferrous metals in the engine, which sits right in front of the compass, inhibit compass accuracy.

Deviation figures are different for every airplane, even among airplanes of the same type. From time to time, especially when radios are installed or removed, technicians determine the deviation applicable to each airplane, and post the results on the *compass correction card,* which is required by the FARs to be placed very near to the compass.

In our Cessna 150, the card is mounted in the bracket that holds the compass. The card notes that when flying in a northeasterly direction, such as 030°, you must subtract 2° from the magnetic heading to arrive at the final figure, which is called the *compass heading*. So subtract 2°. The final result is 028°, the compass heading. This is the actual reading that you want to see on the magnetic compass to make a true course, over the ground, of 053°.

Here's a recap of all of the steps that are necessary to determine the compass heading:

| | | |
|---|---|---|
| 1. Start with . . . . . . . .True course | | 053 |
| 2. Apply . . . . . . . . . . . . . . . .WCA | | −015 |
| *Result* . . . . . . . . . .True heading | | 038 |
| 3. Apply . . . . . . . . . . . .Variation | | −008 |
| *Result* . . . . . . .Magnetic heading | | 030 |
| 4. Apply . . . . . . . . . . . . .Deviation | | −002 |
| Final result . . .Compass heading | | 028 |

Remember the two rules: For variation, add west and subtract east (west is best, east is least). For wind, add right, subtract left.

You'll notice very quickly in your flight training that the magnetic compass oscillates considerably in rough air and during a turn. After a turn, it takes a minute or so to stabilize. However, the DG doesn't bounce around at all and is rock-steady in all normal flight regimes. But the DG cannot sense direction; it's just a dumb gyro that points wherever you've set it. You've already seen that we set the DG to match the reading of the compass before we take off, while everything is stable. In flight, you have to reset it about every 15 to 20 minutes because its precession will slowly drift from an accurate match with the compass heading. Always remember to check the DG against the compass and see if it needs to be set. Even the newest of DGs precess. Once you start flying cross-country flights, you'll use the DG to accurately maintain the desired compass heading, using the compass only as a cross-check and a point of reference to set the DG.

# Maintaining Course by Pilotage

Modern aerial navigation in lightplanes is a combination of three methods, *dead reckoning, pilotage,* and *electronic navigation.* We really don't use any one of the methods by itself, unless we're flying IFR.

The term *dead reckoning* has come into use as a misnomer for what was called *deduced reckoning.* When we drew our wind vector diagram, we began the process of dead reckoning. This term comes from what the pilot is really doing, which is reckoning a heading to fly and the time that it will take to get from point A to point B as a deduction from known facts about the distance between the two points, the speed of the airplane, and the winds. To be absolutely correct, it is "ded reckoning," an abbreviation of the word deduced as ded. But that never looked right, so for years pilots have used "dead reckoning." Some remember the old saying from when it was the only form of long-distance navigation: "If you don't reckon right, you're dead." Dead reckoning, in its purest form, doesn't depend upon looking at the ground and using checkpoints that the pilot can see to monitor the progress of the flight and the correctness of the heading.

Pilotage is the art of navigating by visual reference to points on the ground. We certainly do that, and that is what this section of the chapter will cover. But, we do a little dead reckoning in advance so that we have an idea of what heading will get us to our destination, what our ground speed will be, and how long it ought to take to go from one ground reference point, called a *checkpoint,* to another.

Electronic navigation in lightplanes isn't or, better put, shouldn't be used in a pure form either, unless and until you get an instrument rating and are flying in the clouds, when you obviously don't have any ground references because you can't see them. No competent VFR pilot depends on radios alone to navigate because radios can fail without warning. You must always be prepared to complete the flight by pilotage and dead reckoning, without benefit of the electronic aids to navigation.

Let's plan and fly a different cross-country trip to see how the three methods come together in modern use. Start from Wichita, Kansas, and go to Tulsa, Oklahoma. First, draw the course line on your chart from the Wichita Mid-Continent Airport symbol to the Tulsa International Airport symbol (FIG. 9-8). Then take your plotter, place it on the meridian halfway between the two airports and measure your true course, which you'll see is 140°.

Because you've learned how to properly plan a flight and have checked the weather first, you were given the winds aloft during your briefing. You know the wind directions and velocities for several of the altitudes at which it's practical to fly this trip.

Let's assume that you choose to cruise on this VFR flight at 5,500 feet, where the wind is forecast to be from 270° at 25 knots. That's not squarely on your tail, but the wind will have a tailwind component, which will certainly help. Looking in the performance section of the airplane's POH, you figure that the airplane will cruise at 100 knots at that altitude, using a reasonably efficient power setting.

Next, do your wind vector diagram; it should look like FIG. 9-9. The diagram reveals that the wind correction angle, measured at P, is 12°. The wind today is from your right as you fly this course, so 12° are added to the TC to deduce a true heading of 152°. Your wind vector diagram also gives your ground speed when you measure the line from E to P. This comes out to be 115 knots, which means that the partial tailwind will be giving you a boost of 15 knots across the ground.

Now, looking at the sectional chart and finding the line of variation along the route, you see that the variation is 7° east for this part of the country. Following the second rule of dead reckoning (add west, subtract east), subtract 7° from the true heading. This leaves you with a magnetic heading of 145°.

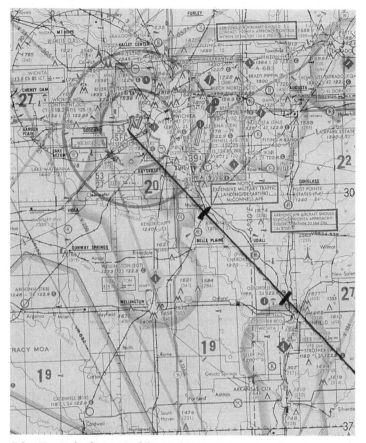

**9-8** *Here's the first part of the Wichita-to-Tulsa course line on our chart. We've selected checkpoints that are 15 miles apart, indicated by the small hash marks perpendicular to the course line. (Not for use in actual navigation.)*

Finally, when you get in the cockpit, glance at the compass correction card and find that, in this quadrant of compass readings, you must steer a compass heading 2° greater than your magnetic heading. You then end up with a compass heading of 147°.

When you use your plotter to measure the course line that you drew on the sectional chart, you'll discover that it is 113 nautical miles to Tulsa from Wichita. Now you can figure your estimated time en route, either by arithmetic using a pencil and paper or more commonly and practically by using the pocket

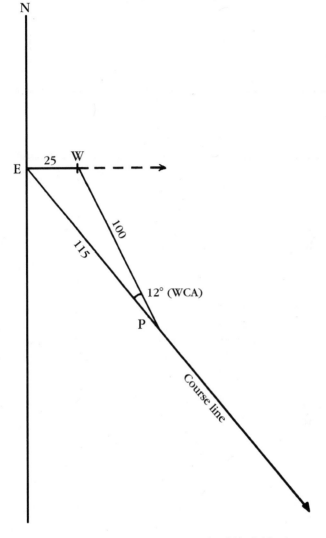

**9-9**  *The Wichita-to-Tulsa wind vector should look like this,
drawn to full scale.*

computer or electronic calculator. One of the finer points of
dead reckoning is to realize that your true airspeed won't be
the 100 knots that the POH shows, over the entire length of the
trip. You will spend some time climbing at a reduced speed,
before you reach your cruising altitude, get the airplane

trimmed, the fuel mixture leaned, and start going at 100 knots. You could be very precise and use other tables in the POH to figure exactly how long the climb will take and what your speed will be while climbing. We do get this exact for instrument flying, but for VFR, we don't.

For all practical purposes, you can call your ground speed for the entire trip 100 knots, and that will compensate for the speed lost while climbing up to 5,500 feet. If the trip weren't so short, the detrimental effect of the climb would be less; it's a matter of experience before you can estimate it closely. At 100 knots, it'll take 68 minutes to fly this trip. To calculate this figure by hand, pencil, and paper isn't difficult. Just divide ground speed into the total distance and multiply the result by 60 to obtain the elapsed time in minutes.

Don't forget how to be precise. Planning a trip like the one we're discussing is easy, and flying it will be, too, because there are so many landmarks to serve as checkpoints and help us correct any minor errors in our dead reckoning. It is a wholly different matter if your flight is over a desert, a swamp, or a large body of water or almost anywhere at night. Under these conditions, there won't be any checkpoints of much use, and those there are will be far between.

So, let's talk about the need to establish checkpoints along your route that are easy to spot from the air. When using pilotage as a part of the total navigational package, checkpoints are vital because they let you see if your compass heading is keeping you on course. Your calculations (dead reckoning) will never produce an error-free result, for several reasons. The winds aloft forecasts are nothing more than forecasts. The actual winds will vary some from the forecast, although the forecast certainly gives us some idea of what to expect. The compass might have an error lesser or greater than the correction card shows. And, finally, you just might possibly make a mistake in your reckoning. Without checkpoints, you wouldn't be able to make the minor corrections needed to keep you on course.

You want to space your checkpoints about 10 to 15 miles apart where possible. Closer than that and you'll overcorrect; farther apart and you can get pretty far off course before doing something about it. Now, back to the wind vector diagram for a minute. The checkpoints will be used while you're at cruise speed, after the climb is completed, when your ground speed should be 115 knots. A moment spent now with your computer tells you that, at 115 knots, you'll travel 15 nautical miles in about 8 minutes.

Take the chart with your course line drawn on it, lay it out on a table or desk, and put your plotter along the route. Look for a landmark every 15 nautical miles or so, and at each one that you select, put a little line, at right angles to the course line. For example, the chart shows that if you are making good your intended ground track, you should have crossed the small village of Mulvane. When you do cross Mulvane, a railroad bridge across a river should be just off of the right wing. Make Mulvane your first checkpoint.

About 18 minutes out of Wichita, you should be approaching the northwest edge of Winfield, Kansas. Make Winfield your second checkpoint because it is easy to identify; the chart shows that there is a racetrack and an outdoor theater northwest of town. The several highways and railroad tracks that converge at Winfield also help to identify it from the air. Continuing on course, your next 15-nautical-mile checkpoint should be a prominent airport, Strother, about 5 miles ahead and to the right of your track.

Picking checkpoints is a matter of personal preference, and another pilot, flying the same trip, might pick different ones. Pick checkpoints that can easily be discerned while flying. Be careful of landmarks like bridges or mines that don't have another feature nearby to ensure that you're seeing what you think you are. Little villages all look alike from the air, so make sure that there is a way to differentiate the one you've selected as a checkpoint. As long as you pick points that you can identify, your points are appropriately spaced, and they keep you on course, choose your checkpoints as you see fit.

## Alternate Airport

Every now and then, you might have to divert from your intended destination and go somewhere else. This problem can be thrust upon a pilot because of deteriorating weather at the intended destination, a dwindling fuel supply, the closure of the airport where you intended to land due to some happening on the ground there, or for a host of other reasons. During your flight test for your license, the chances are very high that the examiner will ask you to demonstrate your ability to abandon your planned flight and proceed to an alternate airport.

Let's assume that the Wichita to Tulsa flight is your checkride and that the examiner suddenly tells you, 5 minutes after passing the third checkpoint, that the weather ahead makes it unwise for you to continue to Tulsa. Your first reaction might be, "OK, can we get back to Wichita?" But the examiner isn't about to make it that easy, so he says, "No, Wichita has just gone below VFR minimums."

Well, because you've been watching your checkpoints, and you know your ground speed, you have no trouble pinpointing your position on the chart. You should be about 8 or 9 miles beyond your last checkpoint, and quickly but carefully placing your plotter's straight edge along your course line, you measure that distance. That should put you over the curved highway that runs east from Arkansas City. Yes, it's up ahead there, where it should be.

Now, knowing where you are, the next step is to check the chart for nearby airport symbols. The closest one shows by the R beside its symbol that it is a privately owned, restricted-use airport that should be used without prior permission only in an emergency. But because you flew right by it without seeing it, it is probably a small sod strip and hard to find out here in the wide open midwest. The next closest public use airport is Strother, your last checkpoint. Strother is now about 5 miles behind and to the right of your current location.

You wisely choose Strother, point it out on the chart for the examiner to see, and turn right, toward it. Simultaneously, come back on the power to begin a normal descent. Even though you can't actually see the airport yet, you know exactly where it is relative to Arkansas City and Winfield. You look at the examiner and say, "We'll be there in about 4 minutes."

This example was easy because there was an airport immediately at hand to use as an alternate. This same scenario could occur over sparsely populated or mountainous terrain where the nearest airport might be much farther away. In that case, the only thing to do is to quickly draw a new course line to the alternate that you select as the new destination. But you'll have to estimate your new heading because it's impractical, in most lightplane cockpits, to draw a wind vector diagram in flight. If you have your pocket computer handy, as you should, and if the winds are significant, do the wind vector solution with the computer. Then, carefully follow the new course line with your finger on the chart until everything settles down, and you're sure that the new heading is taking you to the alternate airport. Doing this as the weather is going sour can be a daunting task.

That's why prudent and wise pilots always plan ahead of time for the possibility of needing to abandon the original plans and head to an alternate destination. If your originally planned flight is a long one, you might need to allow for more than one alternative, depending on where in the course of the trip the decision gets made to go to the alternate. Before you finish your preflight planning, look over your route of flight. Pick out several airports along the way that you could land at if needed. Because airports make wonderful checkpoints, picking them for this purpose also automatically gives you as many alternate fields as possible.

If deteriorating weather is the reason that you divert to an alternate field, the weather forecast was probably significantly in error; you would not have taken off if the prediction weren't for good VFR weather all along the route. When a forecast goes south, and they occasionally do, make sure that the alternate airport to which you're headed still has satisfactory weather conditions. Use your radio and call flight watch to get an update on the current weather and for what will probably be, by then, an amended forecast. It isn't very smart to head for an alternate field, only to have that route blocked by weather at some point.

A very vital part of your flight planning is to ensure that you *always* have enough fuel to carry out not only your planned flight but also a diversion to appropriate alternatives. A recipe for almost certain disaster is poor weather that necessitates diverting to an alternate airport, coupled with insufficient fuel to get there. That's why, when we look at the POH values given for the range of any lightplane, that mileage figure means little to a good pilot. The real range needed for a flight includes the distance to the planned destination plus the additional mileage to any alternate airports, plus a healthy reserve. POH range numbers assume a no-wind condition because the authors at the factory can't possibly anticipate what headwind or tailwind their airplanes will face on any given flight. Take these range numbers with a grain of salt.

Also, *never* trust fuel gauges in any airplane. They are there only as a matter of convenience and should never be counted on to be accurate, which they seldom are. You know, from the POH, the amount of fuel per hour that your airplane will burn at any given altitude and power setting combination, assuming that you properly lean the mixture. The only way to tell how much fuel you have left is by the clock. Always note your take-off time, and unless your loading dictates otherwise, always depart, even for a short flight, with full fuel tanks.

Always have a reserve supply of fuel available in case your planning goes awry. Some pilots are comfortable with 45 minutes of extra fuel, on top of the fuel estimated for the planned trip and the alternate(s). That may be all right in faster airplanes, when 45 minutes of flying time means well over 100 miles of distance covered. But my personal rule, in slower airplanes like our Cessna 150, is to have 1 full hour's reserve fuel at all times as a minimum; it is increased to $1\frac{1}{2}$ hours if my flight is over sparsely populated terrain or at night.

The Cessna 150 carries $22\frac{1}{2}$ gallons of usable fuel. Almost every airplane has some fuel in its tanks that cannot physically get to the engine. Therefore, the important number for you to know is your airplane's usable fuel; total capacity is not nearly so important. Our 150 burns slightly less than 6 gph at normal cruise power settings and altitudes. This is roughly a $3\frac{3}{4}$-hour supply. If you keep 1 hour in reserve, you've got about $2\frac{3}{4}$ hours of cruising time, which gives you approximately a 275-mile range in a no-wind condition.

That's about as long as most people want to sit in a small plane before a stop to stretch their legs. A stop every 2 to 3 hours is also helpful to give you a chance to get an update on the weather, if your trip is a long one. As we said before, running out of gas is unthinkable, so make sure that it doesn't happen to you.

# Radio Aids to Navigation

In the 1930s, the first radio aids to navigation were low-frequency-range stations that emitted only four course legs from the station. The four courses were basically configured so that the "highways in the sky" were each at right angles to the other. This was great if you only wanted to go north, south, east, or west from the station or if you were inbound from one of these cardinal positions. This system didn't work well if you were anywhere else or wanted to go in a different direction from the four courses that emanated from the station. Also, low-frequency radio signals are very susceptible to inference in bad weather, when you need electronic navigation the most.

By the 1950s, the low-frequency system was replaced by very-high-frequency (VHF) omnidirectional range stations, called *VOR* stations. Some people have referred to the VOR system as omni, but the correct term is VOR, and using the right nomenclature denotes a well-schooled pilot.

VOR has gained worldwide acceptance, but it is now in its waning days. A subsequent subsection of this chapter will examine the *global positioning system* (GPS), which will almost surely become the way that things are done in the future. But for now, VOR is still the system used by most VFR pilots and is the one upon which the entire airway system is based. VOR is also the system upon which you'll be tested in the knowledge test that you have to pass before you can take the flight test for your private license.

The full name of the VOR suggests that it is omnidirectional. This means that the stations send out radio signals in all directions so that you can navigate directly to or from a station from anywhere or to anywhere, as long as you are within reception range of the station. Because VORs transmit in the VHF band, the reception range is not very far. VHF signals travel from the station in what is know as "line of sight," as do television and FM radio waves. The radio energy is transmitted from the station's antenna in a straight line, and it does not follow the curvature of the earth, nor does it reflect off of the upper layers of the atmosphere as do lower-frequency radio waves. That's why, on a good day or night, you might pick up an AM radio station hundreds of miles away because it operates in the lower-frequency spectrum, but your TV reception is hardly ever any good beyond 60 to 75 miles from the transmitter antenna.

VOR signals can be received from a little farther out than you would think from drawing an analogy to TV, but that is because we are receiving them in aircraft, which are flying above the ground, where the line of sight signals can still be heard. It's the same principle that enables you to see farther from the top of a hill than you can on flat land. Still, most lightplane VOR receivers don't pick up a signal clear enough for navigation much farther out from the station than about 100 miles, and it's even less if you're flying at the lower altitudes. So, there are many VOR stations in the system to provide adequate coverage throughout the country.

The VOR receiver in your airplane has three main components: a *course selector* or *omni bearing selector* (OBS), a *course deviation indicator* (CDI), and a *TO-FROM indicator* (FIG. 9-10).

Operating a VOR can seem intimidating at first, but it really is easy, and with only a little practice, you'll get the hang of it very quickly. First, let's go into some more basics about how it works. The station transmits its signals out, away from the transmitter antenna. The actual station is large enough to be

**9-10** *A VOR receiver can lead you directly to your destination.
Important parts of a receiver are: course selector knob (A),
omnibearing selector (B), course deviation indicator (C), TO-FROM
flag (D), and receiver tuner display (E). The tuner display for the
communications side of the radio is shown as (V).*

seen from the air as you pass over one. It is shaped like an
inverted cone, large end down and pointed end up; all of them
are painted white.

The signals radiate from the station in the pattern of a
spoked wheel. The spokes of the wheel are called *radials.*
Imagine yourself standing directly at the hub of the wheel, facing north. The spoke that runs north, outward from the hub, is
the 360, or 0°, radial. The one running from the hub outbound
to your right is the 090° radial because it's going due east. The
one running outbound on your left is going due west, so it is
the 270° radial. Naturally, the one running outward from the
hub, directly behind you, is going due south, so it is the 180°
radial. From your nose, all of the way around to your nose
again, there are 360° in the circle, and the VOR station emits
360 radials. This way, you can navigate on a radial outbound
from the station in any direction you wish. You can also navigate inbound to a station from anywhere as long as you are in
reception range.

Similar to highways on the ground that have either names or
route numbers, we have a system for labeling VOR radials.
They are labeled according to the magnetic course of the radial
*outbound* from the station. So, from your position at the center
of the station, you would navigate in an easterly direction by

following the 090° radial outbound from the station. If you were, at a different time, standing on the rim of the wheel, on the east side of it, and wanted to navigate toward the station, you'd need to go due west to get there. In that instance, you'd be flying inbound to the station but still tracking the 090° radial, just inbound on a heading of 270°. In this latter example, 090° has nothing to do with the direction you'll fly to get from the rim of the wheel to the center of the station; that's just the label of the radial that you'll follow. Now, let's get back to operating the system in an airplane.

The course selector, or OBS, is a circular dial that you rotate to set the direction that you want to track, either inbound toward the station or outbound away from it. You *don't* have to worry about the radial labels when setting the OBS. If you're east of the station and want to fly toward it, you know that you'd head 270° to go west. Just set the OBS to 270°.

The CDI is a vertical needle, usually hinged at the top, that swings either right or left to show your deviation from the course that you have set into the OBS.

The TO-FROM indicator is sometimes in a little window on the instrument face and is usually a little flip-flop device that either shows TO or FROM as its display. If it isn't steadily indicating either TO or FROM, you're beyond the reception range of the station that you're trying to use. When it comes to life, it is telling you whether the course that you have selected on the OBS will take you to or from the station from your present position.

Here's the part that is difficult for some people to initially conceptualize—the VOR system senses only your position *from* the station. The radio receiver in the panel of the airplane has no idea in which direction you're actually flying. All that it can do is to tell you two things. First, it will tell you whether the course set in the OBS will take you toward or away from the station. Second, it will display the position of the airplane, relative to the selected course. That is done by the CDI indications, which will be that you are exactly on the course when the CDI needle is centered or off to the left or right of it when the needle is deflected.

Let's take an example and actually plan a flight using VOR to navigate. To make it even simpler, let's plan the same flight from Wichita to Tulsa as before, using VOR this time. Look at the chart and note that the Wichita VOR is about 5 miles northwest of Wichita Mid-Continent Airport. VOR stations are depicted on the chart by means of a blue dot inside of a hexagon and surrounded by a compass rose.

Actually, the Wichita VOR is a *VORTAC*, which is indicated by the three blue "legs" on the hexagon. Although the terms *VOR* and *VORTAC* are often used interchangeably, a VORTAC also provides signals for *distance measuring equipment* (DME) and for tactical military navigation. You can get a DME receiver to go along with your VOR unit. The DME will then display the distance from your position to the station, expressed in nautical miles. Most DME units can also automatically calculate and display your ground speed and the time needed to fly to the station. The DME sends out a signal that is received by the VORTAC station, and then it is retransmitted to your airplane. The DME unit in the airplanes notes the time that it took for the signal to make the round trip and calculates the distance involved. From successive such calculations, it can then figure ground speed and the time needed to fly to the station.

Along with the station symbol on the chart is a blue box that explains the station's radio frequency and its Morse code identifier. In this case, the blue box is at the bottom of the compass rose and says WICHITA, 113.8 CH 85 ICT, followed by the Morse code for ICT.

This information means that the VOR radio frequency is 113.8 MHz; you'll tune your VOR receiver to that frequency to receive that VOR. A military pilot would tune the TACAN receiver in a military airplane to channel 85 to use the station's tactical navigation capability. The identifier for the station, always composed of three letters, is ICT, followed by the Morse code for those letters. Modern VOR receivers have digital tuning, just like modern AM or FM radios do. In former days, when we had to use a variable tuner, like the dial tuner on an old broadcast radio, you would have to listen carefully for the Morse code identifier to make sure which station was tuned in. Although it's still good practice to turn up the volume and confirm that you have the right station, few pilots bother anymore. Most would just put 113.8 into the digital tuner and assume that they have ICT tuned. Always be a pro, and confirm the correct station by listening for the identifier. Frequencies do get changed periodically, and if you have an old chart (another no-no), you may not have tuned in the right station.

Now, draw a course line from the Wichita VOR to the Tulsa VOR. It closely follows the course line previously drawn between the two airports. Near Tulsa, the new route is about 4 miles east of the track drawn for the flight without radio aids

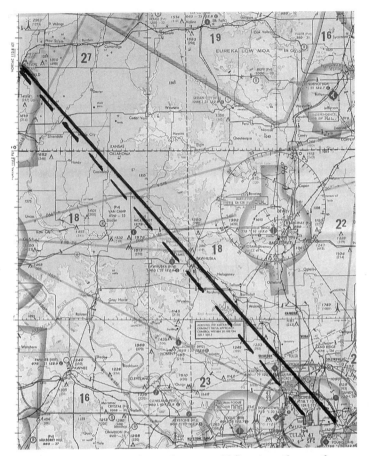

**9-11**  *The dashed line is the track you would fly using pilotage; the solid line is the track to the Tulsa VOR. VORs aren't always located this close to your destination.*

(FIG. 9-11). The course line drawn between the two VOR stations emerges from the printed compass rose around the Wichita VOR at about 130°. Because the compass rose is already corrected for variation at every station's location, 130° is the magnetic course to fly.

Before takeoff from Wichita, tune your VOR receiver to 113.8. Listen for the identifier and then dial 130° into the OBS. Right after takeoff, you'll be headed southeast but somewhat to the north. The CDI needle will be off center to the right. That is telling you that the selected course (130°) lies to the right of your present position. Your goal is to intercept that radial and then fly on it, outbound from the station. To make the interception, turn the airplane about 30° to the right, to a heading of 160°. In few moments, the CDI needle will start creeping toward the center. As it centers, you've intercepted the 130° radial, so take out the intercept angle, and turn back to 130° as your heading. That's it; you've just intercepted a VOR radial.

Now, fly straight on a heading of 130°, and watch the CDI needle to see if there are any needed corrections. If it drifts to the left, your radial is off to your left, and you need to correct slightly to the left to intercept it again and track it. The same goes if the needle drifts to the right, except that you obviously correct to the right. As long as you keep the needle centered, you're tracking the 130° radial outbound from Wichita, heading straight for Tulsa. The TO-FROM window will be reading FROM because, from your present position, flying along the 130° radial will take you from Wichita.

If there is a crosswind present, you'll find that holding a heading of 130° on the DG or magnetic compass won't keep the needle centered because you'll be blown off course by the wind. Just observe the needle, and you'll find that it might take a compass heading of 5 to 10° apart from the 130° to keep the needle centered. Guess what? The VOR has just done your wind correction for you; the difference between your compass heading and 130° is the wind correction angle that needs to be applied to track 130° over the ground (discounting any deviation in the compass).

When tracking either toward or from a station, as long as the TO-FROM indicator corresponds with your direction to or from a station, just make course corrections toward the CDI needle to keep it centered. You should verify proper sensing by checking to see the heading in which you're actually flying and the course dialed into the OBS are within 90° of each other. The pros take small cuts at the correction angle. If your needle is off to the right, you don't just turn circles to the right because, if you do, you'll just orbit out there, off course. What you do is to turn slightly toward the needle. How much you turn and what degree of intercept angle that you establish depend on how far the needle is deflected from center, how close you are to the station, and how strong the wind is. Set up your correction angle and hold the new heading until you see what happens to the needle next. If it starts coming back to the center, you're intercepting the course and you have only to remove some of the correction angle as the needle centers.

If the needle doesn't move at all after you've turned toward it, you're just paralleling the course, and you need a little bit more cut into the course to intercept it. If the needle continues to deflect away from center, you need even more correction to stop the deviation and get back on course.

Because the radials of a VOR go out from the station like the spokes of a wheel, the radials are very close together near the station and very far apart when you are so far from the station that you're at the limit of reception range. In close, the needle gets very sensitive and the correction angles need to be smaller. The results of a correction applied when only 10 miles from the station are a lot more dramatic than they are when you're 40 or 50 miles away.

As your flight progresses, and when you're about halfway to Tulsa, look again at the chart and you'll see that the frequency for the Tulsa VOR is 114.4 MHz. So, switch the receiver to 114.4, and listen for the Morse code identifier to confirm that you've tuned in the right station. The TO-FROM indicator will flop over to TO, and you're now tracking inbound to Tulsa. If you're on course, the needle stays centered.

In practice, there is no need to fly all of the way to the Tulsa VOR itself. Your chart shows that the station is about 4 or 5 miles due east of the Tulsa International Airport, so you call Tulsa Approach Control when you get within 20 miles of the airport. They'll probably give you a suggested heading or two, as the controller sees your position and ground track on the radar. The controller will suggest headings that will both steer you toward the airport and put you into the flow of traffic coming into this busy, airline airport.

VORs can do other things beside allow you to fly from one station to the next. Assume that you are unsure of your position after you've been doing a lot of practice maneuvers and haven't been paying attention, like you should have been, to exactly where you are. Most pilots never get *lost*; they are only unsure of their positions from time to time. If you fall for that prevarication, you're a good prospect for a bridge salesman. In any event, you can use your VOR receiver to pinpoint your location in short order. Tune a nearby station, and just twist the OBS slowly until the needle centers, and the TO-FROM indicator shows FROM. Note what radial the OBS says, and draw a line on your chart from the station that you've tuned, outbound from the station. You are somewhere along this radial.

Then, pick another station on the chart that is located well off to one side of the first *line of position* that you just drew. Make sure that the second station is close enough to receive it at your altitude; if it is not, climb to a higher altitude to increase your reception range. Repeat the process of determining which radial you are on from the second station. Draw that line of position on your chart, and where the two lines intersect is where you are.

# ADF

Another radio navigation receiver is the *automatic direction finder* (ADF). The ADF doesn't actually find any directions, but it enables the pilot to use it to home directly in on virtually any low-frequency transmitter. *Nondirectional beacons* (NDBs) send out a signal that the airplane's ADF can receive.

The station is called "nondirectional" because it does not send out any kind of discreet or directional signal as does a VOR. The signal from the NDB is uniform throughout its compass rose. The ADF receiver in the airplane is composed of two parts: receiver and display head. Sometimes the display head is mounted in the same box as the receiver, but they are usually separate. This display head is circular and shows the points of a compass around it, usually in increments of 10 or 20°. A needle pivots in the center of the display and rotates to point to a direction: 360, 090, 180°, and the like.

When tuned to a station, the ADF needle points to where the station is located in relation to the nose of the airplane. So, if the needle says 360°, the station is directly in front of you. It if displays 270°, the station is abeam the left wing, and so on around the circle. Advanced maneuvering and trigonometry calculations are required to determine a distance from an ADF station, and no one does this anymore; it's not even on the knowledge test for an airline transport pilot certificate these days.

At first blush, it might seem easy to just fly directly to an NDB by putting the station on your nose. But, the NDB doesn't send out directional signals that automatically compensate for wind drift like VOR radials do. So, when you home into an NDB station, you have to learn how to determine and then apply your own wind correction. Most private pilot courses don't even include instruction on the use of an ADF, leaving that subject until a pilot advances to training for the instrument rating.

The beauty of the ADF is that it will tune in on and show the direction to any low-frequency station, including not only aeronautical NDBs but also marine radio beacons and all commercial AM radio stations as well. Also, because the low-frequency radio is not line-of-sight like the VHF band is in which VORs operate, the ADF's range is sometimes hundreds of miles, limited only by the power of the transmitter and atmospheric conditions.

The bad side of ADF is that low-frequency radio transmissions are susceptible to interference from many sources. When there is any thunderstorm activity anywhere near your flight path, the ADF might go nuts, and the needle might swing wildly because those thunderstorms emit tremendous amounts of electromagnetic energy in the form of lightning. The main reason that ADF has stayed around so long in the United States is that the transmitters and receivers are relatively inexpensive, as radio aids to navigation go. The NDBs around the country primarily exist to allow smaller airports to have at least a rudimentary instrument approach for IFR traffic flying into them. An IFR approach is necessary for an airport to handle IFR flights if the weather is below VFR minimums.

In some parts of the world, particularly in South America and northwestern Canada, large and powerful NDBs are the foundation of the airway systems in use. VOR stations have to be close together to make up an airway, and in these remote parts of the world, it's just too difficult and expensive to install and maintain them.

# Global Positioning System

The GPS is taking the general aviation industry by storm, quickly becoming the popular form of navigation. The FAA has proposed a loose timetable to begin eliminating VOR stations and to switch the entire system over to a GPS-based navigational system around 2004. FAA timetables for many improvements over the years have been very optimistic, and this one may be also. But regardless of exactly when it will happen, GPS is certainly the navigation device of the future.

GPS is a system that is based upon a network of 24 earth satellites. Each one transmits a radio signal that is received and processed by a GPS receiver, whether that receiver is mounted in the panel of an airplane, in a pilot's lap, on a boat, in a car, or held in a hiker's hand out in the woods. The entire idea began as a military navigational system that would free military aircraft from any dependence upon ground-based transmitters.

In times of armed conflict, transmitters on the ground are vulnerable and are certainly attractive targets for an enemy to eliminate. In these days of United States interests around the world and possible military action related to those interests, our combat aircraft, ships, tanks, and even foot soldiers often operate in remote areas where there is no ground-based radio navigation system at all. Even though military aircraft are often equipped with inertial navigation systems that do not depend on any outside references to operate, they are not the total or best answer.

So, the military developed GPS to serve its needs well into the next millennium. GPS can also be used by modern, lightweight receivers now being made for a multitude of civilian applications, including aviation. In the military application, GPS is fantastically accurate, allowing a fighter to put a bomb right in the front door of a building. For civilian use, the system is desensitized somewhat, but it is clearly more sensitive and accurate than anything else that we've had.

GPS operates by triangulating the signals received from the satellites. Because the source of the electronic data that the receiver processes is coming from space, several benefits follow. First, GPS is truly global. It works everywhere, from Antarctica to over New York City, over the middle of the Pacific, or the middle of Kansas. It is dependent on nothing on the ground. GPS can also determine an aircraft's altitude because it measures the distance from the satellite. We now have the best backup method for determining altitude, totally independent of the airplane's pressure altimeter and pitot/static system.

While in flight, the GPS unit is not difficult to use. But because it can display so much data, you will have to put some time into practicing with it to become completely at ease with this new system. Tell the unit to find its present position, and in a few seconds you'll know where you are to within a few meters' tolerance. It can be quickly programmed to take you from that position to anywhere on the globe that you want to go, and it will compute the most efficient routing to get there.

While you are en route, the GPS receiver will display your track, ground speed, and time to go until you get where you've told it to take you. The first aviation units depended upon the pilot's inputting the latitude/longitude coordinates of destinations, points of departure, and any points along the way that the pilot wanted identified. Now, most all of the GPS receivers on the market, even those designed to be portable and held in your hands, come with a database. This database can include every airport in the United States, all of the VORs, all NDBs, and about everything else you'd ever want to find. Just let the unit have a few seconds to access the satellites, figure its present position, and it's ready to go. In a flash you can input the identifier of the place you want to go, and the GPS receiver will tell you in what direction to head, how far it is, and how long it will take to get there.

Many of the units now on the market have a moving map display, which puts a little airplane symbol as the cursor on a screen. You then watch the symbol move as you fly along. The database often includes major landmarks such as highways, towns, bodies of water, airports, and other things of a purely aeronautical nature. Some are so full of data that you can call up the scale of the ground display and use them to deliver pizzas.

The more expensive units, designed to be mounted in the airplane's panel, have updatable memory so that the unit can display radio frequencies of nearby airports, FSSs, and ATC facilities. Almost all of them, panel-mounted or handheld, have a feature to quickly call up the nearest airports, in case you need to land in an emergency. If you have an updatable unit, you just order the data card from the manufacturer every so often, plug it into the GPS set, and presto, everything you would ever want to know is a push button away, and the information is current. Just order the card or cards that cover the geographical areas in which you fly, from the central United States to Siberia.

Since the 1950s, aviation radios have been made in a combination called *navcom,* which simply means that a communications radio and navigation receiver are both physically contained within the same black box. This enables the pilot to navigate on the VOR side of the set, while independently being able to use the communications side to talk to someone. Since their inception, navcoms have been combined communications and VOR radios. Now manufacturers are offering navcoms that put together, in one box, the typical communications radio with a GPS receiver, at no really greater cost than before.

GPS will completely replace the VOR system in the near future. The VOR transmitters are aging, and they are becoming increasingly costly to either maintain or replace. Hordes of FAA technicians are required to constantly fix and check them. The FAA must buy the sites upon which VOR stations are put and then spend millions to keep them running. Now a satellite system is in place, paid for by the military and which it will continue to maintain. Civilians, and not only aviators, can get in on the act without all of the costs of the VOR network.

When this replacement comes, we'll have an uncanny and amazing ability to navigate at will across the country. The IFR system will be freed from fixed airways, making direct routing between airports the way to go, saving the time and expense of flying between VOR stations. GPS will additionally allow virtually any airport with acceptable terrain and obstacle clearance properties to have an IFR approach, all free from ground-based radio equipment. You can get in on most of these advantages right now. For about $500, you can buy a handheld unit that has so much capability that as a private pilot you may never tap into it all. Buck Rogers has arrived.

## Airspace Classifications

Progress has always had its price, and sometimes, we don't all agree on what constitutes progress. Up until the late 1920s, pilots flew where, when, and how they felt like it, in whatever weather they were willing to brave and in whatever machine they trusted to leave terra firma. Then, as flying became more popular and accepted, the federal government decided to begin regulating it. First came the licensing of pilots, then the certification of airplanes, and after all of that, the regulation of airlines.

Early in their existence, the airlines recognized that if something weren't done, someday two airplanes might come together in the air with the predictable disastrous result. So the airlines themselves got together and created the first air traffic control system, which had jurisdiction over only the flights of the various airlines that voluntarily cooperated in it.

Everyone else flew at will, but because the totality of aviation was still minuscule, little went wrong. As the airlines grew, they eventually turned over their air traffic controllers and their system to the government, which has operated ATC ever since.

To make a system work that kept airplanes, particularly those flying in the clouds, from running into each other, the government devised the notion that the airspace ought to be

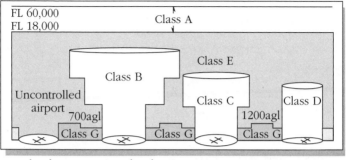

*msl - above mean sea level
agl - above ground level

**9-12** *Airspace classifications in the United States.*

broken up into different blocks, where different rules and procedures would be in force. VFR pilots can identify the various blocks, or classifications, of airspace in which they fly by looking at the same aeronautical charts used for planning and plotting a flight.

In 1993, the entire American system of airspace classification was altered to comply with the classifications used internationally. This system is easier to learn than what we previously had to learn. Descriptive names of the different classes of airspace are gone, replaced now with letter designations of A, B, C, D, E, and G. There is no F in the United States. Let's get into it, and summarize the various classes. First, take a good look at FIG. 9-12.

Class A airspace is that airspace between 18,000 and 60,000 feet (FL180 through FL600). This is where the big guys fly: airliners, turboprops, business jets, and occasionally turbocharged piston engine airplanes. Everything operating in Class A airspace must be under IFR, and there are certain aircraft equipment requirements for flying up there. As a lightplane pilot, this class of airspace, and its operational rules, are of academic interest at most.

Class B airspace is the area around many large city airports where most of the air traffic is airliners. Class B is positively controlled by ATC at all times, and you cannot enter without a clearance from the controller. Many small planes operate in Class B airspace, either going completely through from one side to the other, going to a satellite airport still within the circle of coverage of the Class B airspace, or even taking off from or landing at the major airport at the center of the area. The requirements for operating in Class B include a two-way radio, a transponder, and a device called an *altitude encoder,* which displays the airplane's altitude right on the controller's radar screen.

Access to Class B by a student pilot is highly restricted, but it is wide open to all pilots who hold a private certificate or higher, as long as their aircraft have the required equipment. With more Boeing and McDonnell-Douglas heavies to watch for than they sometimes have the time or personnel for, the controllers just can't have student pilots in there, solo, mixing it up and requiring special handling.

Class C airspace is that area surrounding busier airports that are not quite as large or that don't have enough traffic to justify the restrictions inherent in a Class B designation. Class C also requires a two-way radio, a transponder, and an altitude encoder. The idea of Class C is to identify all traffic within it and to let the controller know what's going on without the aircraft actually being controlled. The controllers must be contacted by every aircraft prior to their entry in the Class C, and entry can be denied if controller workload or any other reason justifies keeping traffic out. When this happens, it's usually for just a few minutes, until a particular burst of traffic is handled, and then the Class C is opened again for new arrivals. Although there is a regulatory difference between Classes B and C, in practice, operations within the two are very similar. In Class B, you must have a clearance; in Class C, you only have to communicate with the controller prior to entering. Student pilots have the same rights as everyone else to fly in Class C, and in fact, quiet a few large flight schools are located at airports within Class C airspace.

Both Class B and Class C airspace have a vertical limit. In most cases, this is around 8,000 feet or so, but it varies according to the primary airport's elevation above sea level and local ATC requirements. So it is possible to overfly Class B and C airspace, but it is mostly impractical to do so in lightplanes.

Class D airspace surrounds an airport that has a control tower and that primarily serves general aviation traffic. Unless prior arrangements are made with ATC, you have to have a two-way radio to be able to talk with the tower to enter Class D. You are not required to have a transponder or altitude encoder unless the airport lies within a 30-mile radius of a Class B airport.

Class D airspace is usually a cylinder-shaped space, about 5 miles in radius from the airport and up to 2,500 feet above it. It is legal and practical to fly over Class D airspace. This class exists for airports that are busy enough to merit a tower to control the local traffic that is taxiing, taking off, approaching to land, and landing but have no reason to limit overflight as long as you're higher than 2,500 feet above the ground level. Check the elevation of the airport on the chart if you want to overfly a Class D— you've got to be more than 2,500 feet AGL, not 2,500 on the altimeter, which would be the altitude above mean sea level.

Class E airspace is virtually all of the other airspace. Class E starts at either 700 or 1,200 feet AGL, depending on the local requirements of the abutting airspace. In Class E, the requirement for day VFR flight is 3 statute miles of visibility, except above 10,000 feet MSL, where it goes to 5 statute miles. You have to be at least 500 feet below, 1,000 feet above, and 2,000 feet horizontally from clouds. Above 10,000 feet MSL, the cloud clearance requirements increase to 1,000 feet below, 1,000 feet above, and 1 statute mile horizontally. While in Class E, you are not required to be talking to any controller and seldom will be when flying VFR. Of course, all of that changes when you're instrument rated and flying IFR. Most of your cross-country flying between airports will occur in Class E airspace.

Class G airspace is not traversed often because most of it only goes up to either 700 or 1,200 feet AGL. This volume of space is about as free as it gets. The VFR visibility requirement is only 1 statute mile, and you are only required to stay clear of clouds, with no minimum distances involved. Above 1,200 feet, cloud separation minimums apply.

Unfortunately, many private pilots promptly forget about the airspace classifications after passing the flight test and just avoid Classes B and C. Some won't even operate into Class D, where there are control towers, preferring instead to fly around what they think is a hassle. Communicating with controllers is not difficult or intimidating after the first few times. Too many private pilots go too far out of their way to avoid that small imposition and, in so doing, waste thousands of gallons of fuel and hours of time each year.

You will have to know the airspace rules to pass both your knowledge and practical tests. It's just not that hard to retain and use that knowledge. If you do, your trips will be more efficient, and the services that the system provides, primarily in aircraft separation, will also enhance your safety.

There are other types of airspace that still carry descriptive names: *special use airspace, prohibited areas, restricted areas,* and *military operations areas* (MOAs). These will be covered in detail in your ground school or home study course, but they are actually pretty simple to explain.

Prohibited areas are just that; you can't fly there, period. They rarely exist, and where they do, they are around someplace where it would be very dangerous to fly, like a gunnery range, or they surround very sensitive government facilities such as the White House, Camp David, and the Capitol.

Restricted areas are areas of airspace to which pilots are denied access at certain times and at certain altitudes. These are often military aviation test sites, military parachuting areas, part-time gunnery ranges, and the like. Danger lurks within the restricted airspace when it is active. When the restricted area is "cold," which means at times other than when active, and outside of the restricted altitudes, there is no restriction to flight operations.

MOAs are not restricted areas, and you may fly through them if you wish. These areas exist where there is intense military flight activity. Fighter pilots training in air-to-air combat or low-level, high-speed operations, and similar military maneuvers, and other military pilots can't be vigilant for a Cessna or Piper popping up in their canopies. These military airplanes are often operating at near supersonic speeds. Because so much military flying is concentrated today at the lower levels, don't think that it's safer to try to sneak through an MOA at low altitude—often that's where the MOA traffic is most intense. Be extremely alert and watchful if you traverse an MOA; stay on your toes and keep your head on a swivel. Avoidance is probably the better option.

# Air-to-Ground Communications

Before you start talking over the radio, you need to learn the phonetic alphabet used in aviation. This alphabet ensures clarity in communications and avoids misunderstandings. These words are used whenever a letter normally would be, such as in the identification number of your airplane. For instance, if the airplane registration number is N4517C, you would say "Cessna four-five-one-seven Charlie," not "forty-five seventeen cee." All airplanes of United States registration have a number that begins with the letter N. In practice, the N is omitted, and it's assumed that you're flying an airplane of U.S. registry. One number, nine, is pronounced as "niner" over the radio; all of the others are said normally. The international phonetic alphabet is easily learned with practice or regular usage.

| | | | | | |
|---|---|---|---|---|---|
| A | Alpha | J | Juliet | S | Sierra |
| B | Bravo | K | Kilo | T | Tango |
| C | Charlie | L | Lima | U | Uniform |
| D | Delta | M | Mike | V | Victor |
| E | Echo | N | November | W | Whiskey |
| F | Foxtrot | O | Oscar | X | X-ray |
| G | Golf | P | Papa | Y | Yankee |
| H | Hotel | Q | Quebec | Z | Zulu |
| I | India | R | Romeo | | |

# Tower Talk

Now that you've progressed this far through this book, you are familiar with most of the terminology that is used during radio communications with air traffic control facilities (FIG. 9-13). As a private pilot, you will primarily talk to three parts of the ATC system: ground control, tower, and approach/ departure control. Air route traffic control centers (ARTCCs) normally deal with en route IFR traffic. Occasionally you might have reason to call an ARTCC, but not very often, until you get your instrument rating. The FSS network is not part of the control function of ATC, but, naturally, you'll deal with and talk to FSSs quite a bit. Let's use an example of some typical talk back and forth with some controllers to see how it works in practice.

**9-13** *The tower of a controlled airport handles aircraft movements on the ground at the airport and in the air in the vicinity of the airport. Be sure to visit a control tower before you complete your training.*

For the flight that we planned from Wichita to Tulsa, the first controller with whom we'll talk is Wichita ground control. After starting the engine, but *before* moving the airplane, we'll call on 121.7 MHz, one of the standard ground control frequencies, and the conversation will go like this:

**Us** "Wichita Ground, Cessna four-five-one-seven Charlie, at Yingling hangar, ready to taxi, VFR to Tulsa, student pilot."

Whenever you first initiate communication with a controller for the first time, remember that there are four Ws to state:

- Whom you are talking to (Wichita ground control)
- Who you are (Cessna four-five-one-seven Charlie)
- Where you are (Yingling hangar)
- What you want to do (Ready for taxi, going VFR to Tulsa)

This is also a good time to let the controller know that you are a student pilot by ending your first transmission with the words "student pilot." You'll be surprised how that will simplify things for you in the beginning.

Remember the four Ws, and that is all there is to starting the conversation. The response from the controller will have important information and instructions:

**Ground control** "Cessna one-seven Charlie, taxi to runway three five. Wind, three six zero° at seven. Altimeter, two niner niner seven. Hold short of the runway."

First, the controller referred to us by the last three numbers or letters of the airplane's number; from here on out, with *that controller only,* we may also abbreviate the number the same way. She told us to taxi to runway 35; runways are always numbered by the first two digits of the runway's magnetic direction, so runway 35 points toward 350°, which is almost due north. The wind is blowing from 360°, which is out of the north, at 7 knots. Our takeoff will have virtually a straight headwind, only 10° off of the nose of the airplane. The barometric pressure, and therefore the altimeter setting, is 29.97.

Lastly, we were told to hold short of the runway, which means that we are to taxi up to it but not go on the runway. She might have had other instructions. Perhaps we might have been told to hold at various points on the airport until cleared to proceed. That frequently happens if a taxi route will take you across other taxiways or runway intersections. Sometimes a controller might tell you to give way to another taxiing airplane. If the controller recognizes your call sign as an airplane based on the field, you might not be given the frequency for the control tower, as ours didn't. If there is any doubt, don't ever hesitate to ask for it.

Whenever you don't understand the ATC's instructions, use the phrase "say again" to request a repeat. This is a common occurrence because some radios are hard to hear, another aircraft might have transmitted at the same time, blocking the controller's transmission, or maybe you just didn't catch it. Again, don't be bashful; even the pros often use "say again."

When you fully understand the controller's comments, your response is straightforward:

**Us**   "Roger, one seven Charlie."

"Roger" is used today to indicate that you've heard and understood what you're supposed to do. You might hear a pilot say "Wilco" instead, which is an abbreviation for "will comply." That's old military terminology and is incorrect in civilian aviation.

We'll taxi to the runway. If you don't know how to get there, ask for a "progressive taxi," which means that you need directions to the runway. Don't hesitate to ask because the controller has no way to know if you know the airport's taxiway layout. If you don't ask, she'll assume that you know where to go and how to get there.

When you've arrived at the runway, you are *not permitted* to get onto the runway itself yet. First, do all of your pretakeoff engine and cockpit checks that we did in our first flight and that your instructor will teach you, using the airplane's checklist. When the checklist is complete, we're ready for takeoff.

Switch the communications radio to the frequency for the control tower, which is 118.2 MHz at Wichita. Listen for a few seconds before transmitting to make sure that you won't block out the controller or another pilot. Then press the mike key and say:

**Us**   "Wichita Tower, Cessna four-five-one-seven Charlie, at runway three five, ready for takeoff." (Remember the four Ws.)

**Tower**   "Cessna one seven Charlie, cleared for takeoff."

That is all there is to it. We're now cleared to taxi onto the runway and take off. Unless the controller tells you to do sometime different, she'll assume that you'll do a normal takeoff, exit the traffic pattern normally, and then proceed on your course to Tulsa. Because Wichita is in Class C airspace, she will probably tell us to contact Wichita departure so that we can be separated from other traffic within the Class C area by a radar controller.

The departure controller will be called by us when the tower tells us to switch to departure. We'll tell that controller who we are, that we've just taken off, and that we're going VFR to Tulsa. We will be told of any traffic that the departure controller sees on the radar scope that might pose a hazard to us. Even though we're talking to a radar controller, we still have the responsibility to look out of the cockpit for other traffic.

Remember to always listen on each new frequency for a few seconds before transmitting; there is only one frequency available to all of the people who want to talk to a particular controller, and it can be a busy party line. Don't block a transmission already in progress. Hold the microphone so that it almost touches your upper lip but doesn't. If you're wearing a headset, adjust the mike on it to the same place. Also, don't yell into the mike; it will pick up your voice properly at a normal speaking volume.

By and large, controllers are nice folks, many of whom are pilots themselves. They do a tremendously complex job very competently. They don't have time for idle chatter, but never hesitate to ask for elaboration if you don't understand the instructions. That's why it's a good idea to identify yourself as a student pilot on each initial call-up to a new facility; then the controller can take more time with you from the outset and perhaps avoid either confusion on your part or the need to repeat instructions. The goal of both the pilot and the controller is to communicate effectively and clearly, so everyone understands, with as few words as are needed and as little frequency time tied up as is practical. This goal will be met if you let ATC know that you are a student pilot.

At some point in your training, you should personally visit a control tower before you take your private pilot flight test. Controllers welcome such opportunities for pilots to see their side of the fence. Telephone the tower office and schedule a visit, or as you taxi in from a flight, ask the ground controller if you can come up. Don't be insulted if the controller begs off a visit at that time because if it is a busy period in their workload, they might not be able to be interrupted. Nighttime is usually a good time to visit most towers, when fewer airplanes are in the area and the controllers can spend some personal time with you, explaining and showing you how the tower works and what is done by the various people in it.

Back to our flight. Notice that Tulsa is also a Class C airspace, and that means that we must contact and establish communications with Tulsa approach control *before* entering the Class C area. So, monitor your flight progress and about 5 to 10 miles before reaching the boundary of the Class C, call up as follows:

**Us** "Tulsa approach, Cessna four-five-one-seven Charlie, twenty-five north, landing Tulsa."

Again, you've followed the four Ws of radio communication by addressing Tulsa approach control, telling the controller who you are, where you are, and what you want to do.

The approach controller will then acknowledge us, probably tell us what runway to expect to land on at Tulsa, and perhaps start giving us headings to fly and altitudes to maintain. His job is to sequence arrivals in the Class C airspace so that each airplane gets into the proper traffic pattern or gets established on the proper approach to the runway(s) in use and avoids excess maneuvering when close to the airport. In addition, he'll give us traffic advisories of other aircraft that he sees on the radar scope that might present a hazard to us if they weren't pointed out, and if we didn't see them. Don't forget that we're always responsible to look for and avoid other traffic—don't depend on the controller to do it for you. When you're given a traffic advisory, tell the controller whether you see the other airplane; when you do see the other airplane and report the sighting, the controller transfers the responsibility to remain clear of that traffic to you.

Within the last few miles, the approach controller will tell us when to contact Tulsa tower and the frequency to use. Again, we'll use the four Ws to call the tower, telling the controller who we are, where we are, and what we want to do, which is to land.

After the tower clears us to land, we'll land on the runway that we're told to use. As we roll out after landing, the tower controller will tell us where to turn off of the runway and then to contact ground control and will give us the frequency.

Following those instructions, we'll roll out and turn off of the runway.

Only after we're clear of the runway and on a taxiway will we slow to a stop and contact ground control. If you're at a strange airport, you might not know precisely where you want to go at the airport. If you want to go to a parking place, tell the controller that you want to taxi to "transient parking." If the airport serves both airline and general aviation users, say that you want to go to "general aviation transient parking." If you do know the name of the FBO where you want to park, use that name as the last W—where you want to go.

And don't be bashful about requesting a progressive taxi; you don't want to taxi along the wrong routes or end up at the wrong place. Worse yet, you don't want to taxi onto a runway or conflict with other airplanes' taxiing. Especially at night, an airport can resemble a meaningless sea of blue, white, red, and green lights on the ground. The controller would always much rather help you with a progressive taxi than to have you aimlessly wandering around.

## Light Signals

What happens if the radio fails while you're talking to a controller at a towered airport? Every tower still has a signaling device called a "light gun." In the early days of aviation, aircraft were routinely controlled at towered airports by using the light gun signals shown in the accompanying table. These guns emit a very bright and highly directional beam of light. By the end of the 1950s, all aircraft using towered fields were required to have a two-way radio, and light gun signals faded from the scene as the normal way of a tower's communicating with pilots under its control. But because every radio has the potential to quit at the most inopportune of moments, the entire air traffic control system has alternate means built into it to deal with this possibility (maybe an eventuality). I've had radios fail and have used light gun signals to finish the job on many occasions.

Airplanes that can fly at night have position lights on their wingtips and tails. The tail light is white, and the lights on the wingtips are red and green. Because color is so important, a part of your physical exam will include a test of your color vision. Very few women have any color blindness, but a surprisingly large percentage of men do suffer at least some

## Light gun signals

| Color and type of signal | Meaning | | |
|---|---|---|---|
| | Movement of vehicles, equipment, and personnel | Aircraft on the ground | Aircraft in flight |
| Steady green | Cleared to cross, proceed, or go | Cleared for takeoff | Cleared to land |
| Flashing green | Not applicable | Cleared for taxi | Return for landing (to be followed by steady green at the proper time) |
| Steady red | STOP | STOP | Give way to other aircraft and continue circling |
| Flashing red | Clear the taxiway/runway | Taxi clear of the runway in use | Airport unsafe, do not land |
| Flashing white | Return to starting point of airport | Return to starting point of airport | Not applicable |
| Alternating red and green | Exercise extreme caution | Exercise extreme caution | Exercise extreme caution |

impairment in their ability to distinguish colors. Recently the color vision requirements were changed by the FAA to include only the ability to see and differentiate aviation red, green, and white. Many doctors still use a different color test that was previously required. The old test consisted of a small book with pages of pastel-colored dots. Those with normal color vision could discern circles and triangles out of the maze of dots, whereas the color deficient could only see the maze of pastel dots, with no figures "hidden" on the page. If you receive this test when taking your physical exam and fail it, ask the doctor to follow the new regulations and administer the test that only calls for your ability to see the bright red and green used in aviation. Most applicants who fail the pastel dot test breeze through the examination for aviation red and green. If you can see traffic lights, you should have no problem passing this part of a properly administered flight physical.

# Common Traffic Advisory Frequencies

A *common traffic advisory frequency* (CTAF) is a radio communications frequency that pilots can use at nontowered airports to communicate with other traffic in the vicinity of the airport, to talk to someone on the ground, usually the FBO's office, or to broadcast their position and intentions when either taking off or approaching the airport to land. The FAA publishes its *Airport/Facilities Directory,* which gives quite a bit of information about each public airport and what is available at the airport in terms of runways and services. This directory also shows the CTAF for each airport. If you don't have an issue of the directory with you, or if you failed to use one before takeoff to see what the CTAF is at your airport of intended destination, don't worry about finding the CTAF for any airport. They are shown on your sectional chart as a part of the data block right beside the airport symbols. There are technically two types of nontowered airports—those with no tower at all and those that have a part-time tower.

At airports that have no tower at all, we used to call CTAF "unicom." You will find that in aviation, just like in many other areas of endeavor, old habits die hard. Many pilots still refer to CTAF as unicom and will even use that word in their call-ups, by beginning with the name of the airport, saying, "Delaware unicom, Ercoupe 2906 Hotel." The best use of

CTAF is to communicate your position and intentions to other aircraft that may be in the vicinity of the nontowered airport. Most often, the CTAF frequency is either 122.7 or 122.8 MHz.

As you approach such a field, intending to land there, when you are about 5 miles away, look up the appropriate CTAF frequency on the chart and make a call. It should go something like this, "Delaware traffic, Cessna 4517 Charlie, five south, landing advisory, please." If someone is manning the FBO's CTAF radio, that person will respond, telling you, in general, what runway is actively in use and, if known, the winds and what other traffic has reported. Don't be surprised if you don't get a reply because many FBOs don't have a person constantly at the radio. Sometimes you will get a response from another airplane in the traffic pattern or taxiing on the airport surface.

When you get close to the pattern, announce your position over the CTAF frequency, include that you will be entering downwind, and say which runway you intend to use. If the wind isn't very strong or if you've flown a distance such that the wind may have changed from its direction at your departure airport, don't hesitate to fly a rectangular pattern at single-runway airports to observe the wind sock and traffic tee before you commit to a runway. If the airport has multiple runways, you can stay at least 500 feet above the pattern altitude, fly over the airport, decide which runway is favored by the wind, and then go out from the pattern, descend to pattern altitude, and enter a downwind leg for the runway that you want to use.

Be aware that most midair collisions occur very close to airports. Keep your head on a swivel and your eyes peeled for other traffic at all times. Don't assume that other pilots will be as careful or as discerning as you are. I've been on final more than once, only to see another airplane on final for the opposite direction of the same runway, headed right at me. Some instructors teach their students to make an announcement, over the CTAF frequency, as they are flying on each of the three legs of the landing pattern. That's fine, and it helps everyone keep all of the other airplanes' positions in mind, especially if the pattern is busy. Use good judgment about whether to broadcast so much. If you fly in a metropolitan area, where several airports, in reception range, may be using the same CTAF frequency, too much chatter clogs the airwaves so much that effective communication is reduced.

When you are departing a nontower airport, use the CTAF to announce when you are getting on the runway for takeoff and say what your departure direction will be, along with the runway identification from which you're leaving. Don't depend on this call to take the place of a careful visual scan of the pattern before you get onto the runway. Never depend on other pilots to have their radios on, to understand what you've said, or to heed the fact that you are in the air too or are about to be. Many pilots fly into nontower airports without turning on their radios, or they keep the volume so low that they don't hear many transmissions. Your best collision avoidance devices are still your eyes.

Before you make any radio transmission on the CTAF, whether approaching or leaving the airport, always listen for a few seconds before you key the mike. If you transmit while someone else is doing likewise, nobody gets through. This same advice goes for anytime that you transmit over the radio, whether it be to a controller or on the CTAF.

Although the CTAF is designed to be used for aircraft to broadcast their positions and intentions on and around the airport, it can serve a few other needs, too. Again, don't crowd a busy frequency with transmissions that are not traffic related. But, if the traffic is light, and the CTAF isn't chattering away, it's permissible to use that frequency to contact the airport to inquire about such things as the services available, to ask the FBO to call a taxicab for you, to see if a passenger has arrived yet, and other such informal things. Remember that the CTAF isn't a telephone, so use good judgment about the type and number of calls that you make.

At some airports, the CTAF is connected to a device that automatically turns the runway lights on at night, increases their intensity, or both. Look in the airport directory to see how many clicks of the mike it takes to accomplish that with the runway lights. I'm one of those pilots who likes to have the lights up full bright, but most others prefer them to be set a little dimmer. When the CTAF controls the runway lighting, as it does at many small airports where the FBO is not open at night, you can turn the lights on, and with the proper knowledge of what is required, you can also set the intensity where you like it, right from the cockpit.

Since the early 1980s, when the FAA was beset with a strike of the air traffic controllers, which led to most of them being fired, many of the smaller towered fields have been reduced to part-time towers. These are general aviation airports, usually classed as reliever airports in larger metropolitan areas. They can be very busy during the day, but their traffic falls off so much at night that there is no real justification to have controllers in the tower 24 hours a day. Quite often, the hours of operation at part-time towers will be from 7 a.m. until 11 p.m; the tower is operational 16 hours per day and closed 8 hours. That way, an entire work shift is eliminated, with the attendant cost savings for the FAA. When you fly from or into an airport with a part-time tower, during the hours that the tower is closed, the tower radio frequency becomes a CTAF. Use it the same way as you would at a nontowered airport, except that you won't be able to talk to anyone on the ground to get a cab, or anything else.

# Multicom

Multicom is the label attached to air-to-air communications between aircraft. For private aircraft, the frequency is 122.75 MHz. You can use multicom to talk to another airplane, while both of you are airborne. In these days of cellular telephones, widespread use of mobile radios, and other forms of portable communications, all too many pilots think that multicom is a wide-open chat site. It isn't. The proper use of multicom is to coordinate group flights of airplanes traveling together and for other legitimate needs for air-to-air communication. We've mentioned cellular telephones, but their use in airplanes while in flight is absolutely forbidden. Their range becomes so broad at altitude that using a cell phone in flight clutters the cell frequency spectrum for a great distance.

# 10

# The Examinations

Obtaining your private pilot's license will be a rather informal proposition, as was your flight training. At some point while learning to fly the airplane, you either attended a ground school over a long weekend or for several evenings at the flight school's facilities, studied in your home, or bought one of the ground school courses now available on video tape. Regardless of how you did it, you have thoroughly absorbed the subjects that we've covered in this book—and some others, too. You now have at least 40 to 60 hours of flight time in your logbook and quite possibly more. You've done most of your flying 1 hour at a time because the learning curve for flying drops off severely after much more than an hour for the usual lesson.

Like most other physical tasks, you've learned to fly mostly by doing. One of my early instructors said that his primary job was to keep a student alive and well while the student taught himself to fly. That is oversimplifying it quite a bit because a good instructor shows you how to do what needs to be done, but in the final analysis, you do have to teach yourself most of the art of flying.

Most average students hit a point, usually after 6 or 7 hours of dual instruction, when it seems that they can't do anything right. You didn't get discouraged when you came to this point because your instructor made you realize that this was a positive sign that you had learned enough to start being critical of your own performance. The instructor also explained to you that the learning curve has flat spots and plateaus in it, when progress seems to slow down for a short time. One day after practicing a few touch and go landings, your instructor told you to taxi over to the ramp, where you were asked to get your student pilot certificate out of your purse or wallet. Then, you were signed off for solo flight and immediately made a few takeoffs and landings alone. This event occurred without warning or ceremony.

The wonderful day of your first solo flight will be burned into your memory for the rest of your life. Every pilot I know remembers every small detail of that short flight, which is usually just two or three trips around the traffic pattern, on a beautiful day without much wind. After all of the sweat, time, and expense, you've done it. After your first solo, there will probably be some sort of ritual, which varies by flight school. At some locales, especially if you're a male, you may get a large chunk of your shirt cut out, and the instructor will take a large marker and write your name, the date, the airplane's registration number, and "first solo" on the scrap of cloth that used to be part of your wardrobe and will ceremoniously hang it on the office wall for all to see.

You'll be able to tell when the time for solo is getting close. The wise student doesn't wear expensive shirts after that, until the great day has come and gone. You'd be smart to have another shirt in your car to wear home. Some flight schools think that this rite has become passé and omit it. When I taught my father-in-law to fly, when he was nearly 60 years old, I didn't cut his shirt; I just made him buy dinner that night for his daughter and her new husband. However the occasion is celebrated, you'll never forget your first solo.

In a rather delightful way, your first solo may be a bit anticlimactic as it is happening. You'd been flying the airplane for weeks, maybe months, while the instructor sat there apparently admiring the scenery and occasionally dispensing some wisdom in a thoughtful, pointed, and maybe even curt manner. That first time alone wasn't that much different than a dozen other flights that you'd recently made, except for two things. Because you trained in a Cessna 150, which has side-by-side seating, you were aware of the instructor's absence immediately. Then, without that extra weight, the little trainer seemed more eager to take off, and it climbed much more spritely than you had experienced before.

After your first solo, you took more instruction in cross-country, night, and instrument flying, plus a few more hours polishing up on the maneuvers required for the flight test. Interspersed were several hours of solo practice in the local area and those great solo cross-country flights when you were always worried about getting lost. Somehow you made it back to your airport every time.

When you reached at least 40 hours in your logbook, and probably much more, your instructor felt that you were ready to join the ranks of licensed pilots. Before you actually got your private certificate, you had to go through some testing.

# Knowledge Test

Before the computer age caught up with flight training, candidates for the various pilot certificates and some of the ratings were required to pass a written test. This test was a multiple choice exam that used a separate answer sheet that was sent to FAA headquarters in Oklahoma City for grading. Within a couple of weeks, the student would receive her grade by mail. It took a 70 percent score to pass. Now, this test is administered using a computer.

Because the test is no longer truly written, its name was recently changed to *knowledge test*. The concept hasn't been altered, only the name and the means of taking the test. You will use a computer screen to read the questions and the possible answers, which are still multiple choice. When the exam is finished, you will know right then whether you've passed; there is no more waiting on a mailed grade.

The knowledge test is taken at the facilities of contractors who have arranged with the FAA to administer the exam. Some of these are at FBOs or flight schools, and others are located at colleges, private schools, or other learning centers. Your local FAA office, known as the Flight Standards District Office (FSDO), can give you a list of the places where you can take the test in your area. You will be asked to pay the contractor a nominal fee when you sit for the exam.

Before you can actually take the test, your instructor will have to sign a form that says you've been given the appropriate instruction to prepare for the test and that you are considered ready to pass it. So, you'll spend some time with your instructor getting ready for the knowledge test. You'll be quizzed as much as is necessary until the instructor is convinced that you know what it takes to pass.

The test has no trick questions, but it is constructed like most multiple choice tests are. There are four possible choices for each question. Because you will have studied the material carefully, you'll easily recognize one or two of the choices as clearly erroneous; but then the others will be much closer, and only one of them is correct. The key to passing this test, beyond the obvious need to understand the subject matter, is to carefully read each question and be certain that you understand it before you try to answer. Some people find it more efficient and simpler to go through the entire test, answering those questions that are the easiest, and then take the time to ponder the questions that take the most thought or require calculations, such as those queries in the flight planning areas.

Because all of the questions have an equal weight in the points attached to them and because the test has a time limit (which is usually more than ample), I like that approach to test taking in a multiple choice exam. I don't want to get hung up early in the test on the more difficult or time-consuming questions, using up time and energy, when I might then become concerned, tired, or running low on time with many of the questions yet to go. Do it however is easier for you, either the way we've just discussed or taking each question in the order in which it is presented on the test.

Bring your pocket computer with you, either the circular slide rule type or the electronic variety. If you use an electronic computer, be sure that you have extra batteries with you. The main reason that I like the old-fashioned circular slide rule type is that you don't worry about batteries. The test will give you all of the excerpts from the mythical airplane's POH, weather information, and other data on which the questions are based.

No notes or study material are permitted in the test area. If you relax and come prepared to pass, you'll have no problems.

## Practical Test

What we used to call the flight test is now called a practical test. This is the flight examination, actually conducted in your training airplane. The person who administers it usually is a designated examiner. On rare occasions, FAA inspectors give a private pilot practical test, but their time is generally reserved for testing applicants for a flight instructor certificate or airline transport pilot license. The FAA people also give the tests that are routinely required for commercial operators running air taxi flights and those for pilots seeking type ratings to fly heavy aircraft and jets.

Some nervousness is normal on any flight test, so there isn't much point in telling you not to be nervous at all. Remember that the designated examiner is a fellow pilot who also went

**10-1** *The flight test. Don't worry about it; some nervousness is normal. The examiner is a fellow pilot who wants to see you do well.*

through this stage of training and licensure, who then went on to become a commercial pilot and a flight instructor, and also who was chosen and additionally tested by the FAA to become an examiner. So your examiner has been through multiple flight tests (FIG. 10-1). The examiner has no quota of applicants to fail. The purpose of the practical test is to ensure that you can perform, in flight, up to the published standards of the FAA's *Practical Test Standards* (PTS). Your instructor will have told you to purchase a copy of this small booklet, so you know not only what areas of flight will be covered during the practical test but also what the acceptable levels of skill are.

The examiner is no more critical than is a good flight instructor. You've satisfied your instructor—she signed the recommendation form that has to be presented to the examiner before the test begins—so you should have no trouble with the practical test. As a flight instructor, I use a very simple standard for recommending a student for a flight test: Beyond the PTS requirements, would I let a nonpilot member of my family fly with this person? If the answer is Yes, I sign the recommendation form; if not, we go back for some more dual instruction.

The first part of the practical test is usually planning a cross-country flight for which the examiner tells you the route that he wants to fly. But this exercise won't be mythical—you'll at least get started on it once you take off. The examiner wants to see you plan all aspects of the flight correctly, and because weight and balance are part of that planning, ask him for his weight if he doesn't volunteer the number. You can't do a weight and balance solution if you don't know your exact cabin load.

Once your flight planning is completed, the examiner will start the oral portion of the test. In this phase, he's looking to see what you know about flight planning, weather, regulations, operating procedures, aircraft performance, and the like. These are subjects that can't be adequately covered in a few short questions and answers while airborne, so expect to spend about an hour, maybe even more, getting quizzed on the ground.

Throughout the exam, both during the oral portion and while aloft, the examiner is not permitted, by FAA regulation, to give you instruction. Sometimes an examiner can offer you some insight, but don't expect her to tell you how to do something right. This is your show, not hers. Don't ever try to snow an examiner; if you don't know the answer to a question, admit it. That is likely to happen, especially during the oral phase. Just tell her how you would get the answer to the question before flying and what sources of information you would consult to find out. No one knows everything, but the wise know where to look to find an answer. You're not expected to be perfect, and one wrong answer or instance of ignorance doesn't mean that you will fail, unless it's so basic as to show that you are too ignorant to go on. Examiners have heard all of the artful dodges before, and they are much more respectful of honesty and judgment than anything else you can imagine.

After the oral is completed, it'll shortly be time to go flying. Before you do, be certain that you perform a good preflight of the airplane, even if the examiner doesn't affirmatively ask you to do it. The examiner will undoubtedly watch your preflight, even if you are unaware that you're being observed. Do the preflight the way you were taught, and use the manufacturer's checklist. If you had to fly to another airport, away from your home base to meet the examiner, do a full preflight just as you would for the first flight of the day in this airplane. Don't ever eliminate or shorten a preflight inspection because you just flew this airplane there a short while ago. The examiner will only be able to see you do one preflight, and that is the one that will be graded.

When you enter the cockpit with the examiner at your side, you should act as if you are already licensed and this other person is a passenger. Use the checklist at every stage of the flight, from before engine start to shutdown after landing and taxiing to your parking spot. Pilots aren't supposed to memorize checklists—that's why they are printed for our use. Good judgment is probably the most important thing that you can impress upon the examiner, and good pilots always use their checklists.

After takeoff, the test will usually begin by flying at least a few miles of the planned cross-country. Here, the examiner is looking to see if your altitude is appropriate for the course being flown, if you can establish yourself on that course, and if you can identify at least the first checkpoint or two. You're also being observed to see if you know how to use the radios and other avionics in the airplane and to determine if you are basically competent at cross-country flying. Once that fact is proven, don't be surprised if you are asked to assume that the weather has just gone down below minimums at your intended destination and to proceed to your alternate field. This shows how you deal with an unexpected situation.

When the cross-country phase is completed, your next testing will cover basic airwork. Now, you'll be asked to demonstrate slow flight, stalls, steep turns, and probably some of the ground reference maneuvers. At some point, probably while you are engrossed in some maneuver, a hand will appear from the right seat, and bring the power back to idle, along with an announcement that the engine just gave up its labors for the day. You will then show how to set up for a forced landing. You won't, of course, actually land in some farm field, but the exercise will go on until the examiner is satisfied that you know how to perform an actual emergency landing.

The next part of the test will probably involve some takeoffs and landings. You may be asked to land at an unfamiliar airport so that you can show that you can handle the challenge of determining which runway to use and how well you can fit into the traffic flow at a strange place. This might even be a towered airport so that your radio communications skills can be tested at the same time. During this phase, you'll also be asked to do some crosswind takeoffs and landings and demonstrate short-field and soft-field techniques.

Sometime during the test, you'll put on the instrument hood that restricts your outside vision and will fly the airplane solely by reference to the flight instruments. The examiner will put the airplane into some unusual attitudes and then ask you to recover to normal flight, while you're wearing the hood.

Before you get all worked up over what is required during the practical test, and fret endlessly, remember that you've done each and every maneuver and encountered every situation with your flight instructor. If you do fail the test the first time, which is highly unlikely, it isn't a black mark against you, but it certainly is one against your instructor. Instructors must renew their licenses every 2 years. If a particular instructor has a higher than normal failure rate of students on flight tests, that instructor will come under some extra scrutiny by the FAA at renewal time. Therefore, your instructor won't recommend you for the practical test until you are ready. Because you've already shown your instructor that you can fly, you'll finish your practical test in the examiner's office as you watch the typing of your newest and proudest possession—your pilot's license.

# Glossary

**ADF**  Automatic direction finder.

**aerodynamics**  The forces, such as resistance, pressure, velocity, and other forces involved in the movement of air or gases around a moving body, or the branch of dynamics and physics dealing with these forces.

**AGL**  Above ground level.

**ailerons**  The primary control surfaces located at the trailing edges of the outer wing panels that, when moved up or down, cause the airplane in flight to bank.

**AIM**  *Aeronautical Information Manual.* An FAA periodical providing basic flight information and air traffic control procedures.

**airfoil**  Any surface designed to create lift, either positive or negative, when moving through the air at a given speed. Examples include wings, control surfaces, propellers, and helicopter blades.

**airspace**  When used in aviation the term means the navigable sky, for all practical purposes, between ground level and 60,000 feet.

**airspeed**  The speed at which an aircraft is moving with relation to the air around it. It may be expressed as indicated airspeed, calibrated airspeed, and true airspeed.

**airspeed indicator**  A flight instrument with a cockpit readout that, in terms of knots or mph, shows the difference between pitot pressure and static pressure. The reading obtained from the airspeed indicator is indicated airspeed.

**alternator**  An electrical device that is driven by the engine and supplies current to the battery and to all on-board electrical equipment except the ignition system.

**altimeter**  A flight instrument capable of displaying the height above sea level (or any other predetermined level), activated by an aneroid barometer measuring atmospheric pressure at the given altitude.

**altimeter setting**  The barometric pressure reading in the small window provided for that purpose on the face of the altimeter.

**angle of attack**   The angle at which the chord line of the wing or any other airfoil meets the relative wind. Angle of attack determines the amount of lift developed at a given airspeed.

**approach**   Airplane maneuver performed to prepare for landing.

**approach control**   The ATC facility monitoring and directing traffic approaching an airport where such a facility is in operation.

**artificial horizon**   A gyro instrument showing the attitude of the aircraft with reference to pitch and roll as compared to the horizon.

**ATC**   Air traffic control.

**atmospheric pressure**   The weight of the air surrounding the earth. Standard atmospheric pressure is expressed as 29.92 inches of mercury, or 1013.2 millibars.

**avionics**   A catch-all phrase for communication, navigation, and related instrumentation in an aircraft. A contraction of "aviation electronics."

**back pressure**   Aft force on the control wheel.

**base leg**   A part of the airport traffic pattern. A flight path at a right angle to the runway, after the downwind leg and before the final approach.

**calibrated airspeed**   Indicated airspeed corrected for instrument and installation errors.

**carburetor heat**   A heating unit located near the carburetor throat and controlled in the cockpit. It is used to melt carburetor ice.

**carburetor ice**   Ice forming in the carburetor throat due to excessive moisture in the air.

**compass, gyro**   *See* directional gyro.

**compass, magnetic**   A compass that, during straight and level flight, automatically aligns itself with magnetic north.

**constant-speed propeller**   A controllable-pitch propeller that maintains a constant rpm by automatically changing the blade angle in relation to engine output.

**course**   The direction of flight of an aircraft across the ground.

**course deviation indicator**   The needle, bar, or other indicator that displays the position of an aircraft relative to a radial or bearing from or to a VOR.

**cross-country flight**   A flight with a landing made at a point other than the initial airport of takeoff, usually farther than 25 nautical miles.

**dead reckoning** A method of navigation by which an aircraft's course and time between two given points is estimated by taking into consideration course, speed, and wind components calculated with a wind triangle. The phrase comes from the term "deduced reckoning."

**density altitude** Pressure altitude corrected for prevailing temperature conditions.

**dewpoint** The temperature to which air must cool without change in pressure or vapor content, in order for condensation to take place.

**DG** Directional gyro.

**directional gyro** A gyroscopic flight instrument that, when set to conform with the magnetic compass, will continue to indicate the aircraft heading for some time, regardless of turns or pitch changes. It tends to develop heading errors and must be adjusted intermittently.

**downwind** In the direction that the wind is blowing.

**downwind leg** The flight path parallel to the runway in the direction opposite to landing. It is part of the standard airport traffic pattern.

**drag** The force created by friction of the air on objects in motion. It must be overcome by thrust in order to achieve flight parallel to the relative wind. Two types of drag are induced drag and parasite drag. Induced drag is created through the process of creating lift. Parasite drag is all drag from surfaces that do not contribute to lift. It increases with an increase in airspeed.

**E6-B** A circular slide rule computer used to compute a variety of aviation mathematics problems.

**elevator** The primary control surface (attached to the horizontal stabilizer) that can be moved up or down to control the pitch of the aircraft. It is a speed control as much as an altitude control.

**FAA** Federal Aviation Administration.

**FAR** Federal Aviation Regulation.

**FBO** Fixed-base operator.

**final approach** The final portion of an airport traffic pattern during which the descending aircraft is aligned with the runway centerline.

**fixed-base operator** A person or organization providing aviation services at an airport: flight instruction, fuel, maintenance, and perhaps more.

**fixed-pitch propeller**   A propeller with blades at a prede-termined angle that cannot be changed or adjusted.

**FL**   Flight level; FL180 stands for 18,000 feet.

**flaps**   Auxiliary control surfaces that are usually located at the trailing edges of the inner wing panels between the fuse-lage and the ailerons. Flaps can be extended and/or turned down to increase the wing camber and/or surface, creating additional lift and drag.

**flare**   A smooth leveling of the aircraft during which the nose is raised at the end of the landing glide and just prior to touchdown.

**flight service station**   An FAA facility that provides weather briefings and other services to general aviation pilots, in person or via telephone or radio.

**fpm**   Feet per minute (rate of climb or descent).

**FSS**   Flight service station.

**generator**   A device identical in construction to an electri-cal motor that, when driven by the engine, generates electrical current and continuously recharges the battery.

**global positioning system**   A system of air navigation in which a receiver mounted in the aircraft receives signals from satellites in orbit, which enable the receiver to electronically calculate the aircraft's position, course to a selected destination, altitude, time en route, and ground speed.

**GPS**   Global positioning system.

**ground control**   An ATC service at controlled airports that is responsible for the safe and efficient movement of aircraft and airport vehicles on the ground.

**ground effect**   Additional lift that takes effect when the aircraft is close to the ground. It is the result of air being compressed between the wings and the ground. Low-wing aircraft are more susceptible to the effect than high-wing aircraft.

**ground speed**   The speed with which an aircraft moves relative to the surface of the earth.

**heading**   The direction in which the aircraft flies through the air, not with reference to the ground. In other words, the direction in which the nose of the aircraft is pointing.

**Hg**   Mercury, as in 30.12" Hg (inches of mercury).

**horizontal stabilizer**   The fixed horizontal portion of the tail section to which the elevator is attached.

**HP**   Horsepower.

**IAS**   Indicated airspeed.

**IFR**  Instrument flight rules due to weather conditions that are less than the minimum VFR requirements.

**inches of mercury**  Units of measurement of atmospheric pressure used to indicate the height in inches to which a column of mercury will rise in a glass tube in response to the weight of the atmosphere exerting pressure on a bowl of mercury at the base of the tube.

**indicated airspeed**  The airspeed that is shown by the airspeed indicator. It is nearly always less than true airspeed, but usually not much different from calibrated airspeed.

**induced drag**  *See* drag.

**kHz**  Kilohertz or kilocycles.

**knots**  Nautical miles per hour.

**kts**  Knots.

**lift**  The generally upward force created by the difference of pressure between the upper and lower surfaces of an airfoil in motion. In level flight, lift is balanced by the force of gravity.

**magnetic course**  The course of an aircraft referenced to magnetic north.

**magnetic heading**  The heading of an aircraft referenced to magnetic north.

**magnetic north**  The location, some distance from the geographic north pole, where the earth's magnetic lines converge.

**magneto**  A self-contained generator that supplies electrical current to the spark plugs in the ignition system.

**manifold**  An arrangement of tubing (on an aircraft engine) with one orifice on one end and several on the other.

**manifold pressure**  The pressure of the fuel-air mixture in the intake manifold.

**MC**  Magnetic course.

**MH**  Magnetic heading.

**MHz**  Megahertz or megacycles.

**millibar**  A unit of atmospheric pressure. *See* atmospheric pressure.

**mixture**  The mixture of fuel and air necessary for combustion in reciprocating engines.

**mph**  Statute miles per hour.

**MSL**  Mean sea level.

**nautical mile**  A unit of linear measure equal to 6,076.1 feet.

**needle and ball**  An instrument that shows the rate of turn of the aircraft and displays whether the aircraft is in a skid or a slip. An older version of the turn-and-slip indicator and turn coordinator.

**nm**   Nautical mile(s).

**parasite drag**   *See* drag.

**pattern**   Airport landing pattern: takeoff, crosswind, downwind, base, and final.

**pilot in command**   The pilot responsible for the operation and safety of an aircraft during flight time.

**pilotage**   Navigation by reference to visible landmarks. Used usually in conjunction with sectional charts on which all meaningful landmarks are shown.

**pitch**   The attitude of the aircraft with reference to a horizontal axis at right angles to the fuselage. In other words, nose-down or nose-up.

**pitot-static system**   A device that compares impact pressure with static or atmospheric pressure and presents the result in the cockpit by means of the airspeed indicator, the altimeter, and the vertical speed indicator.

**pitot tube**   A protrusion, usually from the wing, with a small orifice exposed to the airstream and designed to measure the pressure with which an aircraft meets the air. Also called a "pitot head."

**precession**   The tendency of a directional gyro to gradually become unreliable due to friction.

**propeller**   Two or more airfoil-shaped blades designed to convert the turning force of the engine into thrust.

**psi**   Pressure in terms of pounds per square inch.

**relative wind**   The movement of air relative to the movement of an airfoil. It is parallel to and in the opposite direction of the flight path of an airplane.

**rpm**   Revolutions per minute.

**rudder**   The primary control surface attached to the vertical stabilizer, movement of which causes the tail of the aircraft to swing either left or right. The rudder controls yaw.

**runup**   A pretakeoff check of the performance of the engine and, in aircraft equipped with constant-speed props, the operation of the propeller.

**sectional chart**   An aeronautical chart of a section of the United States at a scale of 1:500,000, which is approximately 7 nautical miles per inch.

**service ceiling**   The maximum altitude above sea level that an aircraft can climb to and then maintain horizontal flight under standard atmospheric conditions.

**skid**   Lateral movement of an airplane toward the outside of a turn. The skid is caused by incorrect use of the rudder.

**slip**   The tendency of an aircraft to lose altitude by slipping toward the center of a turn. The slip is caused by incorrect use of the rudder.

**spin**   A maneuver in which the airplane, after stalling, descends nearly vertically, nose-low, with the tail revolving around the vertical axis of the descent.

**stall**   The inability of an airplane to continue flight due to an excessive angle of attack. The airplane will either drop its nose and thus reduce the angle of attack and regain flying speed or, if forced to retain the excessive angle of attack, the airplane might fall into a spin.

**stall speed**   The speed, at a given angle of attack, at which airflow separation begins and the stall occurs. Aircraft can stall at virtually any speed if an acceptable angle of attack is exceeded.

**stall-spin**   The combination of a stall followed by a spin, a major cause of fatal accidents.

**stall warning**   A buzzer, a light, or both that indicates to a pilot that the aircraft is about to stall.

**static vent**   A hole, usually located in the side of the fuse-lage, that provides air at atmospheric pressure to operate the pitot-static system.

**statute mile**   A unit of measure equivalent to 5,280 feet.

**stick**   Control wheel or yoke.

**TAS**   True airspeed.

**taxi**   To move an aircraft on the ground under its own power.

**torque**   The normal tendency of an aircraft to rotate to the left in reaction to the right-hand rotation of the propeller. Torque varies with changes in power.

**tower**   Control tower at a controlled airport.

**trim tab**   A small airfoil attached to a control surface—usually the elevator and occasionally the rudder—that can be adjusted to cause changes in the position of the control surface under varying flight conditions.

**true airspeed**   The actual speed at which an aircraft is moving in relation to undisturbed air. True airspeed is calibrated airspeed adjusted for actual air density and altitude.

**true course**   Course referenced to true north.

**true heading**   Heading referenced to true north.

**true north**   Geographic (not magnetic) north. The direction to the northern end of the earth's axis.

**turn-and-slip indicator**   *See* needle and ball.

**unicom**   Aeronautical advisory station for communication with aircraft. Unicoms are usually staffed by FBO employees or airport personnel and provide pilots with such information as the active runway, wind direction and velocity, and other conditions of importance to pilots. Unicoms are not authorized to give takeoff or landing clearances, or in any way control traffic, except when relaying word from ATC, in which case any such transmission must be preceded by "ATC clears."

**unusual attitude**   Any attitude of an aircraft in terms of pitch or roll or both that is beyond the normal operating attitude. Recovery from unusual attitudes by reference to instruments is an important part of instrument training.

**vertical speed indicator**   An instrument in the pitot-static system that indicates the rate of climb or descent in terms of feet per minute. It is usually calibrated in units of either 100 or 1,000 fpm.

**vertical stabilizer**   A fixed vertical airfoil on the empennage to which the rudder is attached.

**VFR**   Visual flight rules or weather conditions equal to or better than minimum visual flight rule requirements.

**VHF**   Very high frequency; electromagnetic frequencies between 30 and 300 MHz.

**VOR**   Very-high-frequency omnidirectional radio range; a ground-based VHF navigation aid.

**VSI**   Vertical speed indicator.

**WCA**   Wind correction angle.

**wind shear**   An abrupt change in wind direction or velocity.

**yaw**   The movement of an aircraft to either side, turning around its vertical axis, without banking.

**yoke**   Control wheel; stick.

# Index

Pages shown in **boldface** have illustrations on them.

# About the Author

Jerry A. Eichenberger is a certified flight instructor, rated for single- and multiengine airplanes, and instrument instructor. He is also a commercial pilot, and rated to fly helicopters and gliders. He first learned to fly in 1965 and became an instructor in 1967. He has given over 2,000 hours of flight instruction and has logged over 4,700 hours of flying time. He has owned several airplanes, from classics to twin-engine business aircraft.

Mr. Eichenberger is a practicing attorney in the field of aviation law, representing manufacturers, airlines, flight schools, airports, fixed base operators, maintenance facilities, and individual pilots and aircraft owners. His writings include articles published in *Plane & Pilot News* and *Business and Commercial Aviation*. His previous books are *General Aviation Law*, Second Edition, *Cross-Country Flying*, and *Handling In-Flight Emergencies* (all in the McGraw-Hill *Practical Flying Series*).